GUESSING AT TRUTH

GUESSING AT TRUTH

The Life of Julius Charles Hare
(1795–1855)

by N. Merrill Distad

The Patmos Press / 1979 / Shepherdstown

Library of Congress Cataloging in Publication Data

Distad, N. Merrill.
  Guessing at truth.

  Bibliography: p.
  1. Hare, Julius Charles, 1795–1855. 2. Church of England—Clergy—Biography. 3. Clergy—England—Biography. I. Title.
BX5199.H35D57   283'.092'4 [B] 78-11625
ISBN 0-915762-07-2

© 1979 by N. Merrill Distad. All rights reserved. No part of this book may be reproduced, stored in a retrieval system, or transmitted, in any form or by any means, electronic, mechanical, photocopying, recording, or otherwise, without the written permission of the author and The Patmos Press.

Manufactured in the United States of America

For my wife, Linda Miron

Preface

> *If any foreigner landing in England last year had asked where he should find the man best acquainted with all modern forms of thought here and on the Continent—where he should find the most complete collection of the philosophical, theological, or historical literature of Germany—where he should find profound and exact scholarship combined with the most varied and extensive learning—what would have been the answer? Not in Oxford—not in Cambridge—not in London. He must have turned far away from academic towns or public libraries to a secluded parish in Sussex, and in the minister of that parish, in an archdeacon of one of the least important of English dioceses, he would have found what he sought. He would have found such an one there: he would now find such an one no more. For such was Julius Hare, late Rector of Herstmonceux and Archdeacon of Lewes.*
>
> A.P. Stanley in *Quarterly Review* (June 1855)

Julius Charles Hare is an unheralded figure in the intellectual and literary history of nineteenth-century England, though he achieved eminence in his own day in a career that spanned literature, classical scholarship, university teaching, and the pastoral and administrative duties of a clergyman and archdeacon. Born in Italy to English parents, Hare travelled on the continent, lived for a time at Weimar, where he learned the German language, and acquired the cosmopolitanism which distinguished him among his countrymen.

In his scholarship and his churchmanship Hare was a liberal

and an early member of that circle of divines that has come to be known as the "Broad Church." Hare's special significance as a Broad Churchman was his centrality. His wide acquaintance and friendships with many of the great men of his time, some of whom had been his pupils, gave him a scope for personal influence such as few men enjoy. Hare's influence upon his contemporaries was genuine and pervasive.

As a clergyman Hare sought to promote the ideal of comprehension and toleration within a unified National Church. By minimizing religious tests and exclusiveness, and eschewing persecutions, Hare hoped to see as many Protestant believers as possible comprehended within a Church establishment greater than any known in England since the Reformation. Hare's motives in this were not purely spiritual, but were also patriotic. A fervent nationalist, Hare believed that the pre-eminence vouchsafed England by God would be revoked if she failed to do her spiritual duty. This entailed putting her divided Church in order, providing a Christian education for all her people, and working among civilized and heathen nations alike to promote strong national churches, which could take their place in the coming Kingdom of Christ. These Broad Church ideals were directed against what Hare perceived as selfish individualism, sectarian jealousy, and all-consuming Mammon-worship, that is, *laissez-faire* commercial capitalism. Hare's religious eclecticism, his eagerness within Protestantism to comprehend a variety of theological and ecclesiastical positions within one National Church, made him the archetypal Broad Churchman.

At Trinity College, Cambridge, in the 1820s Hare strongly influenced the young men of the society known as "Apostles," instilled in them a high regard for literature, impelled many to turn to the new literature and scholarship of Germany, and inspired several to pursue careers as scholars. By his example Hare inspired three generations of Trinity men to assign the highest priority to the pursuit of truth.

As a man of letters Hare helped introduce the English reading public to German literature, history, and theology. For this Hare deserves wider recognition than he has received as a pioneer Germanist; he helped transplant German culture into the English intellectual consciousness.

That Hare has been largely forgotten may be attributed to his

PREFACE

having spread himself too thinly over so many fields of endeavour, to having produced translations and polemics, sermons and charges, rather than more substantial works, to the absence of a memorial biography, and to the fact that personal influence, however strong, is seldom the subject of great historical reputations or the monuments raised by posterity.

To seek to resurrect a forgotten man by writing his biography should require no explanation. But the biographical format is so laden with technical pitfalls and restrictions—which Philip Guedalla only hinted at when he located its borders on the north by history, on the south by fiction, on the east by obituary, and on the west by tedium—that the reader may fairly ask for some justification. A monograph of limited scope, one might argue, would be more suitable to a man who was hardly a towering figure upon the historical landscape. The first justification of a biography is partly sentimental: no full-scale life of Hare has ever before been written. Although an official Victorian double-decker "tombstone" biography by F. D. Maurice was projected by Hare's family, it was never produced. Hare's death generated only brief and eulogistic articles, and despite the existence of ample sources, both published and in manuscript, modern scholars have produced only a few specialized studies, confined to the pages of scholarly journals. The very character of Hare's life, with his wide range of tastes and pursuits, renders a biographical treatment appropriate; any attempt to chronicle his life's work and to analyse his influence and friendships by other means would quickly devolve into a catalogue of biographical detail. Julius Hare was an elusive historical figure. He appears fleetingly in scores of biographies and memoirs of his contemporaries, but little is generally known about him. Both to resurrect and to evaluate the life of such a man, biography offers the natural medium.

In the course of my work I have incurred many obligations. Some who warrant particular thanks are the Canada Council for generously providing two research grants in 1971–72; Mr and Mrs Robert Bayne-Powell for their gracious hospitality while I worked on the Bayne-Powell family papers; Philip Gaskell for making me feel at home in the Wren Library; Alphonse Chapeau for placing the Hare-Manning correspondence at my disposal in the Manning

Archive; Richard Helmstadter for patiently sharing his knowledge and his lunch hours with me; Peter Allen for years of help and advice which culminated in his reading of the proofs; and my wife Linda for performing more tasks than she would care to remember.

That I may name many others deserving thanks in the space available, I list them alphabetically and deprived of their titles. In England: Patricia Bradford, John Coulson, E.H. Cuthbert, C.J. Fullerton, Patricia Gill, Mary E.M. Hare, R.G.H. Horne, Leslie Houghton, David Isitt, Trevor Kaye, Lancelot Mason, David Muspratt, David Newsome, David Paton, Heather Peek, Stephen Prickett, Bruce Purvis, Joan Robinson, Robert Robson, Verena Smith, G.W. Stannard, Frank Taylor, Alec Vidler, and T.S. Wragg. In the United States of America: Josef Altholz, William Baker, John Clive, Henry Kozicki, Frank McClain, Thomas Pinney, Charles Robinson, Cleve Want, and John Wiita. In Canada: Brian Heeney, Robin Jackson, Lachlan McNair, Peter Morgan, Peter Munsche, Desmond Neill, Paul Phillips, and Elliot Rose.

For permission to quote from manuscripts I wish to thank Robert Bayne-Powell, Alphonse Chapeau, His Grace the Duke of Devonshire, the Master and Fellows of Trinity College, Cambridge, the Trustees of the British Library, the Cambridge University Library, the Bodleian Library, King's College Library, London, the Manning Archive, London, the Victoria and Albert Museum Library, the Dr Williams's Library, the John Rylands Library of Manchester University, the Hove Sussex Public Library, the North Yorkshire County Record Office, and the National Libraries of Scotland and Wales. In the United States I wish to thank the Trustees of the Columbia University Library and the Public Libraries of Boston and New York City (Astor, Tilden, Lennox Foundation).

I wish to acknowledge the gracious permission of Her Majesty Queen Elizabeth II to consult the Royal Archives in Windsor Castle. Permission to consult manuscripts was also generously given by the late Sir Henry Havelock-Allan, the Fitzwilliam Museum Library, King's College Library, Cambridge, the Leeds University Library, the County Record Offices of Cheshire, Essex, East Sussex, and West Sussex, and in the United States by the Henry E. Huntington Library and by the libraries of Harvard, Kansas, and Yale Universities.

PREFACE xi

For permission to quote from printed works in copyright I wish to thank the University of Alabama Press (E.L. Williamson, *The Liberalism of Thomas Arnold* © 1964), Adam and Charles Black Ltd. (W.O. Chadwick, *The Victorian Church*, volume I © 1966), Cambridge University Press (D. Forbes, *The Liberal Anglican Idea of History* © 1950, and J.W. Adamson, *English Education, 1789–1902*, 2nd ed. © 1964), Curtis Brown Ltd. (M. St J. Packe's *Life of John Stuart Mill*, published by Secker and Warburg, © 1954), Duke University Press (C.R. Sanders, *Coleridge and the Broad Church Movement* © 1942, and W.J. Baker, "Julius Charles Hare: A Victorian Interpreter of Luther," *South Atlantic Quarterly*, LXX, no. 1 [winter 1971], 88–101), John Murray (Publishers) Ltd. (D. Hudson, *Poet in Parliament: The Life of W.M. Praed* © 1939), Oxford University Press (C. Colvin, ed., *Maria Edgeworth: Letters from England, 1813–1844* © 1971), Routledge and Kegan Paul Ltd. (V.A.A. Stockley, *German Literature as Known in England, 1750–1830* © 1929), the John Rylands Library of Manchester University (G. F. McFarland, "The Early Literary Career of Julius Charles Hare," and "Julius Charles Hare, Coleridge, De Quincey, and German Literature," *Bulletin of the John Rylands Library*, XLVI, no. 1 [Sept. 1963], 42–83, and XLVII, no. 1 [Sept. 1964], 165–97), and George Weidenfeld and Nicolson Ltd. (A. Momigliano, *Studies in Historiography* © 1966).

For permission to reprint my own material which originally was published in other forms I wish to thank the Macmillan Company of Canada Ltd. and *Victorian Periodicals Newsletter*.

I should also like to acknowledge the superb resources of the Library of the University of Toronto and of the libraries of its federated colleges. Finally, I wish to thank James C. Holland, my publisher, and Ann Hofstra Grogg, my editor, for making this book a reality. I am solely responsible for any errors which remain.

Brampton, Ontario, CANADA
November 1978

Note on the Text

Julius Hare's phonetic spelling of the past participles of certain regular verbs as if they were irregular—cherisht, equipt, expresst, preacht, punisht—has been preserved in quotations. Hare also discarded the use of the apostrophe to signify elision in the genitive plural. He adopted these "reforms" in the late 1820s, and persisted in them to the end of his life.

Contents

Preface vii
1. Origins and Early Years 3
2. Trinity College, Cambridge 23
3. Law and Literature in London 35
4. A Don's Life 43
5. A Commission from Landor 58
6. Guessing at Truth 70
7. Higher Criticism from Germany 81
8. Germano-Coleridgean Historiography 93
9. Niebuhr's Roman History 105
10. To Italy and Herstmonceux 116
11. Parson and Archdeacon 130
12. Friend and Partisan 149
13. The Broad Church Vindicator 162
14. John Sterling and the Subversion of Faith 174
15. The Church Divided 184
   Abbreviations Used in the Notes 199
   Notes 200
   Selected Bibliography 239
   Index 248

GUESSING AT TRUTH

Chapter 1

Origins and Early Years

The family of Hare was long established in Essex, in the parish of Leigh, Hundred of Rochford. The surviving records indicate that the family was of substance among the local gentry. Parish registers for Leigh are extant only from 1684, making the family genealogy before that date a matter of conjecture. However, the seventeenth-century quarter-sessions records of the commission of the peace establish the existence of two members of the family named John Hare, father and son, and of two more named Richard Hare.[1]

Francis Hare (1671–1740), son of one Richard Hare, raised his family's name from rural obscurity to national prominence. As a Fellow of King's College, Cambridge, in the 1690s Hare served as Tutor to the young Sir Robert Walpole and to John, Marquis of Blandford, only son of the Duke of Marlborough. Hare formed an intimate friendship with Walpole, and also secured the favour of the Duke. These connections along with the subsequent patronage of Queen Caroline, wife of George II, resulted in a meteoric career based upon preferment.[2]

In 1704 Marlborough appointed Francis Hare Chaplain-General of his army in Flanders. As Chaplain-General to the Captain-General, Hare participated in all of Marlborough's campaigns; his journal served as the staff diary of Marlborough's army. In 1707 Hare was appointed to a prebendary's stall at Saint Paul's in London, whereupon he resigned his fellowship at King's College.

In 1709 he married. In succeeding years he was appointed a Royal Chaplain (1711), a Fellow of Eton (1712), Rector of Barnes, Surrey (1713), Dean of Worcester (1715), Usher of the Exchequer (1722), Dean of Saint Paul's (1726), and Bishop of Saint Asaph (1727), and in 1731 he was translated to the see of Chichester. In 1736 only fierce opposition prevented Walpole from elevating him to Canterbury as successor to Archbishop Wake.[3]

But good personal connections, however necessary, are not sufficient to explain Bishop Hare's successful career. He owed this success as much to his academic achievements as to his friends in high places. Hare was renowned for his mastery of Latin, Greek, and Hebrew. Although his attacks upon Bishop Hoadly in connection with the "Bangorian Controversy" led to temporary loss of royal favour and the deprivation of his chaplaincy at court, his prolific scholarship and his patronage of such men as the future Bishop Warburton gained him many admirers. However, Bishop Hare's greatest contribution to his family's history was the acquisition of the ancient estate of Herstmonceux in Sussex, creating a landed base for his family's prosperity.[4]

Shortly after the death of his first wife, Bishop Hare remarried, and so, like Bishop Hoadly, created a scandal within the Church. His bride was Margaret Alston, who brought him rich estates in Suffolk and in Buckinghamshire. However, the family continued to reside at Herstmonceux in Sussex. There the Bishop raised his oldest son under terms of extraordinary severity, forbidding him to use any language but Greek in communicating with the rest of the family. The son grew understandably resentful and rebellious. At his son's majority in 1734 Bishop Hare and his wife moved to their estate near Chalfont Saint Giles in Buckinghamshire, never again to return to Herstmonceux.

Francis Hare the younger, who then assumed the additional surname of Naylor, was left in sole possession of the valuable Sussex estate, free to pursue a life of dissipation. He is alleged to have been a friend of the notorious Sir Francis Dashwood. Whatever the truth of this allegation, Hare-Naylor did have a talent for embarrassing his father, the Bishop. For example, he contrived an engagement with Carlotta Alston, his stepmother's younger sister. Bishop Hare could ill afford another family scandal, and with some difficulty he prevented the marriage from taking place. After the

Bishop's death in April 1740 the couple married. However, the union was a barren one, and upon Francis Hare-Naylor's death in 1775 the Herstmonceux estate passed to his half-brother, Robert Hare-Naylor (1730–99), younger son of the Bishop, by his second wife.[5]

The new heir was well provided for. In addition to Herstmonceux, Robert Hare-Naylor inherited estates in Buckinghamshire, Hampshire, Norfolk, and Suffolk. During the later years of his life he served as a Canon of Winchester. From his Godfather, Sir Robert Walpole, he had received the Sweepership of Gravesend as a christening present. This sinecure paid £400 a year for the nominal duty of making an annual visit to Gravesend and paying the watermen there ten guineas. Moreover, Bishop Hare had insisted that his sons follow his example and marry heiresses. Thus in 1752 Robert dutifully wed Sarah, daughter of Lister Selman, whose estate at Chalfont Saint Peters lay conveniently close to the Hare family's own at Chalfont Saint Giles. This marriage ended with Sarah's premature death in 1763, said to have resulted from eating too many ices when overheated by dancing at a ball.

There were two children by this marriage. Francis Hare-Naylor (1753–1815), father of Julius Charles Hare, was the elder; Robert (d. 1832) was the younger. Robert followed the example of his father and grandfather and entered the Church. He spent his life as Rector of the family living of All Saints, Herstmonceux. Francis, as the elder son, should ultimately have enjoyed a vast inheritance and financial security. But in 1768 his father married Miss Henrietta Henckell. Augustus John Cuthbert Hare (1834–1903), the family historian, claimed that Mrs Henrietta Hare was ruinously extravagant, but he failed to explain how she squandered the money. It may be no more than gossipy family tradition that because of his second wife's extravagance Robert Hare-Naylor began to dispose of family property. In the 1780s estates in Hampshire, Norfolk, and Suffolk were sold. According to A.J.C. Hare, Henrietta Hare's expenditures still knew no bounds, and it was necessary to sell off a farm a year from the Herstmonceux estate to cover the annual deficit.

A.J.C. Hare also claimed that Henrietta Hare abused her stepchildren, and earned their hatred. She took great delight in burning the portrait of their mother. But her most heinous deed was to engineer the destruction of Herstmonceux Castle itself. She resented the fact that the castle would devolve upon her stepson. So in 1777, with the connivance of James Wyatt, the architect, she had the structure declared unsound, and hired workmen to strip and dismantle it. She planned to use the building materials to erect a new house nearby, which could be settled upon her own children. The fabric of the castle proved so strong, despite Wyatt's diagnosis, that much of the material was broken beyond salvage. Nonetheless, the work was carried out, leaving the walls of the castle a hollow shell. Nearby, under Wyatt's direction, Hurstmonceux Place was built. But wickedness was not rewarded. Of Henrietta Hare's seven children, only two daughters lived to maturity, and when her husband died it was found that she had inadvertently built Hurstmonceux Place upon entailed land.[6]

While she despoiled her stepsons' patrimony, Mrs Henrietta Hare forced them to live on allowances of £100 a year. Such a sum was hardly adequate for a boon companion of Charles James Fox, George Selwyn, and Richard Brinsley Sheridan. Francis spent recklessly, and borrowed large sums of money at high interest against his prospects of inheriting the dwindling family estates. Although he tried to avoid the sight of his stepmother, it was during a rare visit to his father at Winchester that Francis first saw his future wife. He met the Shipley family at Twyford House, just two miles from the town.

Jonathan Shipley (1714–88) had been successively Dean of Winchester, Bishop of Llandaff, and Bishop of Saint Asaph. He sired five daughters as remarkable for their intelligence as for their beauty. Young Hare's visit was more than a coincidence. Through his friend Charles James Fox he had met Georgiana, the Duchess of Devonshire. The Duchess, seeing in Hare not only a handsome and intelligent young man, but also one likely to inherit great estates, lost no time in introducing him to her cousin, Georgiana Shipley, the Bishop's fourth daughter.[7]

Bishop Shipley had high ambitions for the future of his daughters. However, the Duchess of Devonshire had taken such a liking to Hare that she arranged meetings between Hare and Georgiana almost daily at Devonshire House. The Bishop was a man of liberal views, and he was at last induced to invite Hare to Twyford to become better acquainted. All was apparently going well until Hare

ORIGINS AND EARLY YEARS

accompanied Georgiana and her parents for a drive. He was overwhelmed by bailiffs, and arrested for debt out of the Bishop's own carriage. Forbidden to return to Twyford, Hare disguised himself as a beggar, and by this means gained occasional glimpses of his beloved. At last the Duchess of Devonshire arranged for the couple's elopement. In 1784 she settled an annuity of £200 a year upon them as a wedding gift, and promised them a small estate in Ireland. The promise of an estate was no more redeemable than the Duchess's astronomical gambling debts, but the £200 a year was a secure, if slim, basis for marriage until Hare came into his inheritance. Both families were indignant, and the bride and groom never saw their fathers again. They left England for Karlsruhe, and after a brief stay in Germany, took up residence in northern Italy. The two decades which the Hare family spent living on the continent had a profound impact linguistically and intellectually upon the Hare children.

Elopement may have been a rash act, but under the circumstances it appeared the only solution to parental disapproval. It was not an impulsive love affair, for as early as November 1782 Sir William Jones, husband of Georgiana's eldest sister, wrote in a letter to Benjamin Franklin of the engagement between his sister-in-law and Hare as though it were formal.[8] In the early 1770s Bishop Shipley had befriended Benjamin Franklin, then in England as Colonial Representative for Pennsylvania. Franklin was a frequent guest of the Shipleys at Twyford, where he began to compose his autobiography. He took an especial liking to Georgiana. She was well versed in Latin and Greek, and had been taught drawing by Sir Joshua Reynolds.[9]

When Franklin left England, and took up his post as representative (subsequently ambassador) to France, he and Georgiana kept up a lively correspondence, though at one point her letters had to be smuggled out of the country. This correspondence was discontinued in 1781. But after her elopement with Francis Hare, Georgiana turned to her old friend for advice: "My dear Doctor Franklin, the kindness and indulgence you have ever shewn . . . encourage me to trouble you on this occasion when I very much want your friendship and advice." She detailed their financial dilemma: "Mr Hare had once the prospect of possessing an exceeding good fortune, but the unkind and unjust conduct of his father . . . joined to his own negligence of his affairs, have so much reduced his expectations, that we cannot hope to live in England with the affluence and comforts to which we have hitherto been accustomed. We naturally, therefore, turn our thoughts to America as a safe and honourable retreat to all those who have any motives for renouncing their native country." Dreaming of a new life in America, Georgiana asked about the prospects for practising law or agriculture in Pennsylvania. She estimated that "at present we can depend on no more than £300 pr ann^m and about £1000 in money; on the death of Mr Hare's father I should hope we can not fail to have at least 10, or 15,000£ to receive." In closing Georgiana spoke of her decision to defy her father's wishes: "It is impossible to express what I feel at quitting my beloved father and mine own dear family. It was long before I could take the resolution & my health suffered so much from the conflict, I doubt whether I shall ever recover it."[10]

Less than two weeks later Franklin wrote with information of Pennsylvania, but he qualified his ability to give any advice: "Not knowing [Mr Hare's] character and disposition it is impossible for me to advise well, or to judge whether sitting down quietly in some cheap part of Europe, and living prudently in two-thirds of your income, may not be preferable to any scheme in America."[11] It was this advice which Georgiana and her husband were to follow, however reluctantly. Weary of Germany, they moved south to Vicenza in Italy. But their experiences in that town confirmed them in their desire to emigrate to America. Writing in August of 1785 Georgiana showered Franklin with another barrage of questions, and complained that "in any foreign country the most we can hope is to live on the little we already possess, paying high for houserent and cheated & imposed upon by all the natives. We are equally weary of this vagabond kind of life & wish somewhere to be permanently settled."[12] Despite their disenchantment with Italy, years passed before they left it.

During the Hares' residence at Vicenza, on 6 January 1786, a son was born. Francis George was baptized in June with his Godmother, the Duchess of Devonshire, in attendance. In 1792 the Hares moved to Rome, where, on 17 November, a second son, Augustus William, was born. He was named for his Royal Godfather, Prince Augustus Frederick, Duke of Sussex, and his uncle, Sir William Jones. In 1795 the family moved to Bologna, but Georgiana retired to the cool

ORIGINS AND EARLY YEARS 9

valley of Valdagno near Vicenza for the birth of her third child, Julius Charles, on 13 September of that year. A fourth son, Marcus Theodore, was born on 9 November 1796, completing that quartet whom Walter Savage Landor later called "the most brotherly of brothers."

Georgiana spent her years in Italy sketching and painting. The intellectual society of Italy's cities suited her. She also took in hand the education of her eldest son. In this she was assisted by two friends made in Bologna. Father Emmanuele Aponte, S.J., was a distinguished classicist who lived in exile in Bologna after his order was expelled from his native Spain. With Aponte lived his niece, Clotilda Tambroni, a well-known scholar who held the chair of Greek in the University of Bologna. Georgiana taught young Francis from the best authors in Italian, Spanish, and French as well as the classical tongues. By the age of four he spoke these languages fluently, and was soon able to read them with ease.[13]

In 1791 the Hares made a lengthy visit to England, about which little is known except that young Francis, while at school, met and befriended young "Harry" Temple, later Lord Palmerston. Bishop Shipley had died in 1788, but Georgiana was reunited with her mother and sisters. Hare's father and stepmother were unrelenting and refused to see him. It was probably lack of money which drove the Hares back to Bologna the following year. Again in Italy they enjoyed the friendship of the artist John Flaxman (1755–1826) and his wife. Flaxman painted portraits of the Hare family, and gave Georgiana help with her own compositions. It was she who commissioned Flaxman's famous line drawings in illustration of scenes from the *Iliad* and the *Odyssey* which won him his greatest renown.[14]

Upon Julius' birth Georgiana wrote to Lady Jones, her recently widowed sister, "My third boy is at present the beauty of the whole family—fine dark eyes and a lovely skin. On Monday we are to have the christening, and a great dinner afterwards. The Duchess of Brissac holds the child, and is to be the only sponsor, for they will not admit of Protestants standing even by proxy, and she is the only Catholic I ever saw whom I could wish to answer for a child of mine. She gives him the name of Julius."[15]

The war in the north appeared to confirm the wisdom of remaining in Italy, as Francis Hare wrote to the Flaxmans in England:

"You . . . are very good to wish us in England; but remember we are now in a country where wheat flour is not yet become an article of luxury; & where a man may powder his hair without a license from government, & what will appear more extraordinary to you Britons, find powder to do it with. Seriously the accounts we receive from all quarters are such that we find no great temptations to return till things are more quiet, & provisions more reasonable. Peace, I still flatter myself, may produce all this, and therefore to the reestablishment of peace are all my wishes turned."[16]

But Italy was not spared the horrors of war, as the military struggle between France and Austria drew armies into the political vacuum of the peninsula. Recovering after the birth of Marcus, her fourth son, Georgiana reported on events to the Flaxmans:

> Flaxman, who like me, is a true friend of liberty & is interested for the real good of mankind—would with pleasure have contemplated the effects and changes produced by the arrival of the French in Italy, & the energy which the Italian character has acquired in eight short months: those men, who were mere automatons under the ecclesiastical government, & never presumed to decide, unless on the merit of a singer, now read Locke & Sidney, and form laws and governments for the benefit of their fellow citizens. . . . Bonaparte is at this moment far advanced on the road towards Rome . . . and the inhabitants everywhere received the republican army with transports of joy, as their protectors and deliverers.

In view of Georgiana's freely expressed republican sentiments, it was safer for her to have been in Italy than in England. She assured the Flaxmans that all their friends in Rome would be perfectly safe, having nothing to fear from Bonaparte, whom she praised extravagantly. Georgiana also described the state of her own family: "My husband grows fat & is always well & in cheerful spirits. My *4* boys are the admiration of all Bologna. . . . The last born . . . I thought deserved a republican name & therefore called him *Marcus* a name so illustrious in ancient Rome. . . . Our family becomes too large to admit of frequent removals, & the calamities of Europe render the man wise, who remains where he can be secure—all these considerations influence us to continue here."[17] But despite the apparent wisdom of remaining in Italy, the Hares soon left for England.

ORIGINS AND EARLY YEARS

In that same year, 1797, Francis Hare's father died, and it was discovered that his stepmother had mistakenly erected Hurstmonceux Place upon entailed land to which he was heir. When news of this reached Italy, Georgiana and her husband resolved to go at once to England to claim their long-awaited inheritance. Young Francis was left in the care of Father Aponte and Clotilda Tambroni. Little Julius and Marcus were entrusted to Betta, an Italian nurse, under the supervision of Father Aponte and the Marescotti family of Bologna. Augustus, then nearly five years old, travelled to England with his parents. His aunt, Lady Jones, offered to provide for the boy's education, and later undertook to adopt him.

The overland journey to England, through Italy, Switzerland, and France, exposed the Hares to the ravages of war. Through it all their republicanism and loyalty to the revolution was unshaken. In charming letters to young Francis, Georgiana described their journey. In the town of Schweitz, at the Wilhelm Tell's *Kapel,* little Augustus kissed the ground where the Swiss hero resisted "tyranny and injustice." From Saarlibre Georgiana wrote: "I never saw your papa better pleased than when we quitted the Austrian lines, and entered the French, and now everything goes well, and he is as happy as possible . . . confessing with me, how much the liberty of thinking improves the human mind, and how much superior is the republican to the automatons we have parted from."[18]

The Hares reached England in October 1797, and were appalled to see the extent to which Mrs Henrietta Hare had ruined Herstmonceux Castle. However, they were greatly pleased by Hurstmonceux Place. With the estate came the additional name "Naylor," which the Hares were obliged to adopt. After paying their respects to friends in London, the Hare-Naylors joined Lady Jones at Bath. There they passed the winter, and, as Georgiana wrote to Francis in Bologna, they enjoyed the company of such people as Pasquale Paoli (1725–1807), the exiled Corsican rebel. The Hare-Naylors' outspoken republicanism may have won them the friendship of Paoli, but Lady Jones feared it would cost them public respectability.[19]

While they were at Bath the Hare-Naylors received regular reports from Bologna in the letters of Francis and Father Aponte. In September 1797 the priest wrote to say that the younger boys missed their parents, but had formed a strong attachment to himself and his niece: "Julius consantly repeated, 'Mama is away, papa is away, but Nono [grandfather, *i.e.* Father Aponte] is at home . . .' As soon as he catches sight of me he runs towards me quite breathless with joy."[20] A month later Clotilda Tambroni confirmed that "the Nono is entirely devoted to Julius, who caresses him even more than he does me."[21] Somewhat later Father Aponte wrote that "Julius interests me most of all, because of his especial devotion to me, for he never sees me without shouting out, 'Nono, Nono,' and he looks at his father's picture, and kisses his tiny hand, calling out, 'Papa, papa.' Then he asks for his letters, and picking out the M, says mama; the P, papa; the N, Nono; the B, Beta; the C, Tilda. Oh! What a beautiful lovable little being he is!"[22] Julius' precocity had already been reported by Francis, who observed that "Jule knows very well all the letters," and "Jule loves especially Dom Emmanuel. . . . Jule is very fond of me. . . . Jule shows great wish to learning, for yesterday, when we went to the library of the college, he did nothing else but want to carry away some of the books."[23] It was prophetic behaviour in one who was in later life known as a bibliomaniac.

But the peace in Bologna did not last long. Following the French conquest Bologna was incorporated into the so-called Cisalpine Republic in 1796, and in the following year as part of the Dipartimento del Reno. At that time Dom Emmanuele Aponte and Clotilda Tambroni were deprived of their university posts and threatened with deportation for refusing to subscribe to a loyalty oath. The revolutionary slogans with which young Francis insisted upon embellishing his letters to his parents only compounded the troubles of his protectors. Father Aponte wrote to Georgiana explaining that these slogans caused letters to be intercepted by the authorities. He acknowledged receipt of £25 but explained that since the loss of their positions they were so penurious that this sum would in no way enable them to repay the debts they had contracted. A week later he wrote again to urge the Hare-Naylors to return to Italy as soon as possible, for all aliens in the Republic as well as those in the neighbouring Romagna were soon to be expelled. Despite these difficulties Aponte tried to be reassuring about the health of his three small charges, saying that Julius and Marcus "become daily more beautiful, more lovable, and more winning."[24]

The Hare-Naylors were already on their way to Italy by the time this last letter reached England, for they arrived at Bologna in June, and reclaimed their sons before the threatened deportation. The Hare-Naylors took their children to live in Padua, where young Francis was tutored by professors of the university. Father Aponte and his niece regularly corresponded with the family. In later life Julius often referred to Italy as his "beloved third native country," the second being Germany.[25]

Although the Hare-Naylors were anxious to return to England, Georgiana's ill health kept them in Italy until the spring of 1799. In a letter to Lady Jones, Georgiana despaired of ever seeing Herstmonceux again, but promised that they would soon depart for home.[26] Georgiana's anxiety about the return to England was at least in part due to the fact that she was once again pregnant. Back in England the family visited Georgiana's widowed mother at Bath. At Hurstmonceux Place on 9 October 1799 Georgiana gave birth to a daughter, Anna-Maria Clementina. After years of wandering and living abroad, the Hare-Naylor family finally settled upon their Sussex estate. This was the most settled, and perhaps the happiest, period which they ever knew. It lasted less than five years.

At Hurstmonceux Place the Hare-Naylors enjoyed the company of Lady Jones, who came each summer with Augustus for a long visit. Their friends Mr and Mrs William Wilberforce and Hannah More also paid them visits. Hare was attracted to Wilberforce out of sympathy for the anti-slavery campaign, and perhaps also because of mutual sentiments of Evangelical piety. Indeed, Georgiana wrote to Lady Jones complaining of the excessive religious sentiment in one of Hannah More's books, and concluded: "We are by nature such lovers of variety, that even goodness and religion should be recommended under various forms in order not to clog. As for me, my religion is as simple as my politics, and as I think the best government that where people are most virtuous and most happy, so in religion, I think the simple study of the Scriptures with the moral duties they teach and the rewards they promise, far more calculated to inspire true piety and cheerful dependence on God's providence, than an inquiry into all those obscure systems of faith, grace, and original sin, on which saints and theologians have written *sine fine*."[27] Like his mother, Julius Hare sought toleration for a variety of religious views, but his approach to the Scriptures was far more sophisticated.

At Hurstmonceux Place Mr Hare-Naylor bent to the literary labours which had occupied him for several years. These included the writing of two plays, *The Mirror* and *The Age of Chivalry*. Hare-Naylor hoped to see his works produced at Drury Lane, and to gain same cash profit. In this he was disappointed. He also completed a lengthy *History of the Helvetic Republic*. He and his wife both found their republican views vindicated in the Swiss Republic. Unfortunately this work proved to be an even greater financial disappointment than the two dramas.

The failure to turn a profit by literary means was of some importance, for the Hare-Naylors were finding their resources insufficient to maintain the somewhat run-down estate they had inherited. Hurstmonceux Place came to them entirely without furnishings, for Mrs Henrietta Hare had taken care to remove everything not physically attached to the entailed land. Despite the frequent receipt of direct and indirect financial assistance from Lady Jones, the Hare-Naylors found it necessary to dispose of the paintings which they had acquired in Italy.[28]

Although Georgiana continued her study of Greek authors and did many works of charity among the villagers of Herstmonceux, she also undertook a large-scale watercolour project. She wished to execute for her children a series of watercolours of all aspects of Herstmonceux Castle, interiors and exteriors, as it was before the partial demolition. She laboured over them so long and so hard that the result, according to her grandson A.J.C. Hare, was nearly total blindness within two years. Indeed, her strenuous labours may well have been the occasion for her blindness. Its cause was more likely hereditary, however, for her mother had lost her sight only a few years earlier. At that time Georgiana had written to Lady Jones, "I have often said, that the privation of light is the only misfortune perhaps to which our nature is liable, which I believe I should never bear with fortitude or patience; here reason, I fear, would lose her influence."[29] But when Georgiana was overtaken by the blindness which she so dreaded, she bore it with all her usual fortitude and patience. However, she keenly felt the absence of her sons from the family household.

Young Francis had been tutored by a German, Dr. Lehmann, and made good progress. But in 1802 Lehmann returned to Germany to accept a professorship in the University of Göttingen. For

ORIGINS AND EARLY YEARS 15

a time the Hare-Naylors considered sending Francis there as a student. But instead he was enrolled in August 1802 at Marischal College in Aberdeen, where he spent the next two years. Lady Jones sent Augustus to board at Mr Stretch's school in Twyford. In January 1804 Julius and Marcus were enrolled at Tonbridge School, under headmaster Dr Vicesimus Knox the younger. Thirty-nine years later it was Julius Hare's lot as Archdeacon of Lewes to fill the vacant headmastership of this school. At that time he recalled his own brief stay there: "The school, the first I went to, & where I stayed some two months, used in those days . . . to be as bad as bad can well be. You have probably heard me say that the sum of the lessons which I had to say in those two months was *ego, mei, mihi, me, me*. Yet I have a pleasant recollection of the place as it was there I first read Don Quixote."[30] Julius fell ill shortly after his arrival at school, and his mother used the occasion as an excuse to bring him home. It was thought that his symptoms were consumptive, but probably Georgiana was merely eager to have one of her sons by her side.

Georgiana's health was now rapidly deteriorating. It was decided that she must move to the continent. In August 1804 Mr and Mrs Hare-Naylor, accompanied by Julius, Anna-Maria, and John Flaxman's sister Mary, set out for Weimar by way of Vienna. They spent the winter of 1804–05 at Weimar, where Mr Hare-Naylor wrote a novel entitled *Theodore; or, The Enthusiast*, for which Flaxman later drew illustrations. Hare-Naylor dedicated the work to the Duchess of Saxe-Weimar, at whose court he spent a great deal of time. Despite her blindness Georgiana found herself at the centre of the intellectual life of Weimar, where the most famous residents were Goethe and Schiller. Henry Crabb Robinson (1775–1867), who then lived in Weimar, recalled many years later: "There came to live at Weimar Mr and Mrs Hare-Naylor, whom I found a very valuable addition to my circle of acquaintances."[31]

It was at Weimar that Julius Hare began to learn German. Georgiana remarked in a letter to Lady Jones "Julius has learned a great deal of German, but is too shy to speak."[32] In the following summer, 1805, Georgiana's health grew worse, so young Francis was summoned from England to join his family. Francis was very much attached to his brother Julius, and undertook entire responsibility for his education. Julius always remembered with affection the lessons with his older brother. Upon Francis' death in 1842 Julius wrote to his sister-in-law, "He was the loving teacher of my boyhood, the kind, generous, unvarying friend and benefactor of my whole life."[33] Francis instructed Julius in literature and introduced him to Greek. Since Francis' German was by all accounts quite good, he probably tutored Julius in that as well.[34] Julius Hare's pupil and brother-in-law, Frederick Denison Maurice (1805-72), felt that the advantage of these youthful studies was that Hare "learned from these foreign teachers the intrinsic worth of the national treasures which so many of us value only for some extrinsic peculiarities, or for the food that they supply to our vanity. He learnt to prize the bequests of the old world as helps in understanding the changes of the times, and in apprehending that which does not change and is not of time; so escaping from the pedantry and frivolity of the merely antiquarian or dilettante scholar."[35] Throughout Hare's life his reading and scholarship drew upon his continental experience, giving his work a foreign dimension which offended many critics.

Shortly after the Hare-Naylor family arrived at Weimar, John Flaxman wrote to announce the publication of his illustrated edition of Homer and to inquire after their health. It was some time before Georgiana could manage to write a reply. "As to our future plans, I can only tell you, we are *in pursuit of health.* . . . all hopes of peace seems [sic] to be at an end, & therefore France or Italy will not suit us, and a warm climate must be sought. Mr H[are] has been just now talking of the *Crimea, Hungary,* or *Madeira.* Now be it known to you, *I will not go to either* [sic]. If I do, we shall never see you more."[36] Georgiana decided in the summer of 1805 that she wished to return to Switzerland, the land of civil and religious liberty which she so idealized. Painfully the family made their way to Lausanne by way of Brückenau. After leaving Weimar they passed near the Wartburg. While visiting the scene of Luther's imprisonment Julius Hare claimed in later years to have "first learnt to throw inkstands at the devil."[37]

In Lausanne, Georgiana's condition worsened steadily. On Easter Sunday, 6 April 1806, she died. Her bereaved husband could not face returning to live at Herstmonceux, which only reminded him of Georgiana. According to his grandson, A.J.C. Hare, "His debts were numerous and his children many, and in the following year

ORIGINS AND EARLY YEARS

he sold the estate of his ancestors."[38] If this act began to alienate Hare-Naylor from his children, the real rift occurred in 1807 when he took a second wife, Anna Maria Mealey (d. 1849), a widow, by whom he had three more children.[39] Thereafter the Hare children looked to Lady Jones and their other Shipley relatives for advice and support. In accord with Georgiana's dying wish Lady Jones took charge of all of the children. Augustus she continued to raise entirely at her own expense. She raised Anna-Maria as her daughter until the girl's early death in March 1813. She also became a second mother to Francis, Julius, and Marcus, and the chief influence in their lives.[40]

According to A.J.C. Hare, Lady Jones was a forbidding person:

> Unlike their own mother, of whose gentle loving-kindness her four sons retained an equal recollection, Lady Jones chiefly showed her affection for her nephews by the severity with which she corrected their faults, while for herself she exacted respect rather than love, and had no sympathy with any demonstration of affection. Her nephews, though devoted to her from motives of gratitude, never ventured to be familiar with her, and Augustus especially suffered in after life from the want of mutual confidence which was thus engendered. In society Lady Jones could be exceedingly pleasant and agreeable. . . . She was very quick in her movements, oldfashioned and peculiar in dress, short in person, and she had sharp piercing eyes.[41]

Her nephews remained closely attached to her until her death in 1829 at the age of eighty-one. This was particularly true of Julius, who remained a bachelor longer than any of his brothers. He nearly always spent part of his summers at Lady Jones' country house at Worting, near Basingstoke, Hants. When he visited London, he usually stayed at her Mayfair townhouse, 73 South Audley Street.[42]

Although it would be hard to over-estimate Julius' attachment to Lady Jones, he was unwilling to accept her judgement in all things; for example, he would not defer to her dislike of things German. When he published his translation of *Sintram and His Companions* in 1820, his aunt was repulsed by La Motte Fouqué's macabre, gothic tale, and said that she wished to see all of Julius' German books burned. He replied "that his patriotism and his faith were in danger, from the materialism which in England was claiming every domain of thought and even of religion itself . . . and that the Germans . . . had at least preserved his intellect, and in some degree his conscience, from this infection."[43] In a characteristicly blunt letter of January 1820, Hare restated this position:

> As for my German books, I hope from my heart that the day will never arrive when I shall be induced to burn them, for I am convinced that I never shall do so, unless I have first become a base slave of Mammon, and a mere vile lump of selfishness. I shall never be able to repay a hundredth of the obligation I am under to them. . . . For to them I owe the best of all my knowledge, and if they have not purified my heart, the fault is my own. Above all, to them I owe my ability to believe in Christianity with a much more implicit and intelligent faith than I otherwise should have been able to have done; for without them I should only have saved myself from dreary suspicions, by a refusal to allow my heart to follow my head, and by a self-willed determination to believe whether my reason approved of my belief or not.

In this rebuke to his aunt one sees the Julius Hare who "never loved or hated by halves,"[44] and who became widely known for his forthrightness in speaking out whether to praise or condemn. One also sees the great intellectual influence of Hare's continental education.

The Hare brothers, as members of a privileged class, were provided with the best formal education available. Young Francis went up to Christ Church at Oxford, but failed to distinguish himself. In truth, he was so well educated and ill disciplined that he held the university and his fellow undergraduates in mild contempt, and gave himself up to hunting and other amusements. Yet he impressed most people with his intelligence and erudition, and Dean Jackson used to say of him that "he was the only rolling stone he knew that ever gathered any moss."[45] This assessment was confirmed by his cousin, Mrs Anna Maria Dashwood, who wrote that "Francis leads a rambling life of pleasure and idleness . . . he *must* have read— but who can tell at what time? for wherever there is dissipation, there is Francis in its wake, and its most ardent pursuer; yet in spite of this, let any subject be named in society, and Francis will know more of it than nineteen out of its twenty."[46] Francis led this existence in London for several years, and then moved to the con-

ORIGINS AND EARLY YEARS 19

tinent, where he recreated the wandering life that he had known as a child.

Augustus was also of an indolent temperament, and although he later did well at New College, Oxford, his performance at Westminster School under Dr Goddard was far from impressive. Julius, on the other hand, possessed the discipline as well as the talent necessary for outstanding academic achievement. Much less is known about Marcus Hare, though he appears not to have inherited his parents' intellectual powers. His mother had written of him, half apologetically, to Mrs Flaxman, "I am not at all uneasy about Marcus, I think I have already more learning and genius IN MY OWN FAMILY! than is fairly their portion, & Marcus has qualities of the heart & temper that perhaps may carry him through the world, better than Greek & Latin."[47] Marcus went to sea, where he pursued a successful career as a naval officer until his death in 1845.

In 1806 Julius Hare was sent to the Charterhouse school, where he spent the next six years. In those days it was located in an old Carthusian monastery in the heart of London, not far from Newgate Prison. Despite its urban location, its monastic architecture gave it a unique charm.[48] Some of Hare's longest-lived friendships were formed with Charterhouse contemporaries. The most famous Carthusian of that day was doubtless Sir Henry Havelock (1795–1857), the great Indian Army general. In his later years Havelock wrote of his Carthusian days, "My most intimate friends were Samuel Hinds, William Norris, and Julius Charles Hare."[49] Hinds was a poet and the heir to a Barbados plantation. Julius Hare travelled with Hinds on the continent in 1819, and later assisted him in publishing his poems. Sir William Norris pursued a successful career as a colonial administrator. Among the younger students at the Charterhouse was Connop Thirlwall (1797–1875), later Bishop of Saint David's. Thirlwall and Hare became lifelong friends. As Thirlwall's biographer noted, "Julius Hare was the ideal companion—friend, literary guide and counsellor rolled into one. Gifted with a superior, if unoriginal mind, which turned instinctively to the best in modern thought, he soon directed Thirlwall to the literature of modern Germany."[50]

The headmaster of the Charterhouse was Dr Matthew Raine (1760–1811), a capable Yorkshireman, who exercised great influence over his pupils, and unfailingly commanded their respect. As one of them noted after his death, he was "a man to be praised as often as he is named, and who was only permitted to die unmitred because his political principles were too liberal to suit the taste of the reigning faction of the day."[51] Raine was a staunch Whig and a gifted scholar.

Havelock's biographer wrote that Havelock "regarded the tuition and associations of the Charter House as having contributed essentially to the formation of his character as a man." Havelock, Hare, and their friends frequently discussed such matters as religion and politics, and they were not lacking in scholarly achievement: "In April [1811] [Havelock] was the fourth in the fifth form; 'of which,' he remarked, 'Walpole, a grandson of Sir Robert, was first; Hare second; John Pindar third; and Havelock fourth. It consisted of some thirty boys, and lower down in it were Connop Thirlwall and Hinds.' "[52]

The curriculum in Hare's day consisted of the same classical studies which prevailed in other public schools, as well as writing and arithmetic.[53] George Grote's biographer, M.L. Clarke, claims that the curriculum under Dr Raine was almost entirely classics, and rather narrowly centred upon Virgil, Homer, and Horace. But here Clarke merely quotes from the experience of Henry G. Liddell (1811–98) at the Charterhouse in the 1820s.[54] In a much earlier book M.L. Clarke cites the praise with which Samuel Parr lauded the school's "solid Greek learning," though here it must be noted that Parr, as a close friend of the headmaster, was not an objective or unbiased observer.[55] This was a period of change for the school. From about 1802 teaching was no longer conducted solely in the great hall, all students sitting in a single classroom. The great expansion of enrolment came a decade or more later, but already by Hare's time the Charterhouse had replaced Westminster as the leading school in London.[56]

The enrolment reflected all levels of society, but children of the commercial middle class and of the landed gentry predominated.[57] The phenomenon of the school peer group and pecking order have been the objects of comment and study at least since the appearance of *Tom Brown's School Days*, the first public school novel, in 1857. Many memoirs reveal the brutalizing and humiliating circumstances under which pupils in the public schools were forced to live

ORIGINS AND EARLY YEARS 21

during the years when they reached their physical, emotional, and intellectual maturity. Only a few years after leaving the Charterhouse, Julius Hare wrote his own cynical observations:

> Public schools destroy that solitude which is almost indispensible for the formation of a great mind. The boy is cast among many others of his own age, whom it is his business and duty to surpass, and he is taught to regard merit, not as positive, but as comparative. His object is to become first in his class, even more than to gain his master's approbation; or at least the latter is regarded as almost synonymous with the former. Hence does he acquire a pernicious spirit of emulation, or rivalry, and of contention.— They also encourage, if they do not produce, selfishness. . . . Now it is quite early enough to be initiated into selfishness, when we are thrown upon the world.—But this is called a necessary preparation for active life, and it is said that without it a young man will enter into competition with those who possess far superior advantages. Now even granting this . . . still that preparation which is injurious to the moral character can never be desirable: and crowds, whether of boys or men, as they produce unwholesome vapours, in the same manner do they generate vices. . . . Again it is urged that a boy ought to be acquainted with vice, in order that he may avoid it; that is he ought to ruin his moral character, or at least his moral delicacy, in order that he may save it. A youth should know nothing of evil, except that it is the opposite of good.[58]

These remarks reveal personal bitterness, and it is tempting to infer secrets of adolescent sexuality in addition to the demoralizing effects of an atmosphere of bullying and violence. However, corroborating evidence is scant. Hare wrote no lengthy or candid account of his Charterhouse days.

In 1811, when Hare and Havelock were in the sixth form, Dr Raine died. His young successor, Dr John Russell, was a man of far different character. He changed many of the rules, and introduced the "monitorial" system of instruction in order to expand the enrolment without hiring more teachers. This accounts for the decline in teaching standards that Liddell and Thackeray described in the 1820s. Russell also changed the congenial character of the school. For his fondness of the birch he has been compared with "Flogging Keate" of Eton and Dr Busby of Westminster.[59] Thackeray satirized Russell as "The Doctor," Headmaster of Grey Friars School, in *Pendennis*. Raine had been ready enough to use the birch when the situation called for it, but evidence suggests that the penitents bore no resentment, even if they could not always feel the punishment richly deserved.[60] Havelock, whose seriousness as a student earned him the nickname "Philos" (Philosopher), was so disturbed by Russell that he at length persuaded his father to remove him from the school. Hare remained only through the end of the next term, and, after six years, may well have left with some reluctance, despite Dr Russell.[61]

Chapter 2

Trinity College, Cambridge

At Michaelmas 1812 Julius Hare was matriculated as a pensioner at Trinity College, Cambridge.[1] His father wrote to Augustus: "I have been to settle Julius at Cambridge, which I have done in a very comfortable lodging. When we were introduced to Mr Monk, the Greek Professor, he told Julius that he had lately had so high a character of him from Mr Russell, that he was happy to make his acquaintance. . . . his tutor . . . assures me that he may live very well upon £160 a year." Then, probably thinking of the abortive career of his eldest son at Oxford, or of his own youth, he added, "His business is to study, not to give wine-parties, and he is perfectly aware, that if he runs in debt, he will be immediately taken from Cambridge. If he gets any scholarships, their emoluments will add to his income, and it will be entirely his own fault if he does not get them."[2] His father need not have entertained such fears, for Julius Hare was already an earnest and upright young man.

Hare entered Cambridge at a significant point in its intellectual history, for it was the beginning of what one writer has termed "the nineteenth-century renaissance," and was marked by the appearance of an "intellectual network" of scientists and humanists, who represented an upper-middle-class "intellectual aristocracy." This elite came to dominate the universities, the Church, and the government of the Victorian period.[3] At Cambridge these men raised the level of scholarship in the traditional curriculum, added new realms of knowledge to the existing academic system, reformed the University root and branch, and exerted a profound influence over several generations of undergraduates. Because Julius Hare was a member of this intellectual network, it is appropriate to introduce the other members.

Hare and his Charterhouse friend George Waddington (1793–1869), later Dean of Durham, entered Trinity College at the same time. Their friend and classmate Connop Thirlwall followed two years later. At Trinity they found a new and valuable friend in William Whewell (1794–1866), the son of a Lancashire master carpenter, who had just arrived as a subsizar. Whewell became one of the prime movers of nineteenth-century science and a great power in the University. A man of diverse parts, ranging beyond science, Whewell was a personal link or liaison between the scientific and humanistic "nodes" of the so-called Cambridge intellectual network.[4]

Richard Sheepshanks (1794–1855) was another new friend who entered Cambridge at this time. He distinguished himself as an astronomer and as one of the founders of the Cambridge observatory. The great mathematician Charles Babbage (1792–1871), inventor of the digital calculator, had matriculated at Trinity College the previous year. George Peacock (1791–1858), later Dean of Ely, took his degree in 1813, but remained as college Tutor and Lecturer in mathematics for a quarter of a century. Through Peacock Hare met J.F.W. Herschel (1792–1871) and J.S. Henslow (1796–1861), who conferred scientific glory upon the neighbouring college, Saint John's. Herschel was a great astronomer and Henslow served as Professor of Mineralogy (1822–27) and of Botany (1827–61), in which capacity he was Charles Darwin's friend and mentor.[5]

In addition to the scientists there were those with other talents. Richard Torin Kindersley (1792–1879), later an eminent jurist, was within the network of friends. So, too, was Henry Venn Elliott (1792–1865), whom Julius Hare came to know more intimately in later life. Among men who matriculated in subsequent terms, Hare was well acquainted with the following: Hugh James Rose (1795–1838), a High Churchman and later a founder of the Oxford Tractarian movement; Thomas Thorp (1797–1877), who served Trinity College as Tutor, Dean, and later as Vice-Master; Thomas Worsley (1797–1885), who migrated to the embryonic foundation at Downing College, and who served as that college's Master for half a century; William Sidney Walker (1795–1846), classicist, poet, and Shakespeare scholar; and Kenelm Henry Digby (1800–80), the romantic mystic and scholar whose long friendship with Hare was little affected by his early conversion to Roman Catholicism.[6]

Among the teaching Fellows of Trinity College in that day two in particular had a great influence upon Hare. The first was James Henry Monk (1784–1856), a Carthusian like Hare, who at the age of twenty-five succeeded Richard Porson in the Regius Professorship of Greek, a post he held from 1809 until 1823. The other was Adam Sedgwick (1785–1873), whose whole career centred at Trinity College after his arrival in 1804. Elected to the Woodwardian Professorship of Geology in 1818, he rose to eminence as a pioneer geologist. Sedgwick was a permanent college fixture. "No dinner party was complete without 'old Sedge' . . . to brighten it up, and help keep everybody in good humour with what Julius Hare called 'the sunshine of his warm heart and of his [unquenchable laughter].' "[7]

From Whewell's letters home during the academic year 1812–13 emerges a picture of what he, Hare, and the other first year men were doing: "We attend lectures on algebra, Euclid, and trigonometry from nine o'clock till ten, and from ten to eleven we are lectured in an oration of Demosthenes. From twelve to one I attend lectures in divinity in three days in the week."[8] In addition to formal lectures and tutorials the serious undergraduates spent much time reading works prescribed, recommended, or independently chosen. An extensive commonplace book in manuscript compiled by Julius Hare has survived. From it much can be learned of his reading and intellectual development.

Julius Hare recorded in his commonplace book lengthy quotations from authors whom he was reading, numerous aphorisms both borrowed and original, some of which later found their way into his book *Guesses at Truth,* and original works of verse, sermons, and oratory. More than thirty writers are quoted or cited in the commonplace book, ancients such as Homer, Plato, and Aristotle, Germans like Goethe, Kant, and Lessing, and Italians like Tasso. The English writers represented range from Shakespeare, Milton, and Spenser to Hare's contemporary favourites, Wordsworth and Coleridge. Bacon, Hobbes, Shaftesbury, and Hume are mentioned primarily as the objects of scorn, but somewhat more sympathy is shown toward Samuel Johnson, Conyers Middleton, and Bishop

Warburton. Hare was also well read in the divines, from the eminent Hooker, Barrow, Jeremy Taylor, and Burnet, to lesser figures such as Cudworth, Reid, Oswald, and South.

Hare even then aspired to a literary career; his opinion of the many mediocre modern writers was acerbic:

> Homer and Shakespeare must ever reign, wherever they are understood. Our code should indeed be as liberal as possible; but the republic of letters should not be exposed to anarchy. We daily see persons, who, fascinated by the gaudiness of some new pretender, quit the good old faith of their fathers, to adopt the heresies, and worship at the shrine of their favourite idol. Scarcely a week passes, which does not usher into the world some upstart Milton with his quarto under his arm, defying all competition, and ready for combat. . . . To adjudge to these various compositions their respective portions of shame, human life would scarce suffice, even had man no more important occupation, than to decide upon the merits of a coxcomb's verses.

Ironically, this diatribe reminds one of Hare's devotion to Wordsworth and Coleridge. Of the former he wrote: "My devotion to Wordsworth is not to be irritated by the flea-bite of a Scotch Philosopher, and it is hardly worth the trouble to level the inequalities which all the blind moles in Edinburgh can raise upon the earth of his glory." Thus, with contemptuous ease Hare dismissed the *Edinburgh Review* for its failure to discern Wordsworth's poetic genius. At another point Hare compared his hero with Lord Byron, and exclaimed: "To take up Byron after Wordsworth is to exchange the empire of the world for the sovereignty of Elba."[9]

Hare took the greatest pleasure in poetry, but mathematics, like all science, he found utterly "heartless." Thus he failed to attain highest honours as an undergraduate. Indeed, he was clearly rationalizing when he wrote that "mathematics are subject to all such difficulties, as must necessarily arise in every train of reasoning in which the means are sacrificed to the end. The mind starting from a known point wanders . . . through a dark and subterraneous passage, and at last emerges into daylight, ignorant how it arrived, conscious that some connection must exist from the fact of its having traced the intervening space. In poetry on the other hand every step is clear, conviction is immediate and complete."[10]

Theological speculations occupy a small but important part of Hare's commonplace book. Hare held an entirely orthodox Protestant view of justification, in which the curse of original sin was mitigated merely by faith in the atonement of Christ. In later years the nature of the punishment prescribed for sinners was a source of great concern to Hare and to other Broad Churchmen. Even this early Hare was convinced that divine punishment must be just, and so he rejected the doctrine of extreme Calvinism: "Horrible enough of itself is the opinion, held by many Calvinists, that God can irrevocably design the innocent to become the inheritors of eternal misery: but even this horror shrinks into insignificance before the notion that he has doomed them to deserve this punishment by sin."[11]

For Hare, God's purposes might be left unanswered, with the confidence that they, like the as-yet-unseen light from a distant star, would eventually become clear to man. Hare, quoting Kant, urged that while it is necessary that one should believe in the existence of God, it does not follow that one must also demonstrate it. To the deficiencies of all arguments for God's existence Hare wrote a defence based on intuition in which he revealed the unsettled state of his own religious belief:

> There is scarcely one English peasant . . . who does not possess a full assurance . . . that there *is* a God. . . . There is scarcely a half-reasoning, all-believing child who does not possess this assurance. *Well do I remember the days when this was my all; and often have I deplored the loss of that childish confidence, and yearned with a painful desire to cast away all the uncertainties of half-knowledge against which my soul is at present struggling, and return from my successless wanderings to that island of the blessed. But it cannot be:—it must not be. Even if it were possible to forget our knowledge, it would be our duty to increase it.*[12]

This dedication to the truth revealed by scholarship, combined with a confidence that religious truth was not inconsistent with reason, characterized Hare's liberal position within the Church. In Hare's day university men were exposed to all manner of religious influences, from free-thought to the piety of the Evangelicals. The spirituality of many Cambridge men was summed up in Lord

Loughborough's remark about subscription to the Thirty-Nine Articles: "It isn't supposed that you believe them, it is only a pledge that you don't hold to any other of the world's superstitions."[13] Those like Hare, alert to the secularist thought of the age and to the new approaches to scholarship being practised on the continent, found their hitherto unquestioned faith challenged, if not shaken. We have Hare's own testimony that the quest for knowledge rendered impossible the simple, childlike faith that is painless because it is never questioned. Such stirrings of doubt prompted Hare and so many of his friends to show great reluctance in taking holy orders to keep their college fellowships.

Hare's commonplace book reveals his intellectual development during his Cambridge years, but there is a dearth of evidence about his social and extracurricular activity as an undergraduate. He appears to have been a member of the Cambridge Union Society, but it is impossible to say how active a member. A speech "On the Question of the Propriety of the War against France," which he prepared for a meeting of the Union in February 1816, has survived. The war in question was the Waterloo Campaign which brought Napoleon's Hundred Days to a close. Hare condemned the campaign for distracting attention from the iniquities of the first peace treaty concluded at the Congress of Vienna. He argued that "the sovereigns of Europe . . . might have otherwise been subjected to a scrutiny which it would have been neither easy nor pleasant to have undergone. . . . It might have been urged . . . 'We have overthrown oppression abroad, and we will not be oppressed at home.' " For Hare, England's role in the restoration of liberty was clear: "In the days of that moral deluge . . . England alone preserved his virtues, as in an ark. For during all this age of universal calamity England has always been free, and safe, and pious and happy. She has stood forth, amidst the perils of the world with almost the immunity of a blessed spirit."[14]

But England's moral rectitude had been compromised by the iniquities of the peace and by the late campaign against the French. Hare asked, "Are we then, sir, to leap headlong from this sublime elevation . . . ? Are we to degrade this Justice by injury, and to desecrate this High-mindedness by oppression? Are we to tyrannize, because France is weak . . . ?" In answer to these rhetorical questions he concluded with a condemnation of the architect of England's moral and diplomatic turnabout, the "tutelary genius of regenerated Europe, . . . this God Castlereagh. . . . I will let him pursue his career of triumph amid the applauses of princes and contractors, while his chariot wheels trample over multitudes, and are dogged by the curses of Africa and of Ireland."[15] These were heady words, and it is difficult to know how much of this speech was heart-felt, and how much was for rhetorical effect. Hare's parents were both ardent republicans, whose unconcealed joy in the French Revolution was not soured by their later opposition to Napoleon. Whiggish, though not republican in his outlook, Hare viewed the French Revolution with Burkean horror, and likened Napoleon to Aaron, for with a magic rod he devoured Europe, and changed its waters to blood.[16] That Hare did not follow his parents in radical republicanism reflects the more conservative influence of his aunt, Lady Jones, whom he knew better than either of his parents, as well as the influences of public school and Cambridge. Moreover, from the vantage point of 1816 the French Revolution appeared in a very different light from that Hare's parents saw in 1789-90.

With oratory such as Hare's the Cambridge Union flourished in its first two years, but in 1817, as the fear of radicalism and revolution increased throughout the country, the government of Lord Liverpool took strong measures, such as the suspension of *Habeas Corpus*. The same fear ripened in the minds of Cambridge administrators when they considered the political debates of the Union. With the government disposed to see sedition everywhere, the Vice-Chancellor of the University, a "rigid and unenlightened disciplinarian," followed suit. On Monday, 24 March 1817, Dr Wood, Master of Saint John's College and University Vice-Chancellor, escorted by Esquire Bedels and Proctors, entered the Union's meeting, and demanded that the members disperse and meet no more. Whewell, the president, rose and met the intruders, saying, "Strangers will please to withdraw and the House will take the message into consideration." Wood was adamant, and Whewell failed to persuade him to allow the completion of that evening's debate. Despite a petition to the Duke of Gloucester, Chancellor of the University, and the advocacy of Henry Brougham in Parliament, the Union fell victim to the hysteria against sedition and blasphemy.[17]

The significance of the suspension of debate in 1817, and of the Union's four-year interregnum existence as a reading club, was that with the removal of this centre of activity, some Cambridge men turned to the study of the German language. Tradition holds that this resort to a hitherto exotic language was undertaken to fill the idle hours. One may properly be sceptical of the notion that undergraduates were driven to German conjugations to fight off boredom. But German did suddenly come into fashion, and its advocate was Julius Hare.

English knowledge of Germany and of German literature remained limited until the end of the eighteenth century for a number of reasons. Lack of significant trade between England and the German states, the high English tariff on imported books, and the difficulties Englishmen encountered in learning German have been cited as reasons.[18] To learn German one virtually had to go to Germany. In England and not least in the universities there had been a repugnance to things German which was linked with Toryism, and which dated from George I's accession in 1714. Ignorance, lack of interest, and prejudice reinforced each other, despite the occasional efforts of some Englishmen to promote German studies. Among these was Hare's own father, whose massive *Civil and Military History of Germany* (1816) is an encomium for things German, though it covers but the latter half of the Thirty Years' War.[19]

English popular imagination was not captured by Germany until the publication in 1813 of an English translation of Madame de Staël's *De l'Allemagne* and the author's celebrated visit to England that same year. Thereafter the best-known exponent of German literature was Thomas Carlyle (1795–1881), whose translation of Goethe's *Wilhelm Meister* had a great success in the 1820s. But Carlyle's work was preceded and paralleled by Germanists of equal stature, such as William Taylor of Norwich (1765–1836), Henry Crabb Robinson, George Soane (1790–1869), and Samuel Taylor Coleridge (1772–1834). These writers and others in the British periodical press brought German literature and thought before an ever-widening English-speaking audience. In this process the *Edinburgh Review, London Magazine,* and *Athenaeum* were particularly instrumental, and the 1820s was the decade of greatest importance.[20]

In the universities George I created the Regius Professorships of History in 1724 with the stated intention of promoting the study of modern languages. Yet a hundred years later the Fellows of Oxford were so ignorant of German that it was said that only three people in the University could read the language. One of them was Edward Bouverie Pusey (1800–82), who had gone to Germany to study theology and oriental languages.[21] Cambridge University was little better equipped. Herbert Marsh (1757–1839), Lady Margaret Professor of Divinity and later Bishop of Peterborough, had a good knowledge of German. The Prussian Marshal Blücher created a novelty upon his visit to Cambridge in 1814; after a banquet in his honour at Trinity, he addressed the gathering in German. Few besides Hare could have understood a word.[22]

When Julius Hare reached Cambridge his scholarly reputation had preceded him. He was well armed with school prizes, won in classical studies, and possessed a knowledge of German and German literature "hitherto unknown in an English undergraduate." This extraordinary knowledge was in part due to his father and oldest brother, who supplemented his school curriculum, made available their own fine libraries for his use, and resisted the censorious objections of Lady Jones. Hare's nephew noted that as an undergraduate Hare was readily befriended by his peers, who were struck as much by his precocious learning as by his ingenuous and rather emotional enthusiasm. "It was perhaps this very openness and demonstrativeness of character which rendered him so peculiarly interesting to his acquaintances, and which made it impossible for him to pass unnoticed. He was often loved, frequently detested, but never ignored."[23] Like his parents, Hare held strong opinions which he was incapable of concealing.

Hare's enthusiasm for German worked slowly but surely upon his friends. In 1818 Thirlwall wrote to an old friend that he had taken up German because "no [other] modern language will so amply repay me for my time and labour."[24] One of Thirlwall's biographers attributed his study of German to the influence of Julius Hare.[25] Another observed that the occasion to do so arose because "with the Union disbanded the only recreation left was reading. Under Hare's direction, therefore, Thirlwall, Whewell, and Hugh James Rose . . . spent the long evenings together studying German."[26] Rose later denounced German theology and biblical criticism as dangerous. Whewell for years thereafter took pleasure in translating German verse. Each was greatly influenced by his German studies.[27]

For the "reading man," as the serious student was called, the degree requirements at Cambridge were relatively modest. In 1809 George Pryme and Charles Blomfield were among the Trinity examiners, and they sought to alter the tradition of asking specific questions about names, dates, and trivial statistical details. The examinations for the B.A. in Hare's day were in two parts, the traditional oral disputation and the written examinations conducted in the Senate House. The former consisted of syllogistic interrogation conducted in Latin, an exercise which had ceased to count for anything by the year 1780, though it was not abolished until 1840. It served only to sort out the honours men from the *polloi*, who took "poll" or "pass" degrees. The written or "Tripos" examination was originally mathematical, but came to include philosophy. By 1808 it was a five-day marathon in which three days were devoted to mathematics and two days to logic, philosophy, and religion.[28]

In 1816 Hare and Whewell took their bachelor's degrees. Whewell placed second in the competition for highest honours, which was a surprise only insofar as he had been favoured to place first. Hare, though he had pursued his classical studies with unbounded energy, had been disdainful of mathematics, and this prevented him from competing for highest honours and the Chancellor's Medal.[29] Both men began soon after to prepare for the fellowship examinations. Hare divided his time between Cambridge and Lady Jones' houses in London and Worting. First-year graduates were not then allowed to sit for the fellowship examinations. But in October 1818 both Hare and Whewell were elected Fellows of Trinity College. Thirlwall was also successful in winning a fellowship. He then promptly left for Rome, where he met Baron Christian Karl Josius von Bunsen (1791–1860), Prussian Minister to the Papal Court, whose English wife, Frances Waddington, was the sister of Waddington of Trinity, and the cousin of Professor Monk.[30] Through Thirlwall, Bunsen later met Julius Hare, and the two became fast friends.

A month after the fellowship examination Hare and Lady Jones were on an outing at Wimbledon where they met Maria Edgeworth, who left an account of the meeting. "I will only tell you who was there . . . Lady Jones—Sir W Jones widow—and her nephew a young Mr Hare. Young as he is he has just accomplished making himself a fellow at Cambridge. . . . quite serious—yet unaffected—his hair as Lady Spencer observed too long and stood up as if with fright ever since reading for the fellowship but he is not pedantic and *is* goodnatured."[31] Miss Edgeworth made it sound as if the examination had been traumatic for Hare. Yet his preparations for it appear less than serious from a letter he wrote to Whewell in Wales only six weeks before the event: "For the last six days I have scarcely opened a book." Hare explained that this was due to his demanding social life, which he described in some detail.[32] After winning the fellowship, Hare had the benefit of a long Christmas holiday in Paris with his brother Francis. Much of the fellowing year, 1819, Hare passed in London and in the country with Lady Jones. He visited Cambridge for the spring commencement, and was much in Sheepshank's company as well.[33]

Eligible young ladies were often mentioned in the youthful correspondence between Hare and Whewell. But love had to be postponed. Difficult decisions faced these young men without independent wealth as they surveyed their career prospects. The security of a college fellowship was a hard-won reward, though it entailed celibacy and in virtually all cases required one to take holy orders. This was doubtless a factor which drove Hare and many of his friends, however reluctantly, to the study of law. Whewell accepted a lectureship at Trinity College in 1818 with a minimum of hesitation. Augustus Hare had already taken up a tutorship at New College, Oxford, and Francis Hare had persuaded Julius to read law. Dutifully Julius entered the Middle Temple at the Inns of Court, where, appropriately, he took rooms in Hare Court. His devotion to the law was brief, but while he lived in London he had the pleasure of the companionship of Thirlwall and Sheepshanks, and the occasion to embark in earnest upon a literary career. One must make generous allowance for hyperbole in the significance which E.H. Plumptre (1821–91), Hare's brother-in-law, later read into this episode in Hare's life: "With [Hare] as with his friend [Thirlwall], it is not difficult to trace in his after life the influence of his legal training in his habit of sifting evidence, his aversion to rash and hasty condemnations, his reverence for the principles of English jurisprudence. In the one character, it may be, these were united more with the coolness and impartiality of a judge; in the other, with the zeal of an advocate who believes in his client. The practical side of a barrister's life, however, had but little attraction for Hare's mind, and he still continued his studies in philosophy and literature."[34]

Chapter 3

Law and Literature in London

Before Hare settled down to study law he embarked on a trip to France and to the Netherlands with his old friend Samuel Hinds. In Brussels he visited his brother Francis, and made a long stay in Paris, where he did not, as Whewell lamented, develop a respect for French politicians or a taste for French brandies.[1]

Back in London, Hare applied himself to the intricacies of the Common Law, but he found this uncongenial. He sought relief from his legal studies in the pleasures of German literature, and set to work as a translator. His choice of material reflects the vogue for chivalric romance and gothic suspense. His first published translation was of Friedrich Heinrich Karl, Baron de la Motte Fouqué's *Sintram and His Companions,* which appeared anonymously in 1820. Hare hoped he would be encouraged by success to follow this publication with a whole series of translations of "the best German romances and dramas," to give English readers "some portion of the delight and improvement" available in recent German literature. He expressed regret that German was known by so few in England, but had hope that it might someday replace French in a proper education. Of the women who would make up a large part of the audience for such a work, Hare wrote: "Nor indeed is it greatly to be desired that language-learning should be extensively diffused among them. The spot wherein woman is most beautiful and most fulfils her duty is her home. And this is no less true of the mind than of the body." For them the works of Fouqué could be recommended without hesitation, "for amongst all works of imagination his are, almost without exception, the healthiest and the purest."[2] In that age of leisure for women of the higher classes, escapism was not yet inconsistent with literature.

As for the story of *Sintram* itself, it is a gloomy tale of murder, guilt, revenge, and redemption set in medieval Norway. Whewell, upon receipt of a copy of *Sintram*, wrote to Hare: "I am extremely glad to receive you in print. I certainly think you might be more worthily employed than in translation but life has room for one such work, and especially when it is to diffuse valuable ideas and feelings, as I know you intend this to do. . . . —I only hope that you will not become one of a Septuagint of translators of German novels/ morals for the conversion of the heathen."[3] Critics who reviewed *Sintram* were not so tender with Hare's feelings.

Hare's translation was extremely literal, and imitated in English the many compound words and word inversions which characterize the German language. This technique, when added to the peculiarly sombre nature of Fouqué's tale, makes uncomfortable reading. Hare considered George Soane's translation of Fouqué's *Undine* (1818) too loose. Soane's different ideas about translation are evident in his comments on Hare's version of *Sintram:* "I know not who the translator may be, but a more unfitting person for the task could hardly have been selected. That he is imperfectly acquainted with the German is the least of his disqualifications; he writes in a dialect which is not always English as to single words, and very seldom indeed as to idiom; what is still worse, he fancies, nay actually asserts, that this barbarous jargon is beneficial. . . . It must be confessed that a more complete victory over the English language has never yet been obtained by anyone."[4] Soane was referring to Hare's defence of his translation innovation, which Hare claimed "must stand or fall, not according to the dogmas of any abstract theory, but only so far as it succeeds or fails in obtaining the sanction of custom, that is, in being vitally assimilated with the body of a language."[5] In considering Hare's version of *Sintram* this question is sidestepped by George McFarland, who makes the limited critical reception of the book appear more favourable that it was in fact.[6] Violet Stockley lists a number of Hare's gaffes in her treatment of *Sintram*, and concludes that "Hare has pushed the principle of literal translation much further than any respect for the genius of the language into which the translation is made allows, and the result is usually a miserable jargon, not always even intelligible."[7] Bayard Q. Morgan, representing a school more sympathetic to experimentation, makes note of Soane's criticisms, but rates Hare's *Sintram* as "not bad."[8]

Hare's innovations were among his most cherished opinions, and were based upon sound philosophical principles: "For no language can ever be the complete counterpart of another. . . . Hence a conscientious translator is perpetually drawn in opposite directions, from the wish to accomplish two incompatible objects, to give an exact representation of his original, and at the same time to make that representation an idiomatic one." As for the apparent excesses and innovations in his version of *Sintram*, "A literal translation is better than a loose one. . . . For copies, whether of words or things, must be valuable in proportion to their exactness. . . . Hence the difficulty of translations, regarded as works of art, varies in proportion as the books translated are more or less idiomatic; for in rendering idioms one can seldom find an equivalent, which preserves all the point and grace of the original." Hare recognized the inherent dangers of translation. He believed that "translations are often injurious to literature. They may indeed be highly beneficial, by promoting that commerce of thought, which is the great end of the intercourse among nations. . . . Very often however a translator goes through his work as a job. . . . Whether from natural ineptitude, or from exhausted interest, he makes no steady strenuous endeavour to realize the conceptions of his author."[9]

The motive of Hare's publishers, Charles and James Ollier, in issuing *Sintram* is clear. The book has many of the same qualities that the reading public admired in the work of "Monk" Lewis and Mrs Radcliffe. The Olliers also had the example of the success enjoyed by Soane's translation of Fouqué's *Undine*.[10] As Thirlwall noted, there was a rage for German tales, which was later stimulated even further by Carlyle's translation of *Wilhelm Meister*.[11] Fouqué was a master of the gothic novella, but the taste for his work waned, and even in the esteem of Hare and Thirlwall he was replaced by Ludwig Tieck (1773–1853), an apostle of the romantic novella.

There was a market for chivalric romances in England, and *Sintram*, though now quite forgettable, was certainly not the worst example of the genre. This in itself makes the limited critical reaction to the work curious. The Ollier brothers had shown better taste in publishing work by Keats and Shelley, but this was not the end of their relationship with Julius Hare. In seeking to introduce German literature to an English audience, Hare and the Olliers found a popular common denominator in Fouqué. However Hare's too-academic approach to translation prevented *Sintram* from achieving popular success.[12]

At the end of 1820 the Ollier brothers published the first number of a journal entitled *Olliers Literary Miscellany in Prose and Verse by Several Hands*. George McFarland says that the brothers naturally called upon Hare for contributions.[13] However, an unpublished letter from Hare to Charles Ollier in 1819 proves that Hare had a hand in inspiring the new periodical: "May I be allowed to suggest to you that considering the number of ingenious young authors with whom you are acquainted, I feel you would not fail of succeeding if you could engage some of them to contribute towards a Journal or Magazine, somewhat in the style of, though of course considerably different from Blackwood's. Notwithstanding the . . . periodical publications that stream forth from the press, I think there is still room for another. . . . I would gladly contribute anything in my power, towards filling up your numbers, at least till you found letters pouring in in floods & had no difficulty except that of selection."[14] The new periodical duly appeared, but Hare's persuasiveness could not make it a success; only one issue was published.

Hare's own copy of the *Miscellany* bears attributions in his own hand. Thomas Love Peacock contributed an essay on "The Four Ages of Poetry." The Ollier brothers themselves contributed some short features, and Hare made three substantial contributions: "A.W. Schlegel on Shakspeare's *Romeo and Juliet*," "On the German Drama, No. I: Oehlenschlaeger," and "The Siege of Ancona: A Romantic Idyll," from the German of La Motte Fouqué.[15] In another letter to Charles Ollier, Hare discussed his translations for the first and susequent issues of the *Miscellany:*

> The last number of the Vienna review contains such an admirable article on Schlegel's dramatic lectures that I think a translation of [a] great part of it ought certainly . . . to be given to English readers. The observations on Shakespeare . . . are

perhaps the most profound and philosophical that have ever appeared. . . . so many of the other magazines have got a knack of murdering articles in Vienna and Leipzig reviews and embalming the skeleton in their pages, that I am very much afraid, if the present article be deferred until your second number some other may have got the start on us.[16]

And so indeed the translation of the Schlegel article appeared in the first issue along with Hare's early appreciation of the Danish writer Adam Gottlob Oehlenschlaeger (1779–1850).[17] Hare's efforts in the *Miscellany* drew praise from Percy Shelley, who wrote to the Ollier brothers from Pisa: "Who is your commentator on the German Drama? He is a powerful thinker, though I differ from him *toto caelo* about the Devils in Dante and Milton."[18]

Hare's literary consciousness and perhaps, too, his ambitions for a literary career had been awakened largely by the works of William Wordsworth and Samuel Taylor Coleridge. Hare was their staunch advocate at a time when both writers were unfashionable. In this taste he had some influence upon his friends and upon his students in the 1820s. Hare had the opportunity to attend some of Coleridge's lectures in London as early as 1817 or 1818, and McFarland feels that he undoubtedly did so. Hare first appeared in Coleridge's correspondence in 1819 as a source of German books, which Coleridge was then avidly reading.[19] In the early 1820s Hare attended the Thursday soirées of Coleridge's friends and admirers at Dr Gillman's house, the Grove, in Highgate. In later years he introduced John Sterling and F.D. Maurice to Coleridge, and both young men were deeply influenced. Sterling became an avowed disciple of Coleridge, but Maurice later disavowed any influence by Coleridge, at least of a theological kind.[20] Hare met Wordsworth during his visits to the Master's Lodge at Trinity College, and they became lifelong friends and correspondents.

Hare's devotion to Wordsworth and Coleridge and their friendship grew with the years. Professor C.R. Sanders said that "of all Coleridge's disciples, one of the most loyal was . . . Hare. No other disciple knew Coleridge better or was better equipped to understand him. . . . He possessed a mastery of German and a capacity for scholarship that enabled him not only to comprehend Coleridge but also to study him against the background of much that Coleridge himself had read. . . . Hare realized . . . in his familiarity with the German language, literature, and philosophy, and in the personal intimacy which he for some years enjoyed with Coleridge, [great] advantages. . . . Yet Hare . . . was very discriminating in what he accepted from Coleridge."[21] Like his commonplace book, Hare's *Guesses at Truth* rings with praise for Coleridge, and for Wordsworth, to whom the later editions were dedicated.[22]

While he was preparing translations for the Ollier Brothers Hare met John Taylor of the publishing firm of Taylor and Hessey. This began a long and significant connection for Hare. Early in 1821 Taylor bought out the proprietors of the recently established *London Magazine,* and Hare soon joined the distinguished group of contributors that included John Keats, John Clare, Thomas Hood, Thomas De Quincey, Charles Lamb, and Henry Francis Cary. Taylor paid contributors at the then-handsome rate of one guinea a page with a half-profit reprint option. Lamb's "Essays of Elia" and De Quincey's "Confessions of an English Opium Eater" first appeared in the *London Magazine.* Taylor played host to monthly gatherings of his illustrious band of contributors.[23] Through Hare's influence Taylor later published books by Thirlwall and Walter Savage Landor.

In addition to new acquaintances in the literary world, throughout two years at the Inns of Court Hare kept up close connections with his old friends. He saw Thirlwall, then at Lincoln's Inn, with great frequency. Hugh James Rose wrote to ask him about German books and German authors. Hare kept quite busy until he fell ill early in 1821. Part of his recuperation that year was a trip to northern Italy, where he visited his brother Francis, so the illness, whatever its nature, was not of long duration.[24]

When Hare returned to London from Milan on Good Friday 1822, his attitude toward his prospective legal career was even gloomier than before. He learned from Whewell that Thorp, writing from Italy, also intended to enter the path of law. Hare would have been sympathetic, but distressed, had he read Thorp's letter which set forth his preferences. Cambridge headed the list, but for the need to take holy orders. At the bottom of Thorp's list was law, "something against which I have not *serious* objections."[25] Thorp, like many of his friends, eventually overcame his reluctance to take orders. Perhaps the study of law was for many of them a necessary factor in this turnabout.

Hare's depressed frame of mind in the spring of 1822 was reflected in his letters. In April 1822 he wrote to Whewell:

> A friend of mine . . . wrote me . . . that he was intending to pay Cambridge a visit for five or six days, and I have therefore desired him to call upon you. . . . He has been a good deal abroad, is an exceedingly good fellow, and you will not think him the worse for his being *what I wish I was, or could see any possibility of becoming, a very excellent parish priest*. For the more I see of Law, as a practical pursuit, the more I feel convinced that I shall never become anything but an asymptote to a brief, and indeed, I fear, that our courses are such as keep evermore receding from instead of approximating to one another; and feel that if it be in my power to do anything *tüchtig* [with competance] anymore, I shall certainly never do anything *tüchtig* here.[26]

This letter is the first indication of Hare's interest in the clerical profession, other than for the sake of an academic fellowship. Whewell replied a fortnight later to respond to Hare's morose view of his prospects at the bar: "I am sorry you don't like the law and the prospects w[hic]h it offers especially if you resolve to take to nothing else—there is one way in which I think you might do something *tüchtig* and w[hic]h I hope you will soon have an opportunity of choosing—I mean infusing good principles of taste and scholarship & if you like to call it so of philosophy into the rising generations of academic youth—I do not venture to say more but I hope that you will receive shortly an explanation of what I mean."[27] Whewell's meaning was unmistakable.

Hare replied the very next day, and Whewell's half-veiled suggestion had clearly lifted his spirits:

> Could I do anything *tüchtig* in the way you have hit out? I am not sure that I might not. But it w[oul]d require some deliberation before such a revolution in my system could be determined upon. . . . At all counts I should like to find phials that must stand to be filled with what I had to pour into them; even though nine tenths of it should evaporate in the process of infusion. But

this is all nonsense; one's business is much more to excite than to infuse; and this is why Plato is worth ten thousand Aristotles & 1000000000000000000000000000000000000000000000000000 00000000000 Locke's. . . . *I believe that . . . philosophy is the true centre of an university education, or at least that philosophy & religion are its two foci which ought ultimately to coincide.*[28]

Whewell's sugestion about a *tüchtig* calling had obviously fallen upon fertile ground.

After all the hinting back and forth, it must have been no surprise to either that Hare was soon able to report to Whewell: "I have received an offer of the classical lectureship from our Master last Friday, and after sundry balancings of pros and cons, and after consulting Augustus who most strongly advised me to accept it . . . I have just closed a letter of acceptance." Eagerly anticipating his new appointment, he offered Whewell condolences, for "you are likely to find annoyance in sufficient quantity, whilst I am muddling the brains which you are attempting to clarify. My fixed purpose however is to be as rational as I possibly can, and that will be quite irrational enough. To be sure it is a tremendous undertaking, and attended with an overwhelming responsibility, to have to teach the flower of England's youth to walk straight in these crooked-going days."[29]

Whewell wrote to congratulate Hare upon his decision. Thirlwall returned to England from abroad in the fall and added his best wishes: "I could perhaps have wished you a somewhat wider channel for your activity, but it is certainly good, and as the course of the world runs to have one at all, especially one which it is possible to enlarge."[30] Thus Hare made his choice. Throughout his life, both at Cambridge and in the Church, Hare's natural role was as teacher. His widespread influence as a teacher was a major contribution to the intellectual life of his times.

Chapter 4

A Don's Life

When Hare returned to Trinity College as a Classical Lecturer in 1822, the undergraduates were divided into three groups known as "sides," each under the aegis of a Tutor and his staff of Assistant-Tutors. Hare was assigned to Whewell's side, where he taught the classics thrice weekly. Although he met with only one-third of the Trinity undergraduates in his classroom, for the next ten years he taught and strongly influenced a large number of remarkable students.[1]

Frederick Denison Maurice went up to Cambridge in 1823, and after the lapse of thirty years still had a clear recollection of Hare's classes: "You will suppose, perhaps, that this was owing to some novelty in his method of teaching. You will inquire whether he . . . gave disquisitions instead of calling on his pupils to construe a book? Not the least. We construed just as they did elsewhere. I do not remember his indulging in a single excursus." Hare's avowed teaching style was Platonic. As his pupils read *Antigone* in the first term,

> the lecturer seemed most anxious to impress us with the feeling that there was no road to the sense which did not go through the words. He took infinite pains to make us understand the force of nouns, verbs, participles, and the grammar of the sentences. We often spent an hour on the strophe or anti-strophe

of a chorus. If he did not see his way into it himself, he was never afraid to show us that he did not. . . .

You will think that so much philological carefulness could not have been obtained without the sacrifice of higher objects. How could we discover the divine intuitions of the poet, while we were tormenting ourselves about his tenses? I cannot tell; but it seems to me that I never learnt so much about this particular poem, about Greek dramatic poetry generally, about all poetry, as in that term.

In the second term the text was Plato's *Gorgias,* and Hare impressed Maurice with his refusal to provide students with a pat analysis:

His anxiety seemed to be that Plato should explain himself to us, and should help to explain us to ourselves. Whatever he could do to further this end, by bringing his reading and scholarship to bear upon the illustrations of the text, by throwing out hints as to the course the dialogue was taking, by exhibiting his own fervent interest in Plato, and his belief of the high purpose he was aiming at, he did. But to give us second-hand reports, though they were ever so excellent—to save us the trouble of thinking—to supply us with a moral, instead of showing us how we might find it, not only in the book but in our own hearts,— this was clearly not his intention.[2]

The rest of the first year was devoted to a single book of Livy's *Roman History.* In the second-year classes Hare turned to the Greek Testament. Of those first year classes Maurice wrote, "To [Hare's] lectures on Sophocles and Plato, I can trace the most permanent effect upon my character, and on all my modes of contemplating subjects, natural, human, and divine."[3] Maurice's appraisal gives a valuable insight into Hare's methods and approach to the classical curriculum. Maurice recorded his first impressions of Hare in a letter to his mother in October 1823: "Our other lecturer, Hare, is . . . a lively lecturer and an admirable classic, and you have no reason to complain in his rooms that you are employed an hour in hearing difficulties demolished in a most triumphant style which you really did not fancy had ever occurred to anyone. I am particularly pleased with his manner, especially that of recommending books bearing upon the subject in question, but out of the regular college routine."⁴ A year earlier Hugh James Rose had remarked in a letter to Whewell that he was curious to hear Hare's lectures, for he was sure that "Plato illustrated by Coleridge with excursuses on Kant will be the least of Hare's feats."⁵

The hothouse intellectual atmosphere provided at Trinity College, the most academically rigorous of the colleges, was not to everyone's liking. Bulwer Lytton, who went up to Trinity academically ill-prepared in 1822, found the formal atmosphere unbearable: "[Trinity's] numbers alone sufficed to revolt the unsocial and shrinking temper that had sicklied over my mind. The enforced routine of lectures, in which I found (proud fool that I was) little to learn, stupified me for the rest of the day."⁶ After a single term he transferred to the less-demanding intimacy of Trinity Hall, and later took a poll degree. W.M. Thackeray was another great writer of that generation who failed to profit from his undergraduate days at Trinity College.⁷ A few years later another sensitive youth, Alfred Tennyson, found the gulf between dons and students distressing. In later years he remembered "a want of love in Cambridge then," and was pleased to believe in its subsequent remedy.⁸

The academic atmosphere at Trinity College extended beyond the lecture hall. Beginning in the 1820s one social institution served as a focus for some of the most brilliant undergraduates. The Cambridge Conversazione Society is—after the Union—the longest-lived of the numerous debating and essay clubs. Founded in 1820 by members of Saint John's College, in subsequent years it was centred at Trinity College, and most of the outstanding Trinity students of later years were members. The membership was limited to twelve, hence the derisive appellation "the Apostles." During the 1850s "the Society," as its members called it, went underground, and maintained a secrecy that prevails to this day.⁹

F.D. Maurice joined the Apostles in 1823 or 1824, and under his leadership the club was reconstituted and raised to a high degree of intellectualism. It was still ostensibly an essay club, which met weekly to discuss a member's essay on some social or moral topic. But under Maurice's influence the members developed a degree of introspection, soul-searching, and self-revelation which they claimed gave them powerful skills of spiritual regeneration.¹⁰ John Mitchell Kemble (1807–57) claimed in 1847 that no society ever existed in which more freedom of thought was found consistent with the most perfect affection between the members, or in which a more complete tolerance of the most opposite opinions prevailed. . . . very few of the distinguished Cambridge men of our time have not been members of it; and it existed to remedy a fault in our education. Its business was to make men study and think on all matters except mathematics and classics professionally considered. Its metaphysical tendency has altered (first at Trinity) the system of university examination itself. . . . To my *education* given in that society I feel that I owe every power I possess, and the rescuing myself from a ridiculous state of prejudice and prepossessions with which I came armed to Cambridge. From "the Apostles" I, at least, learned to think as a free man.[11]

These sentiments echoed in the reminiscences of other Apostles, whose broad-mindedness and desire to consider all shades of belief were rare in an age of strong religious and political partisanship.

This "Apostolic Spirit" enabled men of widely divergent views to maintain respect and camaraderie. Julius Hare and Connop Thirlwall exercised a powerful influence over the early Apostles, and one effect of this influence may be seen in the Apostles' devotion to Coleridge and Wordsworth at a time when the poets were generally unpopular. Thus, Charles Merivale (1808–93) recalled in his autobiography, "We began to think that we had a mission to enlighten the world upon things intellectual and spiritual. We held established principles, especially in poetry and metaphysics, and set up certain idols for our worship. Coleridge and Wordsworth were our principal divinities, and Hare and Thirlwall were regarded as their prophets."[12] But this conveys the un-Apostolic impression that the Apostles were of one mind in such matters. In reality they fell between the two poles of Benthamism and Coleridgeanism. Maurice later recalled that "among the younger and cleverer undergraduates of that day, especially in Trinity, Benthamism was the prevalent faith." Some of the Apostles, like James Spedding (1808–81), remained true to their utilitarian principles. The Coleridgeans included Maurice and John Sterling (1806–44). They hewed closely to the pattern set by Hare, praised the philosophy of Coleridge and Kant, and eschewed the poetry of Byron in favour of that of Coleridge and Wordsworth.[13] It was natural that Hare should take a liking to such precocious young intellects who so readily reflected his teaching and pet notions. Maurice and Sterling later edited the *Athenaeum,* with Hare and numerous Apostles as contributors. This was one means by which Hare's personal connections with them were maintained.

Hare's influence upon the Apostles lay in his approach to the traditional curriculum and in the wider culture that he sought to promote. Just as Benthamism distinguished some of the Apostles, so, too, was it an issue in a wider social context. Upon this issue Hare had strong and articulate feelings. Although he believed that Thomas Hobbes was the English originator of the "ungodly philosophy of enlightened selfishness," he reserved his worst venom for Jeremy Bentham and his followers. Hare thought they failed dismally to understand, in their pursuit of the greatest good for the greatest number, that "the foundation of political happiness is faith in the integrity of man. The foundation of all happiness, temporal and eternal, is faith in the goodness, the righteousness, the mercy, and the love of God."[14]

Because Hare lacked the young Apostles' toleration of antagonistic morals, he saw Benthamism to be merely the latest manifestation of the evil cult of reason of the eighteenth century. This feeling was so intense that it elicited the most powerful and certainly the best-known sermon of Hare's career, "The Children of Light," delivered at Cambridge on Advent Sunday 1828. Hare argued in the fashion of Kant and Coleridge that human reason is highly fallible, and gives rise to self-righteousness. He denounced the delusion that "we are light . . . we were darkness" for having led to the tyranny of reason and the overthrow of ancient institutions. This was true even in England, where the process was merely less destructive. This delusion gave the age its revolutionary character. The Children of Light were deluded by historical ignorance, for "when the mind perceives nothing in the world around it except its own image and reflection [it] . . . will assume with little scruple . . . that all mankind have till now been lying under the same thick darkness, from which they have just escaped, and that all mankind must have been passing in like manner out of the darkness into light, [and] if they have not, *they ought to be dragged or driven."*[15] E.H. Plumptre said of "The Children of Light," "Long as it was . . . and appealing to no emotions of religious terror, or excitment, or partisanship, for the most part a protest against the tendencies of the studies of the University in which he was set to teach, it was felt by many who heard it as marking an era in their own lives, and in the history of Cambridge thought. It was a strong blow aimed at the despotic exclusiveness of a purely scientific course of studies, and at the narrowness of the Paley utilitarianism and Simeon evangelicalism which were then the chief nurture of Cambridge religious life."[16]

The attitudes of Cambridge men to the Evangelical piety of Charles Simeon (1759-1836) were mixed, but one thing many of the Apostles could agree upon was their hatred of Paley's philosophy.[17] When "The Children of Light" appeared in print, Maurice reviewed it in the *Athenaeum*. He lamented the failure of the Church of England to produce a "very great man" since the seventeenth century, but noted, "The sermon before us is the most hopeful omen we have discovered of better things to come . . . this little book gives us a specimen of a union of all the faculties in the service of religion, which needs only to be more extensively applied, to create works worthy of the best age of the Church of England."[18]

With "The Children of Light" Hare expounded the idealism which he shared with Coleridge and which was characteristic of the Broad Church. In the annals of the Broad Church, Hare's "The Children of Light" is analogous with John Keble's sermon "On National Apostacy" (1833), which John Henry Newman (1801-90) said marked the beginning of the Oxford Movement. What set Hare forever at odds with Benthamism was its anti-Christian morality. For Hare love of one's neighbour was a social and religious imperative. Naturally he denounced as evil that creed "which maintains that all morality, if turned inside out, is nothing but an enlightened and well-regulated selfishness, and that this is the only principle powerful enough to make men live and act as they ought." Moreover, Hare felt its true motives were base. He argued that "the current philosophy is merely the reflection of the reigning vice of an age: . . . its chief aim has been to palliate and justify, to establish and diffuse that worship of Mammon, which commerce has been ever fatally apt to propagate and promote."[19]

The political economists or "feelosophers," whom Cobbett denounced, were equally contemptible in Hare's eyes. He professed incredulity at "so trumpery an edifice" as this new "science" which could condemn as evil, because it drove down prices, a good harvest from God's bounty. This "transmuting good into evil" was "satanic alchemy."[20] Hare was scandalized by the economic equation which reduced men to "surplus population." He urged, "Surely there must be something very wrong and rotten in the state of England, when a man, in an economical view, is not worth what he eats and drinks, when a healthy man cannot add more to the stock of national wealth than he withdraws from it for the necessities of his subsistence."[21] At a practical level this creed represented a sinister trend in government administration. With grim resignation Hare wrote, "Ours till lately was a government of maxims. . . . The economists want to substitute a despotism of systems. But who, until the coming of Christ's Kingdom, can hope to see a government of principles?"[22]

Hare and Thirlwall offered students an enriched course of studies. They encouraged their better students to study the works of English romantic poets and German theologians. But they did not shirk their duty to classical authors or allow their students to do so.[23] For Hare and Thirlwall were seeking methodological changes even within the existing academic curriculum. As Professor Momigliano has observed, "They wanted the empirical knowledge of the classical languages characteristic of the English school to be replaced by scientific investigation of the classical literatures as pursued in German universities."[24] Hare and Thirlwall's passion for Germanic scholarship was evident both in their pedagogy and in their scholarly pursuits. But such nonconformity was not a sure route to success in either the University or the Church hierarchy, as both men learned.

For Hare this was the lesson when in 1825 he failed to win election to the Regius Professorship of Greek. Under the terms of Henry VIII's endowment, the chair was filled through election by a small body of college heads and senior Fellows. In 1825 they were Le Blanc, Master of Trinity Hall and Vice-Chancellor; Thackeray, Provost of King's; Wordsworth, Master of Trinity; Renouard, Fellow of Trinity; Greenwood, Fellow of Trinity; Palmer, proxy for Wood, Master of Saint John's; and Croft, proxy for Kaye, Master of Christ's.[25]

The candidates were all Trinity men: James Scholefield, William Sidney Walker, Hugh James Rose, and Julius Charles Hare.[26] Walker wrote a first-hand account in a letter to his mother: "Hare declaimed yesterday. . . . It was of an extraordinary length—an hour and forty minutes,—and my attention was alive and unslackened the whole time. It was indeed a splendid composition; full of research, philosophy, poetic feeling, and virtuous animation,—to say nothing of some efficient strokes of satire. . . . But I hardly know what will happen. . . . nobody can tell how the votes will be balanced. Perhaps Hare has best expectations."[27]

As for the votes, the recollections of Croft, one of the electors, reveal how they were balanced:

> Walker, though perhaps the best Greek scholar among them, was totally unfit on other accounts to hold any office. Rose I considered inferior in scholarship to the other two, besides not having been a fellow of Trin[ity]. Scholefield and Hare were both in my opinion calculated to fill the office with credit, but I thought Hare from his more amiable character & conciliatory manners better fitted to perform some of the duties, that of examiner especially, than Scholefield. I, therefore, upon the whole was inclined to give the preference to Hare.

But Croft proved to be alone in his assessment of the candidates:

> When we met to elect, I marked the voting papers for Hare, the six other electors were equally divided between Scholefield and Rose. . . . The Master of Trinity and Le Blanc certainly voted for Rose, and the third was either Palmer or Thackeray & I am almost certain it was the former. The other three of course for Scholefield. There was therefore no election & we proceeded to another scrutiny, with the same result. Now I knew from the statutes of foundation that if no candidate had a majority of votes in three scrutinies, the appointment would lapse to the V[ice] C[hancellor] and Master of Trinity, who had both voted for Rose. Consequently if I persisted in voting for Hare, Rose, whom I considered the worst of the . . . candidates would be the Professor, I therefore on the third scrutiny voted for Scholefield & thus decided the election in his favour.[28]

While it was not extraordinary for a badly qualified candidate like Rose to find support in such an election, it was peculiar to find the Master of Trinity supporting a non-Fellow against three much better qualified candidates who were also junior Fellows of his own college. This appears to violate all electoral precedents of collegiate loyalty. The reason for Wordsworth's apparently peculiar behaviour was personal favouritism. Neither Hare's political position as a conservative Whig nor his theological liberalism would have elicited much favour from Wordsworth, a Tory and a High Churchman.[29] Wordsworth naturally found Scholefield, a devout Evangelical, unacceptable. Rose, a High Churchman, was on the other hand very congenial to Wordsworth. Dean Burgon referred to Wordsworth as Rose's "fast friend and eager Church patron."[30] Only the previous spring Rose had delivered a University Sermon at Cambridge on "The State of the Protestant Religion in Germany," in which "he had been the first to give warning . . . of the perils to England which lay in the biblical and theological speculations of Germany."[31] This sermon had an impact on High Churchmen similar to that of Hare's "The Children of Light" on Broad Churchmen. In view of Hare's well-known love of German literature and scholarship, the Master's lack of support for him was understandable. Nor was Wordsworth ever afraid to court unpopularity in a partisan cause.

As for Scholefield, the new Regius Professor of Greek, his tenure was long—twenty-eight years—but his scholarship was undistinguished.[32] However, as this whole episode showed, scholarship could be discounted as a qualification in such an election, or at least be made subordinate to considerations of personality, of religion, and of politics.

But such disappointments as this were the exception and not the rule in Hare's college life. The resident Fellows "formed a society whose social charm and intellectual brilliancy has never been surpassed. They differed widely in tastes, in politics, and in intellectual pursuits; but they were united by common interests, by a common devotion to their College and their University, and lived together harmoniously. . . . Some, like Sheepshanks, Thirlwall, Macaulay, Airy, stayed for only a short time; others, like Robert Wilson Evans, Peacock, Hare, Thorp, gave many of their best years to College and University work; while Romilly and Whewell devoted their whole lives to the same objects."[33] This is the picture drawn by Adam Sedgwick's official biographers.

Hare's undergraduate contemporaries Henry Venn Elliott and William Sidney Walker were also elected to college fellowships, as were the most outstanding undergraduates of the early 1820s, Thomas Babington Macaulay (1800–59) and Winthrop Mackworth Praed (1802–39). Hare's good friend Kenelm Henry Digby never became a Fellow, but he was nonetheless a resident of the college for a decade after his graduation as B.A. in 1819. In the Trinity College Library Digby composed *The Broad Stone of Honour; or, Rules for the Gentlemen of England*. Hare was so enamoured of this book that he declared, "Had I a son, I would place [it] in his hands, charging him . . . to love it next to his Bible."[34] Digby was an even greater romantic than Hare, and spurred by this he entered the Roman Catholic communion while in Paris in 1825. The regulations of Trinity College proved flexible enough to allow this wealthy eccentric to reside. He continued in his close friendships at Trinity with those such as Hare, who could only complain that "we do not see a tenth part as much of him as we should wish to do: still even looking on anybody so noble always does one good."[35] Digby was not the only Roman Catholic at Cambridge; he befriended the young Ambrose de Lisle (1809–78), who in turn influenced the conversion of at least one other Trinity man. In light of this and the fact that another Trinity man, Hugh James Rose, called the first meeting of the Tractarian Movement in 1833, one needs only a small exaggeration to claim that the Oxford Movement actually began at Cambridge.[36]

A candid contemporary view of the Fellows of Trinity College was recorded by Hare's nephew, Arthur Penrhyn Stanley (1815–81), when he visited Cambridge. Stanley was introduced to Whewell, Thirlwall, Blakesley, Lodge, Romilly, Kemble, and Christopher Wordsworth, Master of the College. Whewell was talkative; Thirlwall, who fell asleep over a book, was not; and to Stanley's eyes, "They seem very happy all of them together . . . with much less restraint among them than I should think there was among men of the same standing at Oxford." Their "kindness and joviality" struck Stanley, though "with the exception of Wordsworth, I thought them less polished than our Dons."[37]

A far more hostile assessment was given by Richard Hurrell Froude (1803–36), another Oxford man, who wrote impatiently from Italy, where he was holidaying with J.H. Newman in 1833: "Certainly these Cambridge men are wonderful fellows. . . . They know every thing, examine every thing, and dogmatize about every thing; they have paid particular attention to the geological structure of this place, and the botany of that, and the agriculture of another, and they are antiquaries, and artists, and scholars, and, above all, they puff off one another. . . . W[hewell]'s book, and S[edgwick]'s Lectures, and T[hirlwall]'s research, and H[are]'s taste, pop upon one at every turn."[38]

In term the social life of the Fellows of Trinity College included breakfasting and dining either in the Hall or in each other's rooms, of wine parties, and of seemingly endless games of whist.[39] However, not all entertainments were confined to the college precincts. Social evenings in the town were a regular occurrence. The leading Cambridge hostess of the 1820s was Elizabeth Campbell, second wife of Niccolo Maria Doria Spineto, the Marchese di Spineto, who for many years taught Italian in the University. "The Marchesa," as she was always called, held regular musical evenings at their house in Jesus Lane. At these gatherings the Fellows of Trinity College were regular guests. W.S. Walker left an account of one of these evenings: "So to the Marchesa's I went. . . . There was Whewell overwhelming the young simplicity of a little girl with the great guns of his eloquence . . . , and Romilly, with his natural courtesy, and inexhaustible stream of delightful rattle; and Sedgwick, with his north-country naïveté; and Hare and Thirlwall, and I know not who besides. . . . I . . . hastened home, to dream about Eton, and the Egyptian history, . . . and Hare and myself translating Aeschylus."[40]

In addition to the Marchesa's hospitality some of the Fellows of Trinity College in the 1820s enjoyed many memorable evenings in the household of Major-General Sir John Malcolm (1769–1833). His character immediately won him the friendship of the Fellows of Trinity College, whom he first met in 1823.[41] Hare, Sedgwick, and Whewell were soon regular guests at Hyde Hall, and it remained the centre of some of their happiest experiences for four years, until Malcolm was appointed to the governorship of Bombay in 1827. Hare called Hyde Hall "the house in which . . . the life and the spirit and the joy of conversation have been the most intense . . . a house in which I hardly ever heard an evil word uttered against anyone. The genial heart of cordial sympathy with which its illustrious master sought out the good side in every person and thing . . . seemed to communicate itself to all the members of his family, and operated even as a charm upon his visitors. For this reason was the pleasure so pure and healthy and unmixt."[42] The Malcolm children were a special delight to the learned bachelors of Trinity College.

While Sedgwick and Whewell romped with the children, Hare enjoyed the adult members of the household. Lady Malcolm herself so charmed her guests that, as Hare noted, 'there is no chance of tearing one's-self away when once the hostess appears; one can only fly before she comes down for breakfast. . . . it is impossible to leave Hyde Hall without being . . . a sadder and wiser man . . . and if one were not going away, a gladder."[43] Hare's preoccupation distressed his friend Sheepshanks, who wrote to Whewell: "Hyde Hall, why you had better call it Bury Hall or Lost Hall. Julius will never get out of it at all. . . . As it would well become you, I think you should lecture your lecturer upon the vagaries & upon the unreasonableness of men who have no wives of their own gallivanting those of other people. It is confoundedly unfair too[;] marry yourselves gentlemen & *then* make love to your neighbours' wives. That's fair & neighbour fare too."[44] But Hare's strongest affections were aimed at another resident of Hyde Hall.

Miss Mary Manning, known as "Ma-Man," was the Malcolm children's governess, and Hare fell in love with her. Hare's nephew knew her in later years, and left a flattering description of her:

> She was very tall, serene, and had a beautiful countenance. . . . She seemed to have the power of imposing her own personality upon her surroundings, and subduing the life and movement around her into an intellectual as well as a physical calm. She had a melodious low voice, a delicate Scotch accent, a perfectly self-possessed manner, and a sweet and gentle dignity. In conversation she was witty and genial, but never rude. With wonderful power of narration, she had the power of throwing unspeakable interest and charm over the most commonplace things: yet she never exaggerated. All the clever men who came into contact with her were bound under her spell. Whewell, Worsley, Landor, Bunsen, Sedgwick adored her, and did not wonder at my uncle's adoration.

This romantic attachment lasted until Hare's death. In later years many believed that Hare and Miss Manning had once been engaged. She married an Edinburgh physician, who soon afterward died. Later, as the widowed Mrs Alexander, she appeared as a visitor, and still later as a full-time resident of Hare's parsonage at Herstmonceux.[45] This romance had sequels.

It suited Hare's romantic nature to be in love with a series of women. Hare's cousin Anna Maria Shipley was a young widow, and as Mrs Dashwood she was his frequent holiday companion at Worting, at Brighton, and at Bodryddan, the Welsh home of her aunt, Louisa Shipley. Julius Hare and Anna Maria Dashwood were engaged to wed, according to Hare's nephew, who explained their attachment: "[Her] interest in poetry, art, and in Italian and German literature made her conversation exceedingly attractive. . . . Julius . . . was always her favourite cousin, and she was quite devoted to him, but without any prospect of marriage, until he should obtain a living. But the engagement was in itself a great source of delight to him, and for some years he spent as much time as possible at Bodryddan, where Mrs Dashwood continued to live."[46]

Lady Jones was on bad terms with her niece, and opposed Hare's engagement. After Lady Jones' death in 1829, Augustus Hare travelled to Cambridge to persuade his brother to abide by their aunt's dying wishes, and break off the engagement. At length Julius was persuaded, though he and Mrs Dashwood remained the best of friends. Two years later Hare became engaged to Jane, Lady Munro, widow of Sir Thomas Munro (1761–1827), and sister of the Marchesa Spineto. This engagement was said to have lasted for several years.[47] Settled into the *tüchtig* and congenial life of Cambridge, Hare's choice between the bridal chamber and the college combination room was difficult. He betrayed no hurry to marry. In any case among people of the upper classes courtships were long, and men married late in life.

In the vacations the Fellows of Cambridge often travelled abroad. Hare was less avid than some for foreign travel after his trip to Italy in 1821–22. Only in the summer of 1828 did he allow himself a holiday on the continent. Accompanied by W.M. Praed, Hare set off by channel packet to Ostend. One motive for this trip was to visit the Malcolm family and Miss Manning, who were summering in Germany. Hare and Praed travelled from Ostend by horse-drawn barge to Bruges, Ghent, and Antwerp. Praed wrote his sister from Antwerp, "I am to dine to-day with the poets, Wordsworth and Coleridge, and the daughter of the first mentioned. Hare knows both intimately. They are returning from a tour in Switzerland."[48] Afterward Hare and Praed set off on foot up the Rhine valley, often walking thirty or forty miles a day. At Bonn, Hare visited Niebuhr, Tieck, Schleiermacher, and A.W. Schlegel. Hare and Praed walked on to Frankfurt, and appear to have visited Heidelberg as well. After visiting Strasbourg, and posting to Paris, they returned to England after two months' absence. Hare did not travel abroad again until four years later, when he had at last decided to quit Cambridge.[49]

It would be enlightening to know more about Hare's finances. His father's estate was supposed to have been disappointingly small. Francis, the eldest brother, was able to live comfortably on the continent, but he realized the profit from the sale of their father's library, afterwards regularly sold his own book collections, and married a banker's daughter. Before winning college fellowships Julius and his brother Augustus received financial support from Lady Jones, and some of this may have continued for a time afterwards. All four brothers had expectations of inheritance from the estate of their aunt, Lady Jones. But she died intestate in 1829, and her surviving sister, Louisa Shipley of Bodryddan, was sole heir.[50]

The remuneration for Fellows prescribed by the Elizabethan statutes of Trinity College had been eroded to nothing by inflation. But the Fellows divided the annual surplus income of the college by a system of "dividends." Each dividend was £1,000, from which a junior Fellow received £12:10:0. College records reveal an annual average of 16.5 dividends for the period 1821-32; 1821 was a rich year with 24 dividends, while 1823 marked a low with only 10. Therefore Hare's average annual share was £225. There was also an additional emolument for serving as a Classical Lecturer. This sum was negotiable, but according to J.W. Blakesley, writing in the 1830s, it was worth "a hundred or two" beyond the value of his fellowship. Such incomes were handsome ones for unmarried men whose housing and food were also provided. Most of Hare's disposable income over the years went to purchase books.[51] Hare's youthful literary activities were at least partly inspired by a desire for gain. He told Charles Ollier that he could spare time to write only if his work yielded him some profit.[52] What he succeeded in earning by his pen is, however, unknown.

Chapter 5

A Commission from Landor

Julius Hare continued his literary endeavours when he returned to Cambridge in 1822. He served as literary agent and editor for Walter Savage Landor (1775–1864), wrote the phenomenally popular *Guesses at Truth,* and founded and edited the scholarly *Philological Museum.* He also continued his work as a Germanist, translated and introduced works by Barthold George Niebuhr and Jean Paul Richter, and assisted Thirlwall with translations of works by Ludwig Tieck and Friedrich Schleiermacher. In his literary capacity Hare made his most important and lasting contribution to English thought and letters. He also demonstrated several character traits for which he was well known, namely patient and unselfish loyalty to friends, devotion to the scholarly pursuit of truth, and dedication to the principle of free expression. This last became a *sine qua non* of the Broad Church, and often led to difficulty, although Hare's integrity usually won him the respect, if not also the friendship, of adversaries.

Hare undertook to act as agent for Walter Savage Landor while still a law student, and this task occupied him for the rest of the decade. In 1814 Hare's older brother Francis was at Tours, caring for their dying father. There Francis met Landor, a Latin poet and man of letters. Eventually both Landor and Francis Hare became residents of Florence. From their first meeting they took a great liking to each other, doubtless prompted by their mutual passion for scholarship, and by "that excess of overvehemence of speech

A COMMISSION FROM LANDOR

from which neither was free."[1] Landor eventually met the other three Hare brothers, and called them "beyond all comparison the most pleasant family of men I ever was acquainted with."[2]

In 1821-22 Landor was writing a series of dialogues which he called *Imaginary Conversations,* the work by which he is chiefly remembered. The manuscript of the first of these Landor sent off to Longman, the publisher, in the care of Captain C.J. Vyner of the 56th Regiment of Foot Guards.[3] Vyner left Florence in the spring of 1822, and Landor expected his manuscript to reach London by the end of April. But Vyner's route was not direct, and the manuscript was not delivered to Longman until 19 August. In the meantime Landor had written to a puzzled Longman and explained how he wanted his author's copies distributed. Fretful and impatient over the ensuing silence, Landor feared that his manuscript had been lost or even pirated.

At the suggestion of Francis Hare, Landor turned to Julius Hare, and in a letter begged Julius to retrieve the manuscript from Longman, and place it in the hands of another publisher, Mawman.[4] But Mawman was no more interested in Landor's manuscript than Longman had been, once it arrived. Nor were three other publishers to whom Hare submitted it. Julius Hare undertook Landor's commission little realizing that he would not see an end to the *Imaginary Conversations of Literary Men and Statesmen* until he had guided five volumes through the press, dealt with no fewer than eight separate publishers, transcribed virtually the whole of the work in his own hand, and corresponded faithfully and regularly with Landor in Florence. The scale of the undertaking and the amount of time it absorbed over a decade make the publication of Landor's *Imaginary Conversations* a major element in Hare's life, a contribution repaid only with Landor's devoted friendship. Landor admitted that without this help the *Imaginary Conversations* could not have appeared in his lifetime. The magnitude of Hare's work on Landor's behalf constitutes an act of devotion with few parallels in the annals of English letters.[5]

After the five rejections of Landor's manuscript, Hare turned to John Taylor, of the firm of Taylor and Hessey, with whom he was already acquainted as the publisher of the *London Magazine.* Why Hare waited so long to approach Taylor is not clear, and may be thought surprising in view of the ingratiating tone of Hare's first overture to Taylor: "I have been entrusted by my friend Mr. Landor . . . with a manuscript volume wh[ich] he is desirous of having published as soon as possible; and it would give me great pleasure to transfer the MS into the hands of one to whom our literature has been so much indebted. . . . I know of very few works in any language at all comparable with [it] in vigour or raciness either of thought or expression."[6] Taylor replied favourably, and Hare wrote to say that he had dispatched the manuscript and trusted that he had "executed in the best possible way the charge to which I have been entrusted, of finding a good publisher for Mr. Landor. The Conversations have been so long in my hands and in my thoughts, and I have had so much to do in transcribing and arranging them, that I feel the same interest in them as if they were my own, and I deem myself most fortunate in having met with a man who has been led to form a just estimate of Landor's extraordinary powers."[7]

Hare wrote to Taylor a month later to ask for word to pass on to Landor, who "writes often and impatiently."[8] Taylor replied at once to say that he was eager to publish the work provided certain deletions were made, and that he hoped that "a little Curtailment" necessary for the work's commercial success would be possible.[9] Hare replied immediately to Taylor's letter of acceptance:

> I perfectly agree with you . . . that Mr. Landor's Conversations would be considerably improved by the omission of a few passages, and I have state[d] that opinion strongly to their author. I have moreover been authorized by him to make such alterations as I should think indispensible; but you must know enough about authors to feel that I must not avail myself of that authority, except with the utmost delicacy. Still any passages which seem likely to give to[o] much offense, I shall take upon myself to erase or alter. . . . Nor can I mention their affecting the sale of the work as a reason for the omission. Landor has often told me that he is utterly indifferent upon that point.[10]

Taylor then had second thoughts about undertaking the publication, and when pressed by Hare to give specific reasons, he produced a list of passages to which he took serious objection. These included a dialogue between Edmund Burke and Lord Grenville which accused Burke of lack of principle for changing parties; some derogatory comments about William Gifford (1751–1826), editor of the *Quarterly Review;* and a dialogue between Conyers Middleton (1683–1750) and Antonio Magliabechi (1633–1714) in which Middleton argued against the efficacy of prayer.[11] Hare said he thought Taylor's objections quite moderate, and agreed that the attack upon Burke was the most offensive thing in the manuscript: "It was the world that changed not Burke. I have told Landor in so many words that in this dialogue he was indulging in a vulgar calumny, contrary to facts, and that it would materially injure the character of the whole work." Hare said furthermore that he would be happy to dispense with the Middleton dialogue as well, but that Landor had not yet authorized him to do so.[12] A few days later Taylor wrote to Hare to recommend the firm of Simpkin and Marshall as sufficiently lacking in scruples to undertake the publication of Landor's work. At this point Hare suggested, and all agreed, that the offensive passages should be submitted to Southey and Wordsworth, and that they be allowed to pass the final judgement.[13] Hare forwarded Southey and Landor's agreement to this arrangement, and asked Taylor that all objections be sent to Southey. Hare then wrote to Southey, "I was very glad to find myself fortunate enough to agree with you so entirely. . . . Taylor is entering with all his heart into the work. In his last letter he said 'we have not had so much wisdom put into a book since the days of Bacon.' "[14]

At the end of June 1823 Hare wrote to Taylor and reiterated his belief in Landor's right of free expression:

> My principle always is, as I would claim a right to speak out my own opinion, freely and without any restraint, so long as nothing morally wrong is contained in it, in like manner to throw no impediment in the way of a similar freedom of speech in others, however at variance their opinion may be with my own. Many of Landor's . . . I all but abhor. . . . but still I would not prevent publication; but where there is so much good in the volume wish to facilitate it; and trust that the evil the book might produce and the errors it might generate will be purged away. The good must endure and must be great; and we must content ourselves in this world in things good mixed up with evil.[15]

Both Hare and Southey were agreed that the Burke dialogue was one which Landor might later regret if it were printed. In the end this dialogue was scrapped completely. As for Middleton and the efficacy of prayer, Hare, his brother Augustus, and Southey all argued that it was quite unobjectionable. Nevertheless, in the first edition the offending passage was suppressed, but this issue arose again in the following year when a second edition was contemplated. On other passages Hare and Southey were in disagreement.[16]

As Landor continued to forward new dialogues to Hare, Taylor was given fresh opportunities to raise objections. Taylor objected to Lord Chatham the younger being described as "dead drunk," and also insisted that if the word "piss" were not removed from Oliver Cromwell's lips, he would set the printing order at 750 copies, instead of the 1,000 he had planned. Hare agreed that this passage and others besides were coarse, "but they are also very strong & characteristic; and I am afraid that any alteration would very much weaken them."[17]

In the nine-month interval caused by the many editorial disputes it was decided to print the dialogue between Southey and Porson in the *London Magazine*. This was done partly as advance publicity for the book, which was announced in the same issue as "in the press." It was also to please William Wordsworth, whose poetry was flatteringly described in the dialogue. Landor had originally proposed dedicating the work to Wordsworth, who was growing impatient to see it.[18] Afterwards Landor expressed annoyance and disapproval of this serial publication, perhaps feeling that Taylor was merely stalling the book. The following year Taylor offered to print one of the new dialogues in the *London Magazine,* and Hare replied: "Landor has such strange and strong whims, I am afraid to venture it, lest he should say he would rather have his right hand cut off. I wonder that he has never told us he would rather be castrated in body than in mind. Wordsworth mentioned to me that L[andor] was very angry at the publication of the Southey & Porson in the Magazine a twelvemonth ago."[19] In spite of the optimistic announcement in the summer of 1823, the *Imaginary Conversations* still did not appear. In January 1824 Wordsworth again wrote impatiently to Landor: "Many months have I waited for your dialogues & they never appear." He concluded by saying, "I have a strong desire to become acquainted with the Mr Hare whom you mention—to the honour of Cambridge he is in the highest repute there, for his sound & extensive learning. I am happy to say that the Master of Trinity Col[lege] (my brother) was the occasion of his being restored to the Muses from the Temple."[20]

At last, in March 1824, two volumes containing eighteen dialogues each appeared. Before Landor's death these thirty-six increased to one hundred and fifty. Forster, Landor's friend and biographer, claimed that public interest, whetted by the earlier publication of the Southey and Porson dialogue, was clearly demonstrated on behalf of the *Imaginary Conversations*. At Cambridge, in particular, the volumes were the "literary sensation" of 1824. The source of this claim was most likely Julius Hare. For a "literary sensation," Landor had chosen a surprisingly conventional form; the dialogue is a literary device almost as old as literature itself, as the example of Plato will attest. The sensation arose from the outspokenly liberal contents. In Landor's *Imaginary Conversations* historical and contemporary figures discussed topics of literature, philosophy, philology, politics, history, and religion.[21]

When the *Imaginary Conversations* finally appeared, Taylor was preoccupied with securing favourable reviews and large sales. William Hazlitt (1778–1830), then a contributor to the *London Magazine*, received an advance copy of the *Conversations*, and composed a long and largely favourable review for the *Edinburgh Review*. However, Francis Jeffrey (1773–1850), then the *Edinburgh*'s editor, managed to alter Hazlitt's copy before running it. This less favourable review appeared in March 1824, the same month as the *Imaginary Conversations*. Taylor was distressed, but expected worse from the *Quarterly Review* under the editorship of Landor's old adversary Gifford. Taylor therefore suggested that Hare might write something for the *London Magazine* to outflank criticism.[22] The result was an "imaginary conversational review" between Hare and "Frank Hargraves" which very effectively parodied the *Quarterly*'s own reviewing style, and is said to have caused Gifford to modify the hatchet job which he had commissioned from the young reviewer Henry Taylor (1800–86).[23]

The *Imaginary Conversations* sold briskly and by the autumn of 1824 plans for a second edition of volumes I and II, and for the first appearance of a third volume, were well under way. Two of the proof-sheets of the second edition were struck off. Hare then made a final effort to have the Middleton dialogue printed unaltered, but Taylor proved adamant, and threatened to drop the publication entirely.[24] Hare yielded once more, but made his feelings clear in a letter written at the end of November 1824: "The matter is really such a mere trifle. . . . when everything else is amicably settled. . . . do you really think the half dozen words of such importance, as for their sake only to break w[ith] such a man as Landor . . . ? For my own part I see nothing to which it can do harm but the cause of religious hypocrisy, and it will not do that half so much harm as the New Testament does. You will excuse this; but I was forced to assure you that I did not mean to recommend you the publication of any book that can do harm to the cause of true godliness."[25] Taylor was offended to have his scruples dismissed as a "mere trifle," so Hare wrote again, this time showing his knack for conciliation: "You must really have an astonishing notion of Landor's powers, if you think he can dissuade men from prayer by a few words. With all my admiration for him, I think him no reasoner, & could prove him so, if it were worth the while. Nevertheless I feel the sincerest respect for your scruples, as I do for anything that is honest and conscientious. If I have ever said anything which seems to imply the contrary, it is that in the warmth of argument one does not keep due watch over ones words."[26] After proceeding this far with Taylor, defending Landor's literary interests while at the same time assuaging Taylor's attacks of conscientiousness, Hare suddenly found all his work sabotaged.

In a salvo of letters written on 1 and 4 April 1825 Landor ordered Taylor to stop publishing his work, and accused him of withholding payment, of submitting padded claims for the number of copies printed, and of arrogantly assuming that the second edition could be had on the same unfair terms as the first. Furthermore, Landor announced that he was ordering his cousin and attorney, Walter Landor of Rugeley, to bring suit against Taylor. Also on 1 April Landor wrote to Hare to explain his action, and enclosed a copy of the first letter to Taylor.[27]

Ten days later, still angry, Landor wrote to Southey of his chagrin at hearing from Hare that two sheets of the second edition had been printed without his authorization: "It had been my very firm resolution to make a very different contract for this; and above all to stipulate, as he had broken his first engagement, that he should either print all that you and Hare admitted, or nothing."[28] Some

A COMMISSION FROM LANDOR 65

of Landor's complaints were just. Taylor had neglected to answer earlier inquiries regarding the settlement of Landor's share of the profits. Then when Taylor did answer, he excused himself from payment of the £89.17.8 owed Landor because of the possibility of future charges against the balance owing to the expenses of the second edition. The second edition had not been specifically authorized by Landor, much less on the same financial terms as the first edition. Landor's natural impetuosity led him to the conclusion that he was ill-used, but after listening to the malicious advice of William Hazlitt and Leigh Hunt, he became convinced that he was being cheated, and the vituperative second letter to Taylor was the result.[29] On the other hand, while the financial terms of the first edition were unusual, Landor had himself proposed them because the commercial value of the work was unknown, and he more than once assured Hare that he had no pecuniary interest. While Landor never gave specific authorization for the second edition, it had been assumed by Hare and Taylor that a new edition of the first two volumes would naturally follow when the first was exhausted and when further volumes containing new dialogues were ready for the press. Landor had revealed before his naïveté in dealing with publishers, but in this episode he showed his worst side, his quick-tempered petulance.

Hare's reaction to Landor's first letter to Taylor was restrained: "Landor's mortification was that no notice had been taken of two or three letters which he wrote on money matters. If you had written to explain the state of things to him, I doubt not he w[oul]d have been perfectly satisfied. As it is, if you have not written to him on this subject already, I wish very much you would, and would explain the whole state of the case. Otherwise we very probably shall have some more angry letters shortly."[30] When Landor's rudely phrased second letter reached England, the storm broke. Taylor's partner, John Hessey, was furious at Landor. Taylor for his part poured out in a long letter to Hare his amazement and indignation at Landor's outrageous charges and threats, which he half suspected were an excuse employed by Landor to seek a change of publisher: "Many a tradesman is less mercenary than some of those who arrogate to themselves exclusively the Title of Gentleman. I renounce him and all his Works with the greatest Willingness."[31]

Hare responded to Taylor's indignant letter, which was accompanied by a draft copy of Landor's vituperations, with a long reply:

> I must needs think myself personally answerable, as from the beginning I have almost forced you . . . to engage in the publication of his Dialogues. I trust however that you will exonerate me from much blame on this account, as I have always felt . . . esteem for your behaviour throughout the whole of the transactions between us. And as Landor has written in such language upon the subject, allow me to assure you that from beginning to end I have felt convinced that your conduct has been that of a thoroughly upright, liberal, and conscientious man.[32]

The next day, with chagrin at the destruction of his labouriously built arrangements, Hare wrote to Landor to defend Taylor and to share the blame: "On the calmest review of the whole matter, it seems to me that I have been three or four times to blame for delaying to write to you, and that Taylor has been once so or twice; but surely there is no villainy in this, or I must be the fourfold villain."[33]

The same day Hare wrote again to Taylor, and indicated that instead of renouncing the *Imaginary Conversations,* he was ready to begin picking up the pieces:

> I have been writing a very long letter to Landor this morning which I hope will bring him to his senses, and make him acknowledge the wrong he has done you. At all events I have fully explained all that concerns the second edition, and stated how very far you were from being precipitate in undertaking it, and how I almost forced it upon you. . . .
>
> What must I do about the second edition[?] You, I fear, would hardly consent to go on with it, even if Landor were to agree to that. But I suppose if I can find another publisher, he will settle . . . for the sheets already printed. . . . I shall be extremely sorry to be corresponding with any other publisher in your stead, but I am afraid it must be so.[34]

Taylor wrote to Hare in gratitude for the vigour with which Hare had defended him to Landor. Taylor admitted this action surprised him. To this touching admission Hare could not forbear replying:

I am exceedingly glad to find that I could lend you any assistance in dispelling the uneasiness which Landor's letter had excited; and I shall be still more, if, as you say, I have led you to think better of and expect more from your fellow creatures, than you were previously disposed to do. My way has always been to think and hope the best: to be sure, this has now and then led to a little disappointment; but it is commonly possible to diminish this by considering how much is attributable to ignorance of this understanding, or want of thought; and at all events one may turn from a dreary prospect to look at some sunnier one. You must however have rated human virtue very low, if, where no sacrifice was needed, no exertion was to be made, where the stretching out a hand was sufficient to assist a fellow creature in distress, you did not expect that even a hand would be stretched forth.[35]

So ended John Taylor's role as Landor's publisher—Hare had to repeat the dreary task of placing the *Imaginary Conversations*—but it did not end Hare's relationship with Taylor in the publishing of other books. That connection flourished for several more years, and ended only when Taylor left the trade. As for the controversy with Landor, Hare was the one person to emerge with his dignity intact. One can only admire the tact and loyalty he displayed in negotiating with two headstrong characters like Landor and Taylor.[36] But the question remains why Hare so unselfishly devoted time and energy to the interests of someone he had not met, much less someone as irascible and difficult as Landor. The answer is a complex one. At the simplest level the piecemeal and illegible state in which the dialogues were received necessitated their transcription and editing. This might have become the responsibility of a publisher's clerk, except that Taylor's acceptance of the dialogues was conditional, not absolute, and the condition was that Hare supervise the suppression of offensive passages. Thus even when the dialogues were in the hands of a single publisher for a period of two years, Hare was caught up in editorial chores. In the first instance he probably responded to Landor's plea for help out of loyalty to his brother, Francis. Hare formed a high opinion of Landor's work, and his role of fostering literature gave him a sense of pride and purpose. But the task soon expanded to include defending Landor's right to freely expressed opinions with which Hare did not often agree. This protective role helps explain Hare's prolonged, unpaid involvement with the project, and also exhibits his liberal character to best advantage.

Hare's handling of Landor and Taylor was exemplary, and Landor was chastened by the experience, if never quite willing to admit that he was wrong. He was, however, at least willing to give Hare full authority in the publishing arrangements for the *Imaginary Conversations*. Landor realized that if he wished to see them published, he had no other choice. But this delegation of authority came only when Hare protested the utter hopelessness of any other arrangement. "About a new publisher I do not know what to do. As your second letter contradicts the first, your third says you will have nothing to do with either Longman or Constable, and I fear a fourth may come with a new scheme, what am I to do? After having failed once so egregiously, I do not like trusting anything but your express desire."[37] At this Landor conceded authority to Hare, and wrote, "I have no other conditions to propose than that my orthography be preserved, my conversations published unmutilated and twelve copies for my friends from the second edition."[38]

Hare turned the *Imaginary Conversations* over to Henry Colburn for publication. The setting of the second edition of volumes I and II proceeded, and they were issued at the end of May 1826. But to Hare and Landor's annoyance, Colburn failed to issue the third volume simultaneously. Volume III appeared in May 1828 after an unexplained delay of two years. Colburn's lassitude caused Hare to seek yet another publisher to undertake volumes IV and V. This time Hare eschewed experienced publishers, and settled instead upon young William Harrison Ainsworth (1805–82), who was just starting up. As early as March 1828 work on volumes IV and V was under way, and it became clear that their bulk would require another volume, number VI. But before the type was set Ainsworth withdrew entirely from a publishing career to make his fortune as a writer and editor.[39] Again Hare was left to find a publisher. These difficult negotiations cost him much correspondence and several trips to London.

But Hare's travails had not dimmed his enthusiasm, as he wrote to Taylor in November 1828: "The new volumes contain beautiful

A COMMISSION FROM LANDOR

and magnificent things, still better, I am inclined to think, than the former ones. Another scheme we meditate, . . . is to publish a selection in two crown octavos, of all the dialogues fit for female reading, omitting anything in any way objectionable."[40] James Duncan issued the next two volumes in May of 1829, but the sales were disastrously few, and the projected sixth volume did not materialize.

Hare wrote to Landor in July 1829 with a eulogy on the project: "The Conversations are too classical and substantial for the morbid and frivolous taste of the English public, and few publishers, except my friend Taylor, look beyond the saleableness of a work."[41] So ended Julius Hare's years of effort as Landor's unpaid agent. The two did not meet until Landor's visit to England in 1832, but they remained good friends ever after.

Chapter 6

Guessing at Truth

During the years at Cambridge while Hare laboured over Landor's manuscripts he was also engaged in other literary projects. Together with his brother Augustus he compiled a collection of essays, aphorisms, and literary studies which was published by John Taylor in 1827 under the title *Guesses at Truth by Two Brothers.* Though it was published anonymously during his lifetime, Julius Hare was known best as the author of the *Guesses,* which remained in print into the next century.[1]

The *Guesses* covers an enormous range of historical, literary, and moral subjects. But the names most frequently invoked are those of Coleridge and Wordsworth.[2] Professor McFarland suggests that it was the Coleridgean tone of the anthology that recommended it to Taylor. The publisher had issued Coleridge's *Aids to Reflection* just before accepting the *Guesses* late in 1825.[3] Indeed, as the proofs were being corrected Augustus Hare wrote to Taylor to suggest that a set interleaved with blank sheets be sent to Coleridge in hope of eliciting his notes and comments, "which w[oul]d double the value of the book to thinkers, and amply repay my brother & myself for any pains it may have cost us."[4]

In 1838, after Augustus Hare's death, Julius Hare issued a revised edition which he dedicated to Wordsworth as follows:

> For more than twenty years I have cherisht the wish of offering some testimony of my gratitude to him by whom my eyes were opened to see and enjoy the world of poetry in nature and in books. . . .

Then too would another name have been associated with yours ... a name which, I trust, will ever be coupled with yours in the admiration and love of Englishmen,—the name of Coleridge. You and he came forward together in a shallow, hard, and worldly age,—an age alien and almost averse from the higher and more strenuous exercises of imagination and thought,— as the purifiers and regenerators of poetry and philosophy. It was a great aim; and greatly have you both wrought for its accomplishment. Many, among those who are now England's best hope and stay, will respond to my thankful acknowledgement of the benefits my heart and mind have received from you both.[5]

When Wordsworth received his dedication copy he replied to Hare: "I might have thanked you sooner for the Volume and for the honor you have done me by the Dedication. . . . I have contrived to read a great part of the Guesses at Truth, and with great pleasure and profit."[6]

The first series of the *Guesses* appeared in May 1827, but the book had its genesis a decade earlier in Julius Hare's manuscript commonplace book. Not only is the form of the *Guesses* very similar to the commonplace book, but many of the aphorisms and shorter essays in the latter found their way into the *Guesses*. Hare prefaced the 1827 edition with a letter of warning:

> TO THE READER. I here present you with a few suggestions, the fruits, alas, of much idleness. Such of them as are distinguisht by some capital letter, I have borrowed from my acuter friends. My own are little more than glimmerings, I had almost said dreams, of thought: not a word in them is to be taken on trust.
>
> If then I am addressing one of that numerous class, who read to be told what to think, let me advise you to meddle with the book no further. You wish to buy a house ready furnisht: do not come to look for it in a stone-quarry. But if you are building up your opinions for yourself, and only want to be provided with materials, you may meet with many things in these pages to suit you.[7]

Here, then, in book form was much of the same intellectual food which Hare offered to his students at Cambridge, served with the same insistence that the auditors do their own critical thinking. In this form it was available to many who would never see the inside of any university. In a letter to his sister-in-law, Lucy, Hare explained more fully the motives behind the *Guesses:*

> You are a very pretty lady to think one is to write a book for people to read, without thought or attention, when they come in tired from a walk and go to lie down on the sofa. There are plenty of such books; and I am afraid they seldom do much good, and often harm. They weaken the mind, instead of bracing. . . . Especially in a book like the "Guesses", does it seem requisite that the thoughts should be condensed. . . . Only I would try to express every thought correctly, and as clearly as is compatible with brevity. . . . The readers the book is chiefly designed for . . . are young men. . . . and they are the persons to whom I think I can afford the most help, and who want it the most. Women have plenty of good books to read, far better than I could write for them; but young men are inundated with false philosophy, or else fall in a dreary habit of mere mechanical reading.[8]

The production of the *Guesses* in book form took more than a year because both brothers read the proofs, and required numerous corrections and additions to the setting. Moreover, the extraordinarily hot summer of 1826 was not conducive to labour, and was mentioned in the correspondence as a new source of delay.[9]

When at last the *Guesses* appeared, the book's success took the Hare brothers by surprise. Julius dispatched copies from London, where he was staying with Lady Jones, to Whewell and Thirlwall at Cambridge. He also sent a copy anonymously to Richard Sheepshanks, for within a few days of publication Sheepshanks wrote to Whewell with his reactions:

> I can with perfect sincerity admire the spirit & candour of his opinions & the pure language in which they are expressed. I cannot say that in my opinion he has not frequently guessed wrong. But when I think it the work of a gentleman & a scholar he will excuse me when I dissent almost entirely from his political & not infrequently from his ethical maxims. I was for a moment puzzled to think what acquaintance I had who had been thus amusing himself. But a few of H[are]'s characteristic notions and phrases soon convinced me that it could be no one but the veritable Julius. My sister believes she should have discovered

its author without my aid & she of course admires it more unqualifiedly than I do, unqualified admiration not being my forte.[10]

In the autumn of 1827 Southey wrote to a friend, "Of course you have seen the 'Hair-brain'd Guesses at Truth,' by Julius and Augustus. There are some things in it which one wonders that they should have thought worth saying, much that is odd, a little that is paradoxical, but a great deal of sound feeling and sterling sense."[11] Other friends were less harsh.

Hare wrote to John Taylor to call attention to a favourable review of the *Guesses* in the *Athenaeum*, written "in a very manly and amiable spirit."[12] The reviewer was Frederick Maurice, who admired the book and asked, "Why, then, has it not become popular?" Part of the answer, he suggested,

> is, that it does not fall in with the views of any party, or a liberal sect. . . .
>
> Another reason why the "Guesses at Truth" have not become more fashionable is, because they do not profess to be a system. The fault is not that they *are* "guesses," but that they do not *profess* to be any thing else. If you tell a man you are guessing, you leave him the labour of thinking whether you are right or wrong; and labour takes time and trouble, both of which are reserved by our generation for their countinghouses and dinnertables. . . .
>
> It is also comparatively unrenowned for two opposite though not contrary, reasons. The authors do not chime in with the weary "ding-dong-bell" of class doctrines; but they have strong convictions of their own. They do not put forward a system, but they think systematically.[13]

Maurice was, of course, mistaken in his emphasis on the book's unpopularity. In the next decade the revision of the *Guesses* became very much a family industry as Augustus' wife Maria and other contributors brought forth their notes for insertion in future editions. Professor McFarland, writing with a perspective quite different from Maurice's, thinks that it is the book's long-term popularity that requires explanation: "It may well have been that the more common reader between 1827 and the end of the century bought

Guesses at Truth as a prop for his pretensions to cultivation as a Christian gentleman, and it undoubtedly happened that more often than not he found most pleasure and use in its aphorisms, which are seldom effective and seldom the work of Julius Hare. Its popular fate notwithstanding, *Guesses at Truth* is a significant repository of romantic and Victorian literary ideas and attitudes and as such an important link in the history of ideas in the nineteenth century."[14] Professor McFarland is doubtless correct to attribute much of the popular appeal of the *Guesses* to cultural pretentiousness, but he is wrong to exonerate Julius Hare of responsibility for the aphorisms in the book. His commonplace book is replete with such aphorisms, many of which are included in the *Guesses*.[15]

Another of Hare's major literary pursuits while at Cambridge was the editing of the *Philological Museum,* a journal which he and Thirlwall founded in 1831.[16] Their effort was inspired by the *Rheinische Museum* edited by B.G. Niebuhr during his tenure at Bonn University in the 1820s, and by Professor Monk's *Museum Criticum* which appeared between 1814 and 1826. The *Philological Museum* was designed to awaken an interest in the higher criticism, to introduce Germanic scholarship and criticism into England, and to foster classical studies generally. Hare had long been fascinated by the study of language on the comparative model, as an early essay in his commonplace book bears witness.[17] As editors, Hare and Thirlwall sought to gain acceptance for a periodical of limited interest, but high critical standards. Although publication only lasted for two volumes of three issues each, the *Philological Museum* deserves attention not only as a vehicle of the new higher criticism and *Altertumswissenschaft,* but also as a prototype of the modern scholarly journal.

The editor's preface, by Hare, that opened the first volume of the new publication laid great stress upon the absence of any other English journal in the field of philology. Hare registered concern that so much philological writing in English between 1825 and 1830 had been merely translations from German of grammars and dictionaries: "It is not well that we should import all of our knowledge from abroad, and let our own intellects lie waste." He went on to outline a broad editorial policy that, though primarily interested in those "two colossal edifices that stand forth amid the ruins of the ancient world," Greece and Rome, would exclude "no inquiry that comes under the head of philology. . . . Nor will the philology of modern languages be regarded as forbidden ground," nor "dissertations on Oriental literature, when they are not, as such things mostly are, either too heavy or too light." In summary "every subject that concerns antiquity, and can be treated philologically, comes within the compass of the plan." Hare promised that he and his co-editor would demand only "temperance in the style, and soundness in the matter."[18]

Thirlwall sent a copy of the first issue to Baron Bunsen in Rome with a letter which obliquely explained the purpose of the journal: "I am enclosing . . . the first number of a new Philological Journal which we are trying to set up here. The articles signed J.C.H. which you will probably think the best as well as the largest part of the volume are from the pen of my friend Hare. . . . If you are struck by the appearance [in Thirlwall's "Ancaeus"] of an odd mixture of extravagant conjectures with commonplace learning I must beg you to remember that *many things are new in England that are familiar or even stale in Germany.*"[19] Thirlwall exaggerated the number and influence of Hare's contributions, but during the brief life of the *Philological Museum* Hare did contribute major essays "On the Names of the Days of the Week" and "On English Orthography." Both editors contributed numerous translations from the works of Niebuhr, Schleiermacher, Savigny, Buttmann, Delbruck, and Dindorf on various aspects of ancient history.

Perhaps Hare's most important contribution was his persuasive essay "On English Orthography" in which he argued for orthographic reform, and defended the steps he had adopted in his own spelling. Some like Thirlwall and Whewell briefly followed Hare's example, but lapsed in the face of convention. Hare, however, persevered in his reformed spelling for the rest of his life. Hare advocated two reforms, or "renovations" as he termed them. The first and "the one of most frequent occurrence consists of substituting *t* for *ed* in the termination of several preterites and participles, such as *equipt, expresst, punisht.* . . . My object . . . has been to get rid of one of the greatest and commonest eyesores of our spelling." These would harmonize with such irregular verbs as *kept, wept, crept, slept,* and *swept.* Hare believed that the attempt to make Anglo-Saxon verbs conform to continental inflexions arose from confusing monotony in language with harmony. This "renovation" Hare doggedly preserved for the rest of his life, or, as one wit put it, "He *cherisht* until he *perisht.*" Hare also proposed the suppression of silent *e* in certain past participles, but feared that "such is the force of habit, that *reformed* or *reform'd* has a less unpleasant look than *reformd:* though *reformd* agrees exactly with our pronunciation, and the only advantage in the other ways of writing the word is the introduction of an absurdity."[20]

The second reform Hare desired was a restoration of the pure genitive, by suppressing the mark of elision which derived from a seventeenth-century misconception that the genitive *s* stood for *his:* e.g., *the king's sword* equals *the king his sword.* The apostrophe should be *dropt* because there is no elision for it to signify. "Still more absurd is the mark of elision after the genitive plural:" *e.g., soldiers' swords.* Hare did drop the elision mark from the genitive plural in his own spelling, since it occurs infrequently, but he hesitated to drop it from the genitive singular. He justified his concern with such details at great length: "For as no errour, however petty or insignificant, can be allowed to take root and run to seed, but a crop of noxious weeds is sure . . . to sprout up from it, so this very mistake about the nature of our genitives has been . . . injurious to the elegance of our style, . . . and as an idiomatical is always an easy and graceful style, so every departure from idiom . . . renders our phraseology inelegant and clumsy."[21]

The inspiration for Hare's orthographic "renovations" was Landor. In an Imaginary Conversation between Hare and himself Landor created the following dialogue:

> Archdeacon Hare: In some of your later writings, I perceive you have not strictly followed the line you formerly laid down for spelling. . . . It is chiefly in the preterites and participles that I have followed you perseveringly.
> Landor: In more essential things than preterites and participles I ought rather to have been your follower than you mine. No language is purer or clearer than yours.[22]

While preparing Landor's *Imaginary Conversations* for the press, Hare expressed reservations about some of Landor's unconventional forms, such as *sovran* for *sovereign* and *foran* for *foreign.*[23] But in later years Hare adopted these very forms. Hare's notions about orthography were coloured by his characteristic nationalism: while "no true patriot—for our language is . . . a most important part of our country—will think of meddling with it rashly," some reforms were necessary because "when the tongue is paralyzed, the limbs soon follow. No nation hath long survived the decrepitude of its language."[24]

Among the *Philological Museum*'s other contributors were Henry Fynes Clinton (1781–1852), the noted classical chronologist; Henry Malden (1800–76), a classical scholar and college friend of the editors; J.M. Kemble, former Apostle and pupil of Hare and Thirlwall; Henry Alford (1810–71), another Apostle;[25] Thomas Flower Ellis (1796–1861);[26] and John Kenrick (1788–1877), then teaching at Manchester College in York. But the most prolific contributor, after the editors themselves, was George Cornewall Lewis (1806–63). Ten major and minor articles by Lewis appeared in the six published numbers of the journal.[27]

From among the editors' other friends several special features were elicited. Hare persuaded William Wordsworth to submit translations from the first book of "The Ineid," and convinced William Whewell to write an essay on Vitruvius for publication. Hare also took the opportunity to publish two of Landor's Imaginary Conversations from the unrealized sixth volume, as well as some of Landor's celebrated Latin verse. Hare sought contributions from his friend Thomas Arnold of Rugby, but Arnold was reluctant: "You have my best Wishes for your Success, and so far as I have seen of your first Number, I think you will deserve Success. But for myself, I am afraid . . . that I am a very poor Philologist, and my Knowledge is almost too superficial on almost every Point to produce anything worth your having."[28] Four months later Arnold again wrote to Hare: "I like your philological Journal very much, and hope sincerely that it will answer, at least sufficiently to enable you to continue it."[29]

The *Philological Museum* was off to a good start with the phalanx of eminent contributors which Hare and Thirlwall had assembled. The tone of the journal was scholarly, if not downright pedantic. It should have appealed to those who were well-educated in the classics and intellectually curious, and such people would for the most part have been clergymen. The *Philological Museum* was published by Deighton of Cambridge, distributed by Rivingtons in London and Parker in Oxford, and 1,015 copies were issued three times annually, in November, February, and May. Each issue contained several long essays, book reviews, and a number of short notices and "miscellaneous observations."

But despite its many virtues, most copies of the *Philological Museum* remained unsold. The departure of Hare from Cambridge in the spring of 1832 to accept a Church living in Sussex threw the full weight of the editorship upon Thirlwall, and the failure of many contributors to supply promised copy led to a temporary dearth of publishable material. In December 1832 Thirlwall wrote to Bunsen:

> I fully enter into your views as to the important functions which philology might and would discharge in England if it had been cultivated among us as it has been in Germany. But alas! the obstacles both to the cultivation and the application of its resources are at present greater than a foreigner can easily conceive, and its friends have to fight a battle almost against hope. Still the experiment is well worth the trial & god forbid I should despair of the final result. Let our journal only live & I am sure that it would improve & that it would work good.[30]

The following spring Thirlwall sent Bunsen the fifth issue, and noted in his accompanying letter: "I have been keeping [the journal] alive as well as I could in the absence of Hare and some others of our best contributors."[31]

In the autumn of 1833 Thirlwall sent Bunsen the sixth number, and predicted it would be the last, for sales had not improved despite efforts to entice students with essays geared more to the Cambridge curriculum, and Deighton was loath to risk more money on the venture. Unless the Cambridge University Press Syndicate agreed to assume financing, the journal could not go on. Thirlwall was especially grieved at this prospect because the *Philological Museum* was the only effort of the kind in England: "I cannot help thinking that we are in great danger of sinking into that state of general confirmed indifference to this branch of knowledge, which the revolution and the system of Napoleon have produced in France, where I believe a taste for it is generally considered as a kind of eccentric fancy. . . . It is true that we can never come to this point so long as the study of the ancient languages continues to form a part of what passes for liberal education. . . . I am afraid . . . of a growing tendency toward the opinion that such studies are frivolous, or at least of very slight importance."[32]

Thirlwall narrated the final chapter in the journal's demise in a series of three letters to a Scottish correspondent who had submitted an article. Thirlwall explained that although Deighton refused to carry the *Philological Museum* any further, application was made to the University Press for financial assistance. However, the Vice-Chancellor had informed him that no publication grant could be made to a serial which appeared anonymously. Still Thirlwall held out some hope of continuing, but at that point the controversy over compulsory chapel and the admission of Dissenters to degrees erupted, and he left Cambridge.[33]

The *Philological Museum* died, and the diminution of the role of the classics in the university curriculum which Thirlwall anticipated also came to pass. But classical studies in England did not suffer the same fate as Hare and Thirlwall's journal. The Philological Society and such journals as the *Classical Museum* were in later years carrying on in the same spirit.[34] However, the *Philological Museum* stands out for its roster of illustrious contributors and for the high critical standards of its contents. A.P. Stanley observed that while the *Philological Museum* "shared the usual transitory fate of such learned periodicals," it nevertheless "during the period of its existence furnished more solid additions to English literature and scholarship than any other of the kind that has appeared."[35]

In this account of the short life of Hare and Thirlwall's journal, the term "philology" has only been defined vaguely in terms of the journal's contents and the editors' hopes of fostering classical studies in England. The term "philology" was meant to evoke the broad meaning of "logos," of the complete study of ancient literature as a key to the scholarly recapture of the essence of ancient Greek and Roman civilization. This scholarly quest for *Altertumswissenschaft* was a preoccupation of the German romantic movement, and Dr J.W. Burrow has ably shown it to have been the precursor of the field of comparative linguistics. In this scholarly transformation Hare played a direct and seemingly inherited role, for it was his uncle, Sir William Jones, who founded comparative linguistics by his astute assessment of the relationship between Sanskrit, Greek, and Latin. Later Hare's friends C.K.J. von Bunsen and Friedrich

Max Müller, among others, developed a sophisticated comparative linguistics based upon grammatical analysis. The study of language came to be seen as a means of studying ethnology, law, and, of course, the prehistory and early history of man. It was with this enthusiasm for *Altertumswissenschaft,* for philology as a key to broader knowledge of the classical past, that Hare and Thirlwall founded their journal.[36]

Chapter 7

Higher Criticism from Germany

After Hare's return to Cambridge in 1822, his literary activities included efforts to Germanize the English intellectual consciousness. These efforts began in 1820 with the publication of his translation of Fouqué's *Sintram* and of several contributions in the Ollier brothers' short-lived *Miscellany,* and they provide a coherent explanation of much of Hare's literary work in the 1820s. Hare and his friend Thirlwall were moved by what they perceived as the depressed and stagnant state of English intellectual life. They therefore undertook consciously to provide a stimulus by translations from German. Professor McFarland has written that Hare and Thirlwall's Germanizing activities were inspired by a "large and lofty" purpose:

> They hoped not only to acquaint English readers with a foreign literature and thereby possibly to stimulate intellectual and imaginative activity; they hoped also to . . . break down the narrow and static rationalistic and scientific precepts and methods that had determined most of what they had had to learn at Cambridge. . . . Hare and Thirlwall determined to make an attempt, through their translations, to further a reconciliation of reason and imagination and experience and faith so that true vitality and integrity might be restored to thought, to taste, and to belief.[1]

This reconciliation was begun in England by Coleridge and Wordsworth, but the work remained unfinished.[2]

While such a motive is clearly deducible from Hare and Thirlwall's efforts as translators, it must be emphasized that they sought to stimulate English minds to original effort, not to make England an intellectual province of Germany. Hare wrote that if translations from German scholars "do not excite some of their readers to think . . . they might as well have been allowed to remain in the obscurity of their own language."[3] Nor was Thirlwall sanguine about the possibility of imported German ideas effecting the intellectual regeneration of England, as he wrote to Bunsen in 1823:

> Some of the better spirits of the age have expected this regeneration of our literature from Germany & have in consequence attempted to naturalize among us some of the speculations of your philosophers. . . . I am inclined to doubt, first, that it would be possible through any medium to familiarize even our best cultivated intellects with your philosophical theories, & secondly, still more, that by so doing the main object would be accomplished. Such systems would, I think, be always something foreign & uncongenial to our peculiar intellectual character & would therefore have either no general influence, or a wrong & mischievous one, on Literature, Art & Science. It is, as you say, from England, from some original & independent English thinker, that we must expect this restoration of philosophy, which appears unhappily to be still very distant.[4]

There is in Thirlwall's letter a self-conscious nationalism which was a characteristic of the so-called Broad Church. There is also the implicit realization that Coleridge had failed to fulfil the role of a native English intellectual regenerator. For this demanding task no one was better suited intellectually, nor worse suited temperamentally, than Coleridge. He possessed the vision and the familiarity with continental scholarship, but his indolence, improvidence, and addiction rendered him incapable of producing more than notebooks and fragments of the larger work required.[5]

Both Hare and Thirlwall persevered as translators, and it is instructive that they both should have produced translations of Tieck's *Novellen* in these years. Hare's earlier fondness for Fouqué reflected a susceptibility to stories of the fantastic and the gothic, which were so much in vogue in England and Germany. In Tieck's *Novellen* Hare and Thirlwall found what they believed to be the most authentic strain of such romantic elements.[6]

Hare told Charles Ollier that he was anxious to find a rapid means of diffusing new tastes and principles among his countrymen. *Olliers Literary Miscellany* was a failure. Hare also considered contributing to the *Quarterly Review* because of its wide circulation.[7] But instead he found a waiting vehicle for his translations in the *London Magazine*, published by Taylor and Hessey, which became one of the principal organs for the dissemination of German literature in England. In 1823-24 Thomas Carlyle contributed a series of articles upon "Schiller's Life and Writings," and Thomas De Quincey, another regular contributor, often wrote on German subjects. In the spring of 1824 Carlyle's translation of Goethe's great novel appeared anonymously at Edinburgh under the title of *Wilhelm Meister's Apprenticeship*. In a letter to Taylor, Hare noted with irritation his inability to obtain Carlyle's *Meister* at Cambridge.[8] De Quincey, however, experienced no such difficulty in obtaining the book. In the August and September issues of the *London Magazine* he unleashed his "Goethe, as Reflected in His Novel, Wilhelm Meister," a savage appraisal of author, book, and translator.[9] Carlyle appears to have taken this, the worst review of his translation, with adequate good humour. But Julius Hare did not, and resolved to write a reply in the form of a defence of Goethe and a clarification of *Wilhelm Meister*.[10] Goethe's novel was the paradigm of the *Bildungsroman*, or apprenticeship novel, which also flourished in English literature. Reception of the original novel in 1798 had been as cool as it was limited in England; William Taylor of Norwich referred to it as a "comic novel." Carlyle's version was more warmly received.[11]

Hare had a high regard for the abilities of De Quincey, whom he called "the great logician of our times," but in attacking Goethe, De Quincey had gone too far.[12] Hare was an admirer of Goethe and was well acquainted with *Wilhelm Meister*. Only months earlier he had contributed to the pages of the *London Magazine* a translation from that novel of Mignon's famous song, "Kennst du das Land."[13] Hare began his reply to De Quincey, but soon bogged down, for he was at that time still disputing with Taylor over the censorship of Landor's dialogues, as well as counselling Thirlwall over his translations, in addition to his own teaching duties.[14] Hare apparently finished his article in December 1824, but at the beginning of 1825 Taylor and Hessey sold the *London Magazine*. Hare's article never appeared. He showed his annoyance over the matter in letters to Taylor during the following spring. Hare did cross swords with De Quincey in print a decade later, defending Coleridge, not Goethe.[15]

Later in 1825 another periodical outlet appeared for publishing the defence of Goethe. But it was not the Goethe essay that appeared, but rather a translation by Hare of one of Tieck's *Novellen*—*Die Liebezauber*, or *The Love Charm*.[16] W.M. Praed joined with Charles Knight, the popular publisher, Macaulay, and several others in 1823–24 to produce *Knight's Quarterly Magazine*, which died after six issues.[17] Early in 1825 Praed and Henry Malden persuaded Charles Knight to resurrect the journal, which was then simply titled the *Quarterly Magazine*. The first and only issue of this journal appeared in August 1825, and contained Hare's translation of Tieck's *The Love Charm*.[18] Hare then submitted his Goethe essay to Henry Malden for inclusion in the second issue of the *Quarterly Magazine*. Malden wrote to Charles Knight regarding Hare's essay: "The article is a masterly piece of elaborate criticism, better than any literary criticism which has appeared in any English review for the last half-dozen years. It is a kind to stamp at once . . . a very high character, on a new publication. . . . I wish to show that men may be . . . liberal thinkers in politics, without being raving democrats, without reviling everything old, without renouncing the imagination . . . and without being despisers of God and of all religion. I wish too, that our magazine may be thoroughly and heartily religious without cant or affectation. Such a character Hare's article will go very far to give us."[19] After this wonderful build-up of anti-Benthamite fervour, it is disappointing that the proposed second issue never appeared. Presumably the sales of the first issue prompted Knight to drop the project.

Hare's translation of Tieck's *The Love Charm* was reissued anonymously in 1831 by Edward Moxon in a single volume that also contained translations by Hare of two more *Novellen* by Tieck: *Der Alte vom Berge* and *Pietro von Abano*.[20] These three tales, which have the requisite quantity of medieval romanticism and the supernatural, received a glowing review in the pages of *Fraser's Magazine*.[21] Tieck later wrote that excellent translations had been made of several of his *Novellen,* and at the time of his death in 1853 he owned several volumes of such translations including two copies of Hare's versions in the 1831 Moxon edition.[22]

For the 1831 publication of *The Love Charm* Hare revised the 1825 version to conform to his recently adopted orthographic reforms, which gave the two versions a dissimilar appearance. When James Hogg helped De Quincey compile his *Selections Grave and Gay* (1852), he suspected that *The Love Charm* of 1825 was De Quincey's work, though De Quincey rejected the authorship. But after De Quincey's death Hogg nonetheless included it in his *Uncollected Writings of Thomas De Quincey* (1890–92) upon the authority of Charles Knight's recollections. David Masson had done likewise in compiling and editing De Quincey's *Collected Writings* (1889–90). Only in 1937 did Hans Galinsky overturn the false ascription of Hare's translation.[23]

While Hare's authorship of the translation of *The Love Charm* in the *Quarterly Magazine* long went unacknowledged, a later version of the same tale was incorrectly ascribed to him. The superficial similarity between Hare's 1831 Moxon version and the translation which appeared in *Tales of the Phantasus,* published by James Burns in 1845, led the standard authority on German literature in English translation to give Hare the credit.[24]

Hare probably undertook his translations of Tieck's *Novellen* as a relaxing pastime. Thirlwall certainly did so, turning to Tieck as a relief from his labours in rendering into English Schleiermacher's treatise upon the Gospel of Luke (1821). Hare was involved in both these projects, and they also led to yet another attempt at censorship by the publisher John Taylor.[25]

Biblical scholars in eighteenth-century Germany undertook to analyse the Holy Scriptures objectively, as though they were dealing with any other work of history or literature, and in this way to reach conclusions about authorship, chronology of composition, and sources of information.[26] This was not an entirely new procedure, but harkened back to French critics of the late seventeenth century, like Richard Simon and Pierre Bayle.[27] Nonetheless, the boldness with which this biblical research was expounded flew in the face of the still-prevalent doctrine of the divine inspiration of Scripture. This doctrine was especially entrenched in England, where, in the three decades following the "godless" French Revolution, orthodoxy was identified with conservatism and social stability, sound churchmanship with good citizenship. In that era social critics and political radicals were often atheists, and like Thomas Paine and William Hone were likely to be prosecuted for "seditious blasphemy." Dominated by such attitudes the Episcopal Bench remained conservative and the curriculum at the Universities remained narrow.

Hare and Thirlwall were as anxious to break down the prejudices inhibiting English speculative theology as they were to attack the stagnation which they perceived in other areas of English intellectual life. Not surprisingly the means chosen was the translation of German theological scholarship. The attack upon rigid thinking became an aim of the Broad Church, and brought that band of liberal Anglican Churchmen into a series of controversies in which their orthodoxy was impugned. This drawn-out struggle culminated in the 1860s with the trials of Bishop Colenso and of some of the authors of *Essays and Reviews* (1860) for heresy. Hare did not live to witness this debacle of the Broad Church, or perhaps he, like Thirlwall, would have regretted that honest intellectual speculation appeared to have grown out of control.[28] Hare was a participant in the earlier battles of the Broad Church. In this role he defended his German friends, Niebuhr and Bunsen, and he and Thirlwall helped to introduce the German higher criticism to the English reading public.

The first exposure in English of the new German *Bibelkritik* was the publication of an English translation of J.D. Michaelis' *Introduction to the New Testament* (1793–1801) by Herbert Marsh, later Lady Margaret Professor of Divinity at Cambridge. Marsh had studied under Michaelis at Leipzig, a most unusual background for an English divine. His translation included his own extensive notes and a dissertation on the origin and composition of the first three Gospels. This was the first modern English scholarship on the so-called synoptic problem, that is, on the interrelationships of the first three, or "synoptic," Gospels.[29] Marsh's divinity lectures at Cambridge were popular and well attended. It is probable that Hare and Thirlwall heard them, and were thus inspired to an interest in biblical philology. Even without this stimulus, their interest in Niebuhr's history might naturally have led them to Schleiermacher's great work upon verbal, biblical inspiration. Their familiarity with Marsh's work is clear from the title of Thirlwall's translation: *A Critical Essay on the Gospel of St. Luke. By Dr. Frederick Schleiermacher. With an Introduction by the Translator. Containing an Account of the Controversy respecting the Origin of the Three First Gospels since Bishop Marsh's Dissertation* (1825).[30]

The controversy referred to in the title was over the source of common elements in the first three synoptic Gospels, Matthew, Mark, and Luke. One school of thought maintained that there had once existed an *Urevangelium* or "source Gospel," from which the Gospels of the New Testament had been in part drawn. This notion was reminiscent of the Marcionite heresy of the early church. Marcion (fl. 2nd century A.D.) had distinguished between the Hebrew God of the Old Testament and the Christian God of the New, and created a church which acknowledged two deities, but only one Gospel to which Marcion added the Epistles of Saint Paul. In early *Urevangelium* theory the Gospel of Marcion was presumed to have derived from an original Gospel in the same way as the Gospels of the New Testament. However, the Gospel of Marcion later proved to be merely the Gospel of Saint Luke heavily altered. A more telling threat to the *Urevangelium* school represented by Friedrich Schleiermacher (1768-1834) was the hypothesis of J.K.L. Gieseler (1792-1854) that common elements in the synoptic Gospels resulted not from transcription from a common source, but from established phrases and imagery which had grown up in the age of apostolic preaching before the evangelists wrote.[31] Schleiermacher offered a careful refinement of the *Urevangelium* theory in his essay on Luke. He maintained that instead of supposing that the evangelists drew only upon each other's work, or upon a single *Urevangelium*, it was more logical to assume that there were numerous Gospel-like narratives antecedent to Matthew, Mark, and Luke. Multiple versions of the life of Christ would have grown up as a part of the proselytizing process of Christian preaching. The relatively refined and finished Gospels of the New Testament, asserted Schleiermacher, would have been the work of authors who "had collected by diligent research an extraordinary treasure of detached narratives from all parts of Christ's public life."[32] In a letter to Hare, Thirlwall lamented that reconciling these points of view was the hardest task he faced in writing an introduction to Schleiermacher's essay.[33]

While such critical speculations seem easily justified in the name of scholarship, they bore a tinge of heresy, which timid-minded English divines, raised upon such dogmas as the Mosaic integrity of the Pentateuch, and the originality of the divinely inspired synoptic Gospels, found quite distasteful. If there was anything more offensive to believers in divine inspiration than the notion of a "source Gospel," it was the promotion by translation of the work of a man who posited scores of such heretical documents. Although the first great controversy over Broad Church orthodoxy lay a decade in the future, Thirlwall was well aware of the risk even in translating such a work for anonymous publication.[34]

Thirlwall in his introduction, which traced the background of textual criticism and controversy over the Gospels, approached the problem of prejudice head on: "Before however we enter upon the proposed inquiry, it may appear to some readers necessary to apologize for the controversy itself, by shewing . . . that it is neither dangerous nor useless. . . . as it cannot be concealed that German theology in general, and German biblical criticism in particular, labours at present under an evil name among our divines." Then in a note he was even more specific about those to whom he alluded: "The last warning against the infection of German divinity was raised by Mr. Conybeare, in the Bampton Lectures for 1824. The candour and earnestness displayed by the author increase our regret that his studies had not led him to feel the necessity of acquiring the German language before he undertook that work, and that he was snatched away before he had an opportunity of enlarging and correcting his views. . . . although . . . Mr. Conybeare's book is directed against that school, it does not contain one of the modern names which everyone at all acquainted with the literature of Germany has been accustomed to respect as the chief ornaments of its theology."[35] Thirlwall was celebrated for his sense of irony, but here he engaged in unbridled sarcasm, against a man who died the previous year at the untimely age of forty-five. It might have been this discourteous assault upon the dead that Coleridge had in mind when he wrote of the book to his nephew: "Have you seen or heard of the translation of Schleiermacher's Essay on St. Luke's Gospel . . . ? It will make the Bamptonists, Hulseans, &c shake their ears."[36]

The reaction set in quickly enough, for within two months of the publication of Thirlwall's translation, Hugh James Rose was attacking German theology, and Schleiermacher in particular, from the pulpit of Great Saint Mary's, Cambridge, where in May 1825 he served as Select Preacher.[37] Rose's assault had a sequel more than twenty years later. In February 1848, when Caroline Fox (1819–71), the Quaker diarist, had translated some of Schleiermacher's sermons, she showed them to F.D. Maurice, who replied,

> There is one consideration in reference to the wisdom of publishing these sermons at the present moment which I would submit to you. . . . The Bishop of St David's very injudiciously translated, about twenty years ago, Schleiermacher's book on St Luke. . . . In consequence of the rumour that Thirlwall would be made archbishop, all the most revolting passages in this treatise . . . have been carefully hunted out and paraded in the newspapers as exhibiting the deep-seated rationalism and blasphemous temper of a man whom an English bishop had delighted to honour.[38]

But between the critical blasts of 1825 and 1848 the *Saint Luke* received disappointingly little critical attention for a work of such importance. Schleiermacher had intentionally written a difficult book as "the best mode of keeping off improper readers," and no translation, however excellent, could entirely compensate for this.[39] Among those who did read the book, a number must have reacted like Maria Hare, Julius' sister-in-law: "I have been reading a little of Schleiermacher. . . . Schleiermacher, I think, clearly has a right feeling *himself,* and only wishes to account for the discrepancies in the best way he can, believing in the main points as divinely taught. But I suspect the effect upon most would be rather of creating doubt than of satisfying it."[40] But the sad truth was that the book failed to reach much of an audience at all. Crabb Robinson remarked, "I believe [it] has fallen dead-born from the press."[41] Many were therefore left to learn of and pass judgement on Schleiermacher's "heresies" by hearsay. In the autumn of 1828 Schleiermacher made a brief visit to London, where he met Thirlwall, and the German theologian was overheard to say, descriptively and prophetically, "My dear Mr. Thirlwall, I am very happy to see you. I dare say you had a difficult time with my Lucas."[42]

Hare not only introduced Thirlwall to Schleiermacher's treatise, but played an important role in the publication of Thirlwall's translations. Schleiermacher's *Saint Luke* first appeared in 1821, and Thirlwall undertook his translation sometime in 1822 or 1823. It was slow going at a time when his principal occupation was the study of law. By the spring of 1824 the translation was completed, and Thirlwall began to compose his lengthy introduction with the help of many books borrowed from Hare.[43] After three months, the introduction far from completed, Thirlwall wrote to Hare: "I am afraid you will think I have not made so much use of your books as I ought, for I have as yet done nothing more than trace in my mind the general plan of my introduction, and have committed nothing to paper. I hope, however, that my stay at Cambridge will produce some visible fruit. It will at all events determine the amount of service I shall be able to render to Schleiermacher's book."[44]

By October 1824 Thirlwall had made real progress, and wrote to Hare: "You will probably be much surprised to hear that my Introduction . . . is not quite finished. I still want some of the materials. . . . I should like you to see what I have done, which will give you a tolerable notion of the whole. . . . In the meanwhile, partly to relieve the dryness of some of these investigations, I have filled up some of my leisure hours with translating those two exquisite pieces of Tieck's 'die Gemälde' [*The Pictures*] and 'die Verlobung' [*The Betrothal*]."[45] Thirlwall had not yet found a publisher when he wrote to Hare: "Can you ascertain before you leave town whether Taylor would like to publish Tieck's 'novellen'? I believe I cannot well avoid offering the other bargain [Schleiermacher] to Whittaker, as there is a sort of family acquaintance between us, and he has often expressed a wish to publish something of mine."[46]

Hare did speak to Taylor, but failed to follow instructions precisely, for the publisher evinced a strong interest in Schleiermacher's book. Hare notified Thirlwall accordingly, and urged him to give serious thought to allowing Taylor to publish it. Thirlwall reported to Hare that "of the 'Schleiermacher' nobody certainly has as good a right to dispose of as yourself, *to whom I am indebted both for the knowledge of the book itself and for almost all of the materials of my Introduction.* I found Taylor at home . . . I sent him my manuscript of the 'Novellen' . . . when I called . . . upon Thurs-

HIGHER CRITICISM FROM GERMANY 91

day I found that he had only read a quarter of the first novel. . . .
I was not much surprised to observe that the impression he received
was not the most favourable."[47] The very next day Thirlwall wrote
again to Hare to recount Taylor's brighter attitude toward the
Tieck translations: "I have been spending almost all morning with
Taylor. . . . what he had read had produced the natural impression of delight and admiration which I thought it could not fail to
make. He also liked the 'Schleiermacher' very much, and will send
it immediately to the press."[48]

Just as the publication of all of Thirlwall's translations appeared
amicably settled, Taylor suffered another attack of religious qualms,
as he had done with the Landor dialogues. Again Thirlwall wrote
to Hare: "I begged to know whether his motive for declining the
publication [of Tieck's *Novellen*] was that he thought the work unsaleable, or whether he had any other. He assured me that it was
solely a conscientious one. He had received and imparted a great
deal of pleasure at the public reading of the novel, but the result
of his own reflections and the suggestions of his friends was that he
should be doing *an injury to the cause of godliness by publishing
it.*"[49] Thirlwall claimed to be neither surprised nor upset by this
behaviour. He said he would merely let the Tieck translations lie.
Taylor may have felt that the wider, female audience of the Tieck
Novellen offered greater scope for moral damage than the limited
scholarly audience for Schleiermacher's book. Thirlwall for his part
was most interested in seeing the Schleiermacher essay published,
for it was the more important work intellectually.

A fortnight later Thirlwall wrote again to tell Hare that proofsheets of the Schleiermacher essay would be sent for his scrutiny.
Hare's letters to Taylor show that he gave the Schleiermacher
proof-sheets a good deal of attention.[50] The letters also reveal that
Hare reacted amicably to Taylor's sudden refusal to publish the
Tieck. This is curious, for the incident occurred at the same time
that Hare was disputing Taylor's religious scruples over Landor's
Middleton dialogue:

> I am heartily glad . . . that your objection to Tieck's tale was
> not one of principle, or as I should call it, of prejudice. For I
> began to fear it was impossible we should ever agree upon any
> single subject; and though I like difference of opinion, yet where
> there is no agreement at all there can be no sympathy. Had you

sent it back from scrupulousness, I must have given up hope of your ever printing the Middleton, and should only have been surprised at your ever having printed anything but the Evangelical Magazine and its kin.[51]

It might be asked now, as it certainly was asked by critics at the time, if no thought was ever given to the popular mischief which might result from such scholarly speculations as Schleiermacher's, however innocent and pure their motive. Hare was concerned upon social as well as religious grounds to maintain the credibility of the Bible. It was for precisely this reason that he believed that books such as Schleiermacher's should not be ignored. Starting with the confident assumption that scriptural truth was not inconsistent with reason, Hare argued for the higher criticism, or "neologism," as the critics called it:

> The subject is indeed one of great difficulty and delicacy because the faith of so many simple good people will be grievously disturbed, when they find that their notion of inspiration is untenable; but still it is of great importance that the truth sh[oul]d be spoken; & I fear that the state of compromise is, as it ever must be, fruitful of . . . infidelity. Indeed, the light must & will come; & it would seem that one is rendering good service in letting it in by degrees, so that people may not be blinded by its influx when it does come.[52]

The events of the next few decades fully justified Hare's fears for the light's blinding effect upon faith.

Chapter 8

Germano-Coleridgean Historiography

The new German higher criticism was not confined merely to biblical exegesis, but was a sweeping trend in scholarship which brought a fresh approach to all literature and history. It began as a reaction against rationalistic scholarship, such as the histories of David Hume and Edward Gibbon.[1] It has therefore been hailed as a part of the romantic movement. Friedrich August Wolf (1759–1824) of the University of Halle, overhauled Homeric studies with his *Prolegomena ad Homerum* (1795). The history of the Greek and Roman world was revised by new approaches in the works of Barthold Georg Niebuhr (1776–1831), August Boeckh (or Böckh) (1785–1867), and Karl Otfried Müller (1797–1840).[2] The story of the development of the new German historiography and its incorporation with English historical thought is complex.[3]

The German historical method represented by Niebuhr and his *Römische Geschichte* (1812) has been acclaimed as an intellectual watershed and for initiating a revolution in the writing of history.[4] Niebuhr's work brought together a number of scholarly principles which were not really new. He dwelt in his history upon the critical evaluation of sources, especially of traditional accounts such as Livy's history, which included compilations of myths and apocrypha. He demonstrated the utility of a philological approach, using language itself as historical evidence. And he maintained an "evolutionary" interpretation of the history and development of all human societies, under which practical comparisons might be drawn between nation and nation, epoch and epoch.[5]

A healthy scepticism toward one's sources in the writing of history is as old as Herodotus, who prefaced his more incredible anecdotes with personal disclaimers. Serious textual criticism of sources flourished in Renaissance Italy. In seventeenth-century France critics such as Richard Simon and Pierre Bayle turned their attention to biblical inconsistencies and spurious lives of saints.[6] But the immediate predecessor of the German *Historismus* was the Italian scholar Giambattista Vico (1668–1743), whose *Principi Di Scienza Nova* (1725) anticipated all aspects of the German school.[7] To the destructive criticism of the French scholars Vico attached a methodological structure which emphasized the critical evaluation of sources, the value of etymological analysis, and an evolutionary unity of social development that is comparable in all societies.[8]

At the time that Vico's book first appeared the French Academy of Inscriptions witnessed a running controversy over the probity of the sources of early Roman history.[9] Out of this controversy came Louis de Beaufort's full-scale sceptical treatise on the sources of early Roman history, published in 1738.[10] Despite such antecedents Niebuhr was loath to acknowledge any earlier work in the field of early Roman history or critical methodology.

Niebuhr's work was a reaction against the Scottish "conjecturalist" school represented by Adam Ferguson, and the "rationalist" school of Hume and Gibbon. Both schools drew upon Locke's principles to posit a kind of uniformitarianism of the human mind, seeing man in all times and places to be the same psychological creature, and viewing social development as a continual, linear progression toward material and moral progress. This "idea of progress," which became such an article of faith among the general public, was characterized in the late eighteenth century by the phrase "march of mind."[11] The strength of the conjecturalist and rationalist historians lay in analysing institutions and laws; their weakness lay in narrating and analysing human behaviour. For Hare, however, the enlightened eighteenth century did not represent the zenith of human progress: "As we draw toward the close of the [eighteenth] century, we sink into the slough of Rationalism . . . which had done little more than skim the froth of history, and dissect the carcass of philosophy."[12]

At base, then, a psychological theory separated the Germano-Coleridgeans—a title coined by J.S. Mill—from the rationalist historians, a belief in the evolutionary development of the human mind as opposed to Locke's theory of the eternal uniformity of men's minds. But the Germano-Coleridgeans also rejected the notion of linear progress, or the "march of mind."[13] In the *Guesses at Truth* Hare included a lengthy essay in which he examined in detail the origins and growth of the "march of mind" through the works of authors such as Condorcet, Herder, and Hegel. The whole creed of progress became entangled with the Mammon-worship and materialism that Hare so often condemned, and made that false doctrine still more pernicious:

> We may perceive how baseless and delusive is the vulgar notion of the march of mind, as necessarily exhibiting a steady, regular advance, within the same nation, in all things. . . . when the intellectual and moral energy of a nation has declined, that decline becomes perceptible after a while in the very lowest branches of trade and manufacture. Civilization[14] will indeed outlive that energy, and keep company for a long while with luxury. But if luxury extinguishes the energy of a people, so that it cannot revive, its civilization too will at length sink into barbarism.

In ridiculing the rationalist doctrine Hare hinted at the Vician, Germano-Coleridgean notion of cyclical development with periodic decay: "Are we really more enlightened than our ancestors? Or is it merely the flaring up of the candle that has burnt down to the socket, and is consuming that socket, as a prelude to its own extinction? Such at least has been the character of those former ages of the world, which have prided themselves on being the most enlightened."[15]

The well-being of materialists and the idea of progress of those who attributed to mechanical invention the upward progress of civilization could lead only, Hare thought, to ungodliness:

> All who worship means, of whatsoever kind, material or intellectual, . . . all who forget that it is still the Lord of Hosts, who breaketh the bow, and knappeth the spear in sunder, and burneth the chariots in the fire,—all who are heedless of that *vox populi*, which when it burst from the heaving depths of a nation's

heart, is in truth *vox Dei* . . . —all who conceive that the well-being of a people depends on its wealth, . . . all who dream that mankind may be ennobled and regenerated by being taught to read,—all these, and millions more, who are besotted by analogous delusions . . . may be numbered among the idolators of the golden calf.[16]

This affected tone gave Hare, like Carlyle, the appearance of a biblical prophet "alone in the moral wilderness of civilization."[17] Hare followed Coleridge and the tradition of Vico and Niebuhr in seeing human will and character as the agency through which history was formed, but it was nonetheless subject to God's all-embracing providence. To the Vichian-Niebuhrian notion of cyclical development, Coleridge fused the principle that history is a process governed by the presence of ideas, and that human actions may thus be explained as movements in the direction of the realization of those ideas.[18]

The so-called romantic school of historians offered opposition to the rationalists; Sharon Turner rekindled interest in the Teutonic societies of the Middle Ages with his massive work on the Anglo-Saxons, and the extremely popular *History of England* of John Lingard introduced a new standard of objectivity into English historical writing.[19] But this "romantic" history was too particular and antiquarian; it did not offer any useful generalizations. Its methods were sound, but its scope and aim were not "philosophical."[20]

Hare in his essay on the idea of progress led the way in calling for a more philosophical history: "The philosophical idea of the history of the world will be, that it is to exhibit the gradual unfolding of all the faculties of man's intellectual and moral being . . . under every shade of circumstance, and in every variety of combination. . . . In a word, *the purpose and end of the history of the world is to realize the idea of humanity.*"[21] This notion is derived from Coleridge, but it is no surprise that Hare's search for a "Christian Thucydides" ended in Germany.[22] Hare noted that "during the last fifty years, the idea of history as an organic whole, regulated by certain laws inherent in the constitution of man,—as a macrocosm analogous to the microcosm contained in every breast,—has been a favourite subject of speculation with the Germans."[23] He felt that the German critical methods would provide a middle course between the blind faith of orthodox believers and the scepticism of the eighteenth-century rationalists.[24]

The Germano-Coleridgean outlook offered a view of the past at once more subtle and richer in texture than the rationalist view. In history, unlike science, the simplest explanation is not automatically to be preferred. Hare was cognizant of the complexity of history, as he remarked in a long "dialogue" on history and poetry in the *Guesses at Truth:*

> The field of observation is so vast and unsurveyable; so much of it lies wrapt in a thick, impenetrable darkness, while other portions are obscured by the mists which the passions of men have spread over them, and a spot here and there shines out dazzlingly, throwing the adjacent parts into shade; the events are so inextricably intertwisted and conglomerated . . . that a perfect, consumate history of the world may not unreasonably be deemed the loftiest achievement that the mind of man can contemplate; although no one . . . will dream that it could ever be accomplisht, except by an intellect far more penetrative and comprehensive than man's.

Where the rationalist and romantic historians were content to analyse institutions and narrate events, the Germano-Coleridgeans like Hare sought explanations of the motivation of human behaviour. This was by no means easy, as Hare observed in his dialogue:

> But surely it is a part of the historian's office to explain by what principles and passions the persons in his history were actuated.
> Undoubtedly; so far as he can. Sundry difficulties however impede him in doing this, which do not stand in the way of the poet. A historian has to confine himself to certain individuals. . . . Nor can the historian place his persons in such situations, and make them so speak and act, as to set off their characters. He must keep to those circumstances and actions which have chanced to gain the most notoriety, and for which he can produce the best evidence.[25]

While Hare and his fellow Germano-Coleridgeans found the system and methodology of Vico and Niebuhr to their taste, it was not their aim to erect a theoretical philosophy of history. The reader is left to infer a great deal from their writings. Hare, unlike Thirlwall and Arnold, wrote no formal works of history. Nonetheless, an explicit exposition of the method of Niebuhr emerges from Hare's writings, particularly from the *Guesses at Truth*.[26]

Hare promoted Vico and Niebuhr's theory of cyclical social development, but he emphasized the importance of religion and divine providence in the process: "The natural life of nations, as well as of individuals, has its fixt course and term. It springs forth, grows up, reaches its maturity, decays, perishes. Only through Christianity has a nation ever risen again: and it is solely on the operation of Christianity that we can ground anything like a reasonable hope of the perfectability of mankind; a hope that which has often been wrought in individuals, may also in the fulness of time be wrought by the same power in the race." Thus Christianity offered some hope of amelioration despite Hare's belief that "the ultimate tendency of civilization is toward barbarism."[27] A nation's progress through its life cycle was not as strictly regulated as in a living organism, for "it is subject to manifold vicissitudes, interruptions, and delays; ever advancing on the whole indeed, but often receding in one quarter, while it pushes forward in another; and sometimes even retreating altogether for a while, that it may start afresh with greater and more irresistible force."[28] There was no absolute impetus or time-table to compel this development. To maintain otherwise would be to destroy divine providence and fall into an ungodly determinism.

The practical result of such a cyclical scheme was to permit comparisons and generalizations between different societies, and thus further man's understanding of the past and the present:

> A nation has a living, organic growth, which manifests itself in its constitution, and in its various institutions . . . the two great witnesses that the history of the world brings forward, to show the wisdom and permanence of organic constitutions, expanding and developing themselves along with the growth of the nation, and continuing the same . . . are Rome and England. Both indeed had to pass through diverse critical trials, and the wilfulness and selfishness of man tried to suspend and arrest the organic development of the Constitution; and Rome at last perish, when that development seemed to have become a practical impossibility. But each is the witness for true political wisdom, Rome in the ancient world, England in the modern.[29]

For Hare, who lived in England at what he saw to be the high-tide of its maturity, the significance of the analogy with Rome was obvious. But it was only valid to draw comparisons between comparable periods in the histories of nations. To do otherwise would produce invalid and fruitless analogies.[30]

Moreover, the people of past ages had striven to realize the ideas of their respective nations to the best of their ability. Nothing was more unhistorical or anachronistic than to fault them for their apparent ignorance, much less to follow the practice of the rationalist historians in heaping scorn and ridicule upon men and societies which they could not understand. Hare wrote that

> every age has had a certain portion of truth, a certain quantity of knowledge, assigned to it, which it was to increase, but which it could only increase step by step, and from which it could not bound forward at once into the position designed for its remote posterity. Hence it is an injustice and foolishness to blame the writers of former times, because their fashion of speech, of thought, of feeling is in many respects unlike our own, or because they have not the same clear insight into truths, which we may count among the most precious parts of our possessions, yet for which we may perhaps be in no slight measure indebted to their patient and persevering cultivation of the inheritance they had received.[31]

Nations remained discrete entities even if their stages of growth were comparable. For the rationalist historians the "march of mind" imposed a sense of internationalism in human history, since according to Locke all human minds were basically alike, regardless of race or language. The Germano-Coleridgean view, on the other hand, made an analogy between nations and individuals. For Hare and his fellows the concept of nation as the basic unit of history, of nationality as supremely important, fostered a nationalistic historiography. The fundamental differences between nations Hare saw reflected most clearly in their national literatures.[32]

Niebuhr's method of writing history drew heavily upon pre-literary sources such as ballads and epics.[33] Utilizing such sources required imagination, and Hare felt that a poetic imagination was a great aid to a historian's understanding. In Hare's dialogue on history and poetry his young acolyte protests that "the historian's facts are true; the poet's are acknowledgedly ficticious. When I have read Herodotus, I know for certain that Xerxes invaded Greece; after reading Homer, I am left in doubt whether Agamemnon ever sailed against Troy." To which Hare replies: "And what are you the wiser for being certain of the former fact? or what the less wise for being left in doubt about the latter? Your mind may be more or less complete as a chronological table: but that is all. The human, the truly philosophical interest in the two stories is much the same."[34] But even though Hare thought that every historian must be in part a poet, he was keenly aware that mere imagination about the past was not sufficient. Still necessary for the accurate reconstruction of the past was philological analysis.[35] The short-lived journal which Hare and Thirlwall produced at Cambridge endeavoured to promote philology as the key to the unfolding of *Altertumswissenschaft*, because for Hare "philology, in its highest sense, ought to be only another name for philosophy. Its aim should be to seek after wisdom in the whole series of its historical manifestations."[36]

The Germano-Coleridgean demand that truly "philosophical" history seek to explain the motivation behind human actions made it incumbent upon the historian to recreate the thoughts, ideas, and emotions of the people of past ages. Therefore

> a historian . . . has something else to do, besides relating naked facts: a file of newspapers would not be a history. He has to unfold the origin of events, and their connexion, to show how they hook and are linkt into the "never-ending still-beginning" chain of causes and consequences. . . .
>
> Moreover, as the theme of history is human actions . . . brought about by the agency of man, he has not merely to represent them in their maturity and completion, as actually taking place, but as growing in great measure out of the character of the actors and having their form and complexion determined thereby. So that human character, as modifying and modified by circumstances, man controlling and controlled by events, must be the historian's ultimate object.[37]

This notion that the historian's task is to "rethink the thought of the past" is still accepted methodology, and received its clearest and strongest modern formulation in the work of the late R.G. Collingwood.[38]

In the act of rethinking the thought of the past the perspective of the historian was a matter for concern; one must contemplate the whole in order to comprehend it, Hare argued in his dialogue on history and poetry:

> Were you to live inside a watch you could neither use it, nor know its use. Were our sight fixt on the inner workings of our bodies, . . . we should have no conception what a man is or does, or was made for. Sorry too would be the notion of the earth pickt up at the bottom of a mine. In like manner, to understand men's characters, one must contemplate them as living wholes, in their energy of action or of suffering, not creep maggotlike into them, and crawl about from one rotten motive to another, turning that rotten with our touch which is not so already.[39]

Hare believed that the interpretations of rationalists and utilitarians, that human actions are governed by "well-regulated selfishness," resulted from a too-limited perspective.

When one turns from questions of method to examine philosophic structure, it appears that the principal systematic flaw in the Germano-Coleridgean philosophy of history lies in the irreconcilability of three of its main tenets: the organic growth of the nation on an analogy with living bodies, the agency of free human will in the determination of events, and the role of divine providence with the capacity to intervene in human affairs.[40] A cyclical system of social development can easily lead to a form of determinism where events unfold beyond the power of God or men to control. The Germano-Coleridgeans countered this tendency by insisting that man is a moral being with freedom of will and the power to control events.[41] But this insistence only produces a homocentric system, unacceptable to Christians. Therefore the Germano-Coleridgeans, who were profoundly religious, maintained as an absolute presupposition the concept of divine providence in human affairs. To admit the possibility of divine intervention was theoretically untidy, but was compatible with religious faith. However, the Germano-Coleridgeans were practical men, not philosophers or system builders.[42]

As Churchmen the Germano-Coleridgeans looked to the past partly for what it told them about the present, and what they perceived alarmed them. Hare believed that a high level of civilization need only prove a prelude to renewed barbarism should religious faith prove wanting. And it was clear to Hare and his friends that religion was under attack in many quarters: "Even in the last dozen years . . . the Antichristian spirit has become stronger and more audacious and subtiler [sic] than ever; and it is now waging open war against the name and existence of Christianity. . . . But even this is better than to lie embedded and suffocated, or to sprawl and crawl about, in a slough of Rationalism." The Mammon-worship that was growing in England as a partial consequence of industrialization threatened to create a new, material barbarism, and this, Hare and Thomas Arnold feared, could lead to class warfare and social dissolution.[43]

The need to make the truth known, to warn society of the danger of a renewed age of barbarism, was only too clear to the Germano-Coleridgeans. But while Hare rendered good service in translating Niebuhr's history, he was not himself a practising historian. It was left to men like Thirlwall and Arnold to naturalize the idealistic concepts of the German *Historismus* in works of English historical scholarship.[44] The relationship between Hare and Thomas Arnold has never been clearly analysed, nor all of the significant correspondence printed, even in Stanley's admirable life of Arnold. Among the more recent works of scholarship devoted to Arnold, E.L. Williamson in *The Liberalism of Thomas Arnold* makes only a grudging acknowledgement of Julius Hare as Arnold's friend, and dismisses him as "lacking in the power of independent thought and memorable expression which would have enabled him to meet the religious needs of the time."[45] This appraisal is uninformed and unfair; it ignores Hare's popular volumes of sermons, his charges and pamphlets on Church affairs, and his phenomenally popular *Guesses at Truth*.

Arnold and Julius Hare's brother Augustus were both members of the Attic Society while undergraduates at Oxford. It was through Augustus that Arnold met Julius Hare.[46] In 1821 Arnold became a contributor to the *Encyclopaedia Metropolitana*, for which he produced articles on Roman history. During this time he realized the importance of Niebuhr's *Römische Geschichte*, and resolved to learn German that he might read it.[47] Arnold's first task was to obtain a copy of it, for German books were not common in England. In the summer of 1824 he wrote to Julius Hare about his researches and Niebuhr's history. Hare replied that a set of Niebuhr's work could be had from Deighton in Cambridge, and volunteered to advance the money and himself dispatch the books to Arnold. Arnold accepted Hare's offer, and a friendship developed over the next few years by correspondence. This consisted largely of Hare's recommendations of works by German authors, and Arnold's pleas for advice and counsel: "I am well aware of my own Ignorance on many of the Points which I have already touched upon in the Encyclopedia. . . . my Progress has been so very limited, that it will be a real Kindness in you to name any of the Points on which you doubt the Correctness of my Statements. Remember that any Hints or Corrections you will take the Trouble of giving me, will be most welcome, and I shall be very heartily obliged to you for them, as I am for what you have given me already."[48]

Early in the 1820s Arnold began work on a critical edition of the history of Thucydides, whom he regarded as highly as Niebuhr. He several times turned to Hare for help and advice: Arnold wrote "to trouble you once more with some Questions relating to my difficult Occupations, for which I know no Man who can answer them so well. . . . there are many Points on which I fear I am so ignorant as not even to know how much I do not know; and you would confer on me a real Favour by suggesting any Questions whether historical or philological which you think that an Editor of Thucydides ought to discuss. . . . your Knowledge is far more extensive and accurate than mine, so that you have it in your Power very measurably to assist me."[49] Arnold's scholarly labours, which he called his "amusement between nine and ten at night," proceeded slowly. Three years passed and Arnold wrote again to Hare seeking the loan of two manuscripts from libraries in Cambridge in order that they might be collated for his edition of Thucydides. Again Hare obliged, and the manuscripts were placed at Arnold's disposal for several months.[50]

After Arnold assumed the headmastership of Rugby in 1828, he hired as a master one of Hare's best students from Trinity College, James Prince Lee (1804–69), who later became Bishop of Manchester. Arnold's enthusiasm for Lee is reflected in many of the letters which he subsequently wrote to Hare. As Arnold admitted, Lee prejudiced him in favour of hiring Cambridge men.[51] Hare proffered Arnold loyal and devoted friendship, in which he gave far more than he ever took. In later years Hare enjoyed visiting both Arnold and Wordsworth in Westmoreland.[52] After Arnold's premature death in 1842, Hare remained a devoted friend of Arnold's widow, and took in hand the preparation of the third volume of Arnold's *History of Rome* for publication. In his preface to that volume Hare lamented that Arnold, like Niebuhr, should have been cut down in mid-passage before his scholarly work was completed, so that it must ever remain fragmentary. As for continuing it, "It would be as easy to complete Cologne cathedral." Hare ended with a posthumous tribute to Arnold:

> We are so bound and shackled by all manner of prejudices, national, party, ecclesiastical, individual, that we can hardly move a limb freely; and we are so fenced and penned in, that few can look out over their neighbour's land, or up to any piece of sky, except that which is just over their heads. Many too of our ablest men in these last years, instead of seeking after truth with loving patience and candour, have rather employed their best faculties in decking out their favourite idol with all the finery and tinsel which they could scrape together, and in burning incense before it, until they are wrapt in a mist, and count the glare of their tapers more glorious than the noonday sun. At such a time it is especially wholesome and refreshing to find a man like Dr. Arnold, who loves the truth, and seeks it, and speaks it out. . . . O that his example and his teaching may arouse others to a like zeal in the same holy cause![53]

Arnold's early death was a grievous blow to Hare, who wrote to John Kenrick, "It is a satisfaction to me to find that you concur in my opinions of [Arnold's] third volume; for I have sometimes doubted whether the personal interest I have been led to take in it might not have caused me to estimate it too highly. With reference to his position at Oxford and in the English Nation and Church, it is impossible to estimate the loss sustained by Arnold's death too highly."[54] With Arnold's passing Hare lost a good friend, and the Germano-Coleridgean school of historiography lost one of its leading exponents.

Chapter 9

Niebuhr's Roman History

After his return to Cambridge in 1827, Thirlwall needed little prompting from Hare to collaborate on a translation of Niebuhr's *Römische Geschichte*. They must have begun work promptly, for the first volume was published the following year, by Hare's old friend John Taylor. In 1827 Rivington had published a two-volume translation of Niebuhr by Francis Augustus Walter. Taylor was not dismayed when a rival translation appeared first. In fact he wished to see a more elaborate scholarly apparatus in his English edition than the few notes that Hare and Thirlwall added to identify sources unnamed in the original. But Hare refused, saying "though nothing would be easier than to pile up ordinary references; and to build a theory of some kind or other, I should be unwilling to let anything of the kind into the same volume with Niebuhr. At all events my acquaintance with him has made me too well aware of my own ignorance, not to shun anything which might bring us into contrast."[1]

Niebuhr's first two volumes had appeared in 1812, and his subsequent appointment as Prussian envoy to the Vatican prevented him from completing his third volume for more than a decade. Proofs of the first volume of Hare and Thirlwall's translation were sent to Niebuhr, who had meanwhile been revising his work for a second German edition. He promised to send his revisions to his English translators. Hare wrote to Taylor early in 1828, quoting Niebuhr's comments on the English proof-sheets: " 'It is astonishing and wonderful how you have expressed all and everything, the whole and every particular thought, with the exact shade of feeling with which I wrote. Just such a translation had I conceived to be possible, but had not hope that I was destined to meet with it: just such a one did I wish for, or none. No thanks can express what I owe you: through you my history belongs to your nation and your literature as much as to Germany.'" Hare was flattered by these remarks: "This is to be sure a proud recompense for all the trouble we have spent upon him: and I trust that in another edition the translation will be less unworthy of what Niebuhr says of it. Of course I need not say to you, what would be necessary if I were writing to Colburn, that I would not for the world have any use made of Niebuhr's expressions in advertising the work."[2]

Taylor anticipated a wide and favourable reception for the book, but just to be sure he sent his colleague James Duncan off on the eve of publication to promote it among provincial booksellers.[3] Niebuhr received his copy, and expressed his reaction candidly to a friend: "It is not absolutely free from faults; with respect to which, it is singular that they do not occur in really difficult passages, but in perfectly clear ones, so that they can only have arisen from inattention: but these are trifles; on the whole the work is masterly, and a perfectly genuine representation of the original." While he was pleased by the English rendering of his history, the state of England in her life's cycle distressed and depressed Niebuhr even more than Hare. Referring to favourable reviews of the English translation Niebuhr wrote: "Were my old affection for England unchanged, it would give me intense pleasure to stand in such high estimation there. My principles . . . are adopted there without reservation, and will take root too firmly to be extirpated. But my heart has become estranged from England; the period of her glory has passed away: . . . the whole moral condition of the nation is degenerating, although to a great extent, this is as much its misfortune as its fault." Niebuhr concluded by noting that he had just completed the revisions for the second edition of his history, which in addition to being liberally sprinkled through the text, extended its length by forty pages.[4]

By the autumn of 1828 the first edition of the first volume of the English translation had been sold out. As Niebuhr wrote to his friend and fellow historian Savigny: "In England, the first edition of the translation, consisting of a thousand copies, is already out of print, and my translators are about to translate my [new] edition. In England, my results triumph without opposition."[5] There was opposition, but it was slow to marshal. Meanwhile, publisher and translators in England received the revised German edition to discover that it was entirely rewritten, and that, instead of being able to press on with their translation, they faced the necessity to retranslate the first volume. Nonetheless Hare expressed his eagerness to undertake the work at once, if another edition of the first edition would be wanted.[6] Taylor's enthusiasm for the project was undiminished. The revised translation of volume I appeared the following year, 1829, but volume II did not appear until 1832.

In spite of brisk sales, critical attention came to Hare and Thirlwall's translation rather slowly. In June 1828 a favourable review of the German editions of Niebuhr's history appeared in the *Foreign Quarterly Review*. The reviewer, Thomas Keightley (1789–1872), noted: "The long-expected translation of the first volume, . . . by Messrs. Hare and Thirlwall, has made its appearance, and it gives us the highest pleasure to be able to bear out our almost unqualified testimony to the fidelity, ease and spirit of its execution."[7] In July 1830 a "contemptuous" notice by Shelley's friend Thomas Jefferson Hogg (1792–1862) appeared in the *Edinburgh Review*, and was said to have distressed the journal's editor, Macvey Napier.[8]

Macaulay, whose writings show a disregard for the Germano-Coleridgean method, wrote Napier regarding Hogg's review:

> The article on Niebuhr contains much that is very sensible; but it is not such an article as so noble a subject required. . . . The appearance of the book is really an era in the intellectual history of Europe, and I think that the *Edinburgh Review* ought at least to have given a luminous abstract of it. The very circumstances that Niebuhr's own arrangement and style are obscure, and that his translators have need of translators to make them intelligible, to the multitudes, rendered it more desirable that a clear and neat statement of the points in controversy should be laid before the public.[9]

So Macaulay did acknowledge Niebuhr's history as an intellectual milestone. Robert Southey criticized Niebuhr's history for its dearth of narrative. Instead of straightforward narrative exposition, Niebuhr strung together dry analytical essays. Hare acknowledged the problem of readability in later editions of the *Guesses at Truth:* "Histories used often to be stories. The fashion now is to leave out the story." Nonetheless, Hare defended Niebuhr's form in almost the same breath: "Some minds are too rapid and vehement and redundant to flow along in lucid transparence; some have to break over rocks, and to force a way through obstacles, which would have dammed them in."[10] Niebuhr was not without critics in Germany. Landor wrote to Crabb Robinson about an encounter with A.W. Schlegel: "Among other novelties, he remarked that Niebuhr was totally unfit for a historian; and that the battle of Toulouse was gained by the French; a pretty clear indication that he himself will never rise into the place which (he tells us) Niebuhr ought not to occupy."[11] But the worst criticism was still to come.

In the January 1829 issue of the *Quarterly Review,* John Barrow (1764–1848) reviewed A.N. Granville's *St. Petersburgh: A Journal of Travels to and from That Capital.* In the text Niebuhr was linked with the rioting of German university students. The reviewer noted that Niebuhr's political opinions had since undergone considerable change. To this review the editor, or perhaps the author, added a footnote regarding Niebuhr's alleged change of opinion:

> We wish we could say the same as to his absurd and shallow doctrines of another class—but these remain; and, by the by, we think his last translators, two clergymen of the Church of England . . . might have as well *remarked* . . . on some of the most offensive paragraphs which have appeared since the days of the Philosophical Dictionary. . . . Pity that such talents should be wasted on the drudgery of translation—and pity still more that the works rendered by such a hand should in any instance be pregnant with crude and dangerous speculations.[12]

This vicious attack upon Niebuhr and upon the character of his translators could not be ignored. But was it entirely unexpected?

In June 1825 Thomas Arnold had reviewed the original German edition of the *Römische Geschichte* without eliciting a whisper, since his audience remained blissfully ignorant of the "wickedness" hidden in the German text.[13] Once supplied with the English text English religious partisans were bound to turn their sights on a scholarly work with such significance for biblical as well as historical studies. Arnold was himself sensitive to the scepticism implicit in such works. As he wrote to Hare: "I adhere to my own Judgement about Müller . . . and though my Reverence for Niebuhr is such that I hardly like to say it, I think that even he was not exempt from that same Defect [excess scepticism]. I wish that some Man would give some good Criteria to distinguish between what is mythical & what is historical in ancient Writers. That the Domain of the latter was unreasonably extended in Times past, I am well aware, but I think that the Reaction is now going too far on the other Side."[14] The challenge of the *Quarterly Review* had to be met, so Hare at once set about composing a sixty-page *Vindication of Niebuhr's* History of Rome *from the Charges of the Quarterly Reviewer.* To Hare's lengthy rebuttal Thirlwall added a three-page postscript. This polemical pamphlet became known at Cambridge as "Hare's bark and Thirlwall's bite."[15]

In his vindication Hare termed the *Quarterly Review* essay a baseless attempt to ruin the reputation of a distinguished foreigner and to prejudice the English reading public. It was inevitable, Hare thought, to find bad reviewers among the good, but in this case the reviewer did not even trouble to read the translators' preface, or he would not have made his groundless accusation that the translators appended notes at whim to Niebuhr's text. Hare noted with irony that the very same journal had earlier published a favourable review of Niebuhr's history. In the meantime Niebuhr's political and religious principles had been declared sound in the *Foreign Quarterly Review* and the *British Critic & Theological Review.*[16]

Regarding the charge that Niebuhr was a religious scoffer, Hare admitted, "What his religious faith may be, I know not: that is to say, so far as regards the peculiar doctrines and mysteries of Christianity. . . . This much however I do know, that it is very possible in Germany, under the present aspect of religious feeling and knowledge, to unite a fervent faith in Christianity, with considerable doubts and scruples about the historical value of certain passages in scripture." Such a bold admission of the implicit significance of the German *Historismus* for biblical criticism would have damned Niebuhr in many eyes. But Hare concluded, "One thing I feel perfectly sure: with that religion which manifests itself chiefly by evil-speaking, lying and slander, Niebuhr never has held and never can hold any communion."[17]

The sarcasm of Hare's concluding remarks anticipated that of Thirlwall's brief postscript. After concurring with Hare's lengthy vindication, Thirlwall denied that such a labour as translating Niebuhr was either drudgery or a waste of time. Such descriptions, suggested Thirlwall, should rather be used to describe the mercenary activities of journalists whose pens served partisan ends. Indeed, "when I see it made the instrument of a religious, political or literary proscription, forging or pointing calumny and slander to gratify the malice of hotter and weaker heads against all whom they hate and fear, I have now before me an instance of what I consider as the lowest and basest intellectual drudgery."[18] The attack upon Niebuhr was only a foretaste of the attacks which the Broad Churchmen suffered in the coming decades, and was only the first occasion for a retaliatory pamphlet from Hare.

Several copies of the vindication were sent to Niebuhr in Bonn, and Niebuhr wrote of his translators' efforts: "They have been obliged to answer for themselves, since their prospects of patronage and promotion in the Church were endangered, as I foresaw would be the case. . . . The defense is written in a most affectionate spirit as regards myself. . . . Further, with many readers, their extreme veneration will inevitably produce a reaction."[19] Hare also sent a copy of the pamphlet to William Wordsworth, who promptly replied, "Your *Vindication* is triumphant—the obnoxious passage would never have been worth a moment's notice but for the vehicle which conveys it to the world."[20] But Wordsworth, like Niebuhr, feared for the effect that such slanders might have upon the careers of clergymen. Arnold's reaction when he received his copy was less critical: "Let me add with regard to Niebuhr, that Bunsen assured me that he was a sincere Christian. . . . But Mr [Hugh James] Rose, and I fear he but represents a numerous Class in England, considers any critical Inquiry into the Genuineness of the Books of either Testament, and much more any different Notions about Inspiration from what he has been accustomed to entertain, as Symptoms of Infidelity; with him Opinions must go in the Lump; he insists upon all or nothing."[21] Orthodox High Churchmen, Evangelicals, and the radical fringe were equally sensitive to any threat to their notions of the divine inspiration of Scripture. But for the notoriety that Niebuhr's book received in the major reviews, religious partisans might have been slower to attack it.

Religious criticism was not the sole species of opposition to Niebuhr's *Römische Geschichte*. In Germany "almost all the subsequent works on the subject are either founded upon his researches, or are occupied to a great extent with criticism of his conclusions, and with reasons for rejecting or doubting them."[22] The work of Becker and Marquardt on Roman antiquities, and the Roman histories of Schwegler, and of Gerlach and Bachofen disputed nearly all of Niebuhr's conclusions. Thomas Arnold's *History of Rome* is the most self-conscious English example of Niebuhr's method in practice, and important, too, is Thirlwall's *History of Greece*.[23] Perhaps the most able English critic of Niebuhr's methodology was George Cornewall Lewis. He remained wary of Niebuhr's conclusions, and was a critic to be reckoned with, for he was an accomplished Germanist, well acquainted with the work of Niebuhr and other German historians.[24]

Lewis' criticism was not committed to magazine polemics, but to his massive and systematic *Inquiry into the Credibility of the Early Roman History* (1855):

> The great cause of the multiplicity of opinions, which characterizes the recent researches into early Roman history, is the defective method, which not only Niebuhr and his followers, but most of his opponents have adopted. Instead of employing those tests of credibility which are consistently applied to modern history, they attempt to guide their judgment by the indications of internal evidence, and assume that the truth can be discovered by an occult faculty of historical divination. . . . It is an attempt to solve a problem, for the solution of which no sufficient data exist.
>
> The consequence is, that ingenuity and labour can produce nothing but hypotheses and conjectures, which may be supported by analogies . . . but can never rest on the solid foundation of proof.

Lewis' criticism was not only an apt description of the writings on the subject, but a fundamental protest against the evidence of internal, philological analysis which was the hallmark of German methodology. For Lewis the proof of historical hypotheses could only come in one way: "Historical evidence, like judicial evidence, is founded on the testimony of credible witnesses. Unless these witnesses had personal and immediate perception of the facts which they report, . . . their evidence is not entitled to credit."[25]

Although Lewis' book appeared immediately after Hare's death in 1855, Hare must have examined a draft copy, for it was precisely this argument of Lewis' which Hare addressed when he wrote:

> at the bottom . . . is . . . the supposition that we have the evidence of eyewitnesses to the facts. Throughout your friend [Lewis] reasons upon the principle of our common law, that all secondary and hearsay evidence is not only to be rejected and set at nought, when opposed to direct ocular testimony[,] but is in every case little to be relied on; a principle, into the legal worth of which this is not the place to inquire, but which, if applied with any strictness to history, will soon reduce it to a bundle of dry sticks, which a boy ten years old might grasp in his hand.[26]

Hare knew that to admit Lewis' legalistic test of evidence would paralyse the writing of history and biblical exegesis. He was therefore at pains to reject Lewis' criticism as a fruitless obstacle to scholarship. In the end, however, this dispute over the credibility and admissibility of sources could not be resolved until the new field of archaeology brought to bear a corroborative class of historical evidence in the form of artifacts.

Despite criticism of the Hare and Thirlwall translation of Neibuhr's history, it was soon in wide circulation as a university text. Thanks to Arnold's enthusiasm it was even used among the schoolboys at Rugby. Many students of Hare and Thirlwall at Cambridge, including several of the Apostles, were influenced by it, and went on to write histories of their own. Dean Merivale's *History of the Romans under the Empire* (1850–64) is a conspicuous example. J.M. Kemble became the foremost expert on Anglo-Saxon historical texts. Henry Alford applied the German techniques he learned from Hare and Thirlwall to the editing of the New Testament. George Long (1800–79) became a prolific author in the field of Roman law and Roman political economy. John William Donaldson (1811–61) presented Franz Bopp's Greek grammar in an English version entitled the *New Cratylus* (1839), collaborated with G.C. Lewis in translating Müller's *History of Greek Literature* (1840), and was the principal author of the *Theatre of the Greeks* (1836), which applied the new methodology to literary history.[27] Even the work of students who did not become historians or philologists bore the influence of Niebuhr thanks to the teaching of Hare and Thirlwall. For example, Tennyson's poetry has been shown to embody the Germano-Coleridgean philosophy of history.[28] When William Smith (1813–93) edited and published a *Dictionary of Greek and Roman Biography and Mythology* (1843), among the thirty-six contributors the largest identifiable groups were seven "Arnoldians" from Oxford, five of Niebuhr's successors at Bonn, and four men of Trinity College, Cambridge.[29]

Hare and Thirlwall's translation of Niebuhr's history ended in 1832 with the publication of the second volume. Thereafter one detects a loss of energy on the part of the translators, faced with the prospect of translating the long-delayed third volume. Hare's departure from Cambridge in 1832 effectively ended the project. When the third volume still remained untranslated six years later, Arnold wrote to chide Hare, "I think that you & Thirlwall have much to answer for in not having yet completed your Translation of the third Volume of the History. It is only when the Volume shall have become generally known that English Readers will learn to appreciate Niebuhr's Excellence as a Narrator."[30] Finally, in 1841 the task of translating the third volume fell to Leonhard Schmitz (1807–90), a pupil of Niebuhr's.[31]

The translation of Niebuhr's history was the most important task of Germanizing undertaken by Hare and Thirlwall, in the course of which they made perhaps their greatest contribution to English thought of that era. Both men warrant more than the brief mention they have hitherto received in the history of Anglo-German intellectual and literary relations. As for the long-term significance of Niebuhr's history, its power to provoke may be counted in its favour. Ancient history was later transformed under the impact of the discoveries made by Schliemann, Layard, and other "diggers," but to Niebuhr goes the honour of providing the chronological watershed of ancient historical scholarship. The Germano-Coleridgean philosophy of history, and the notion of an impending "crisis of civilization" that it produced lost momentum and currency; Germano-Coleridgean historians lost the battle with the "idea of progress" and the "march of mind."[32]

Hare's contributions to the foundling journal called the *Athenaeum* complete the story of his Germanizing. At the beginning of 1828 the erratic publisher James Silk Buckingham (1786–1855) founded the *Athenaeum* in collaboration with the publishers Henry Colburn and Charles Knight. Buckingham met F.D. Maurice and John Sterling through political clubs; the two young men visited the *Athenaeum*'s offices regularly, and soon became contributors.[33] In May 1828 Colburn sold his interest in the *Athenaeum* to Buckingham, and on 30 July 1828 Buckingham sold the journal to Maurice, Sterling, and "half a dozen friends" to effect a merger with the *London Literary Chronicle*. During the early years of the *Athenaeum* its circulation was small, its advertising revenues minute, and its life precarious, though it grew in strength and survived into the twentieth century. The small syndicate of proprietors appears to have consisted of Cambridge Apostles, for in July 1828 R.C. Trench wrote to J.M. Kemble that "Maurice and that gallant band of Platonico-Wordsworthian-Coleridgean-anti-Utilitarians still keep with undiminished sway at the helm." Still later he wrote, "That paper, the Athenaeum, which, by the by, is entirely written by Apostles, should it obtain an extensive circulation, is calculated to do much good. It is a paper not merely of principle, but what is almost equally important, of principles—certain fixed rules to which compositions are referred, and by which they are judged. In this it is superior, not merely to contemporary papers, but to the reviews of the highest pretension."[34] Hare, too, spoke of the *Athenaeum*'s "high philosophical and moral principles," but he should have been biased in its favour inasmuch as Maurice wrote highly laudatory reviews in its pages of the *Guesses at Truth* and "The Children of Light."[35]

Filling the columns of a densely printed weekly literary paper was no small task, and Maurice was happy to turn to Hare for help. Shortly before he handed the editorship over to Sterling, Maurice wrote to Hare to acknowledge his assistance: "I . . . return you my most grateful thanks for the valuable communications you have sent to the 'Athenaeum', and for the most kind language with which you accompanied those communications, and for your promise of further favours. . . . How much this pleasure is heightened to my friend Sterling and myself by the kindness proceeding from yourself could only be understood, if we could explain how many of our better tastes or feelings we trace to the effects of your instructions at Cambridge."[36] The contributions which Hare made to the *Athenaeum* were slight, but served as an important bridge toward his later friendship with Maurice.

The first of Hare's contributions to the *Athenaeum* was a translation from Jean Paul Richter's "Vision of a Godless World," which like Hare's other contributions was signed "J.C.H."[37] This macabre devotional work was supposed to shock one from sceptical thoughts, and had a powerful influence. Years later Maurice recalled it, and quoted from it at length in a review of Renan's *Vie de Jésus*.[38]

Throughout the spring of 1829 Hare contributed to the *Athenaeum* a series of five installments on German authors under the general heading of the "Museum of Thought."[39] In May 1829 the *Athenaeum* published Hare's translations from Goethe's "Poetic Epistles," and in October 1829 his version of Goethe's "Alexis and Dora" formed his last contribution to the journal.[40] Eighteen years later these verse translations, along with Hare's rendering of Schiller's epigrams, were reprinted in a collection of *English Hexameter Translations* edited by William Whewell.[41] Hare's important efforts to make German thought and literature better known in England virtually ceased upon his departure from Cambridge in 1832.

The decision to become a country parson marked another stage in Hare's life. With half his years behind him, he embarked upon a new career. But in little more than a decade as a translator he had already made a major contribution in introducing the English reading public to German works of history, theology, and literature. As a Churchman and parish priest he also made his mark, but the time consumed in so doing left him with few moments which he was willing to spare for the congenial pursuits of literature.

Chapter 10

To Italy and Herstmonceux

In 1826, at the age of thirty, Hare took holy orders that he might retain his fellowship.¹ This was not a surprising step, nor did it indicate a continuing commitment to a career in the University. As early as 1822 Hare had expressed his eagerness to become a good parish priest, and in 1829 he was appointed chaplain to the sixth Duke of Devonshire, probably through the influence of the young Lord William Cavendish, who had been Hare's pupil.² The appointment appears to have surprised Hare: "My Lord, Allow me to return your Grace my most grateful thanks for the honour you have been so good as to confer upon me, an honour as unexpected as it was totally unmerited. . . . It is a matter of peculiar gratification [to] me to have become the chaplain of the Duke of Devonshire, when I recollect the obligations my family have already been under to your noble house, when I reflect that my mother was blest with the kindness and . . . the friendship of that Duchess of Devonshire whom everybody admired and loved."³

There is no evidence that Hare's chaplaincy was more than honorary. Despite Hare's comment about the unexpected nature of the appointment, it may not have been wholly unsolicited. If Hare were ever to marry, and he was then still engaged to Anna Maria Dashwood, a Church living was necessary. The advowson of the old Hare family living at Herstmonceux was held by Francis Hare, and his intention was to present his brother Augustus to the living as soon as it fell vacant. However, when that time came, the candidate was not Augustus, but Julius Hare.[4]

That Augustus Hare should succeed to the rich living of Herstmonceux had been the cherished wish of Lady Jones. They quarrelled over his reluctance to take orders, though he was eventually ordained in 1825. In July 1829 Augustus married and settled in the poor parish of Alton Barnes, Wiltshire, a living in the gift of New College, Oxford. When his uncle, Robert Hare, Rector of Herstmonceux, died in February 1832, Augustus was unwilling to give up his living at Alton Barnes. He acted to persuade Julius to leave Cambridge and accept the Herstmonceux living. Now that Julius was again engaged, to Jane, Lady Munro, he was even more susceptible to persuasion.[5]

At the end of August 1831 Julius Hare wrote to his sister-in-law Maria: "If, when Herstmonceux becomes vacant, you still prefer remaining where you are, it will then be my duty to think about taking it. . . . I am always averse to forming plans, to making decisions about the future . . . and more especially in the present state of England, how impossible it is to calculate what will be the state of any living in England, or whether there will be any livings at all, next year!"[6] Indeed, it was partly a reaction to Julius' depressed state of mind which led his brother and sister-in-law to apply pressure over the family living. Maria Hare remarked in a letter to her sister: "Julius . . . is much more communicative than Augustus, and more generally conversable. But with all that mildness of demeanor and character, I am surprised to hear him so violent on politics, &c. I think he will be obliged to end by living in Germany, he is so much annoyed by the present system of things in this country—by the overpowering commercial spirit which fills everything. . . . He does not conceal his dislike for people when he feels it, and is not near as cautious as Augustus is."[7] During this same visit Maria wrote in her diary her impressions of a sermon that Julius delivered in his brother's church at Alton Barnes, and she concluded: "I long for him to be thrown more into the world, that, by mixing with different classes of society, his theories may become less visionary."[8] Maria was convinced that the rectorship of Herstmonceux would "be a means of calling forth all Julius' power for the good of others."[9]

Julius, however, had serious doubts about his ability to adjust to the proposed change from Cambridge to a rural parish: "It would be a sad exchange to give up my beautiful rooms, my friends whose converse strengthens and steadies my mind. . . . for the dismal solitude of that great, big house, with . . . not a soul nearer than . . . Brighton, with whom I should have a thought in common." But this loss was not his greatest fear about such a change:

> I speak with the utmost sincerity, when I say I do not think I should make an efficient parish priest. I know not what, but there is an incapacity about me for conversing with the lower orders; part of it may be constitutional; habit may have increased it; the very nature of my pursuits, of my studies and speculations, withdraws me more than others from the commerce of ordinary thought. I find a great difficulty in carrying on a conversation except with a very few of my friends: my thoughts don't seem to move in the same line as theirs, my views, my interests, seem to be so different; it is hard to find a point of union. This grows upon me year by year. I know not how to check it; and I fear I should never learn to talk to the poor as they ought to be talked to; in time, perhaps, I might learn to preach to them; but that you know is a very small part of what a parish priest has to do.[10]

Julius' brother Augustus was remarkable for his ability to preach and to minister to his congregation in their everyday speech without appearing to patronize them. Julius admired his brother for this skill, and correctly predicted that his own inability to communicate with the common people would prove his greatest handicap as a parson.[11]

Despite his diffidence about parochial work, when his uncle's death brought him the Herstmonceux living, Julius Hare was resigned to the need for change. Julius wrote to Maria, "Whether Herstmonceux is to be a paradise to me or a wilderness, or, as is more likely, something between the two—my lot is now cast. I am to quit this goodly college, with all its goodly inmates, and to take up my rest there, in all probability for life. . . . I agree entirely with you, that 'a life of mere literary activity is not all that is required from a minister of Christ's church'; . . . it aught always to be combined with *practical activity*."[12]

TO ITALY AND HERSTMONCEUX   119

Also in the spring of 1832 Hare at last met Walter Savage Landor, who came to England on a visit. Upon meeting Landor, Hare resolved to accompany him to the continent and to spend a year in Italy before settling down as a parson.[13] Landor's trip to Cambridge coincided with a six-day stay by Augustus and Maria Hare, whom Julius had long begged to visit him. After returning from Cambridge, Maria wrote to Lucy Stanley:

> Julius's rooms at Cambridge are most perfect, looking as they do down that glorious avenue . . . his walls literally lined and papered with books, except one side, over the fire-place, where Raphael's "Madonna and Child", and two or three other good pictures are. I fully enter into his feeling of the unworldliness, the freedom from care, the leisure afforded by such a life, and with him the warmth of friendship keeps alive the affections, which, in general, must lie dormant in a college; yet I shall be much surprised if, after two or three years of his country life at Herstmonceux, Julius has not received more of real happiness than in many years at Trinity.[14]

Hare suffered from another of his periodic illnesses in the spring of 1832. Travel was good therapy, however, and in July 1832 he journeyed to the Lake District to visit Wordsworth. Hare's mind was brimming with plans for his continental tour, and he tried, without success, to persuade Wordsworth to accompany him. Before Hare left England he was formally presented to the Herstmonceux living. During his absence he retained the services of the incumbent curate, George Matthews. Hare did succeed in persuading his good friend Thomas Worsley to join him and Landor, and on 1 October 1832 the three set off by channel packet for Ostend.[15]

From Ostend the three companions made their way to Munich by way of Ghent, Antwerp, Liège, Cologne, Bonn, and Frankfurt. In his travel diary Hare entered numerous comments about the scenery, which prompted him to marvel, "We call this life a vale of troubles, and we turn in thoughtlessness away, from the numberless pleasures that nature strews along our path." He also noted with distaste the English-built steam engines which disfigured some of the scenery, and which he believed "fated to be the destroyers of picturesque beauty." On this trip Hare was the complete tourist, and allowed his romantic imagination free rein. He used every opportunity for sight-seeing, while Worsley busied himself with sketching, and Landor was preoccupied with food. The hardships of travel, such as preparing tea without kettle, pot, or cups, Hare believed "give a kind of zest to travelling."[16]

In Bonn the travellers visited Hare's half-sister, Georgiana, and she invited A.W. Schlegel to join them. In Frankfurt the travellers passed by the house where Goethe was born, and paid their respects.[17] Hare found the Germans "a most amiable, kind hearted people," and despite his eagerness to reach Italy, he was reluctant to leave Austrian territory "even without considering the sorry substitutes that Italy affords for [citizens]. In Germany I always feel at home, almost . . . more so than in England." But he soon grew to love the Italian peasants and to praise them above their English counterparts. After leaving Venice the party reached Florence on 25 November 1832. For three weeks Hare and Worsley were Landor's guests. Hare examined the churches, and visited every picture gallery, public and private, to which he could gain access. His diary is especially full of praise for the work of Raphael.[18]

Bidding Landor farewell, Hare and Worsley reached Rome by way of Sienna on 20 December. Hare had written that "Landor . . . goes far beyond any person I ever knew in exaggerating the impressions of the moment & depreciating everything else in comparison." In praising Rome, Hare fell into the same hyperbole: "Of all the cities in the world Rome is by far the most delightful . . . one of the objects which I have been longing all my life is . . . to see this mistress of the world, this capitol of Christendom, this eternal City." In Rome, Hare met Bertal Thorwaldsen (1768–1844), the Danish sculptor, whose work he especially admired. He also called upon Nicholas Wiseman (1802–65), the future Cardinal-Archbishop of Westminster, who was then head of the English College in Rome.[19] But, most important, Hare at last met Baron Bunsen, Niebuhr's successor in the Prussian delegation at Rome.

Hare and Bunsen became fast friends, and during his stay in Rome hardly a day passed that Hare did not spend some time in Bunsen's company.[20] Bunsen was an amiable gentleman, an accomplished scholar, and a theological liberal. As Niebuhr's close friend and successor he was the natural object of friendship of the English

Broad Churchmen. Thirlwall, Arnold, and Hare all returned from Italy to extol their new friend's virtues. J.W. Blakesley, Fellow of Trinity College and former Apostle, exemplified this reaction when he wrote, "In my opinion, a man who knows Bunsen may all but dispense with knowing the rest of the world."[21] Certainly Bunsen was the perfect guide to the wonders of the Eternal City, which his seventeen-year residence had enabled him to master.[22]

While in Rome, Hare was asked to deliver a sermon in the English Chapel. He chose as his text Matthew XI:7, "What went ye out into the wilderness to see?" and caused a stir among the Anglican congregation by preaching against the idleness of many visitors to Rome.[23] On 21 February 1833 Hare and Worsley set off from Rome for Naples, which they reached two days later. During a month spent in Naples they enjoyed the company of Henry Francis Cary, visited Pompeii and Herculaneum, and climbed Mount Vesuvius.[24]

Throughout his tour Hare showed a great interest in the liturgy of the Roman Catholic Church. He attended vespers and Christmas Eve mass at Saint Peter's: "This is one of the things for the sake of witnessing which I have for many years been anxious to come to Rome." He was pleased by the music, the pageantry, and the absence of pews, but felt the exclusion from the services of lower-class Romans in favour of foreigners showed a "want of devotion" and "tended to give the whole the character of a mere spectacle . . . which in religion is above all things disgusting." On another occasion Hare went eagerly to see a nun take the veil. He visited Monte Casino and other monasteries, and commented favourably on the spirituality and habits of the monks he met there: "The courteous affability . . . is a thing characteristic [also] of a Catholic priest: that religion, as Digby boasts, is certainly singularly effective in inculcating good and gentle manners." Hare admired the priests for their active roles in society, especially in the education of children. At the church of Saint Anthony in Rome, Hare was moved by the sight of the cattle-blessing ceremony: "Letting the animal creature partake in the blessings of Christianity is exceedingly pleasing, and, if not expressly prescribed, at all events is not repugnant to the Bible for they shared in the evils of the fall." Hare returned from his tour with vivid impressions of Romanism, some of which were decidedly friendly: "There is," he wrote, "something in every manifestation of real religious feeling, however deluded it may be, that I cannot but revere."[25]

Returning to Rome on 30 March 1833, Hare again enjoyed the company of Bunsen, who had just received the long-awaited third volume of Niebuhr's history. Hare read Bunsen's copy, and noted: "This will be a most arduous task for me to engage in as soon as I get back to England." It was so arduous that he never did translate the third volume. Leaving Rome was painful, but Hare was satisfied with the fullness of his trip's achievement: "I have seen the finest pictures in the world, the finest statues; I shall never again see such beautiful scenery as that around Naples. Life seems to have presented me at once with a cup brimming over with all its pleasures." Indeed, he worried that it had been too complete: "All the things that from my boyish days I have most longed to see and do, I have seen and done: and it seems as if 'earth had nothing more to show'—nothing at least that I am ever likely to see: for Athens and Jerusalem I can never hope to set eyes on. All other objects that I may hereafter fall in with, when regarded entirely as objects of taste, will be inferior to what I have seen already." Still, there was some consolation in the acquisition of half-a-dozen Renaissance paintings with which to decorate the walls of Herstmonceux Rectory.[26]

After following the line of Hannibal's march, Hare and Worsley reached Florence, where their host, Landor, desired them to spend a month. But after only five days with Landor they were once again on their way, having met Ralph Waldo Emerson at Landor's table.[27] Hare and Worsley visited the marble quarries at Carrara, and parted company at Genoa. Worsley's health had broken down, and he set off for sea-bathing and sketching at Nice. Hare soon departed for Milan. From Lombardy, Hare went to Switzerland where he visited Lugano and Zurich. Heavy snows in the Saint Gotthard Pass that June forced him to cross on horseback. His destination was Bonn where his half-sister nursed him through a rheumatic attack brought on by his exertions in travelling. There he encountered his former pupil, John Sterling, who was in Germany to learn the language and to study theology.[28] In earlier years Hare had urged him to pursue a clerical career, and Sterling gave evidence that spring of being eager to do so. Hare therefore offered

TO ITALY AND HERSTMONCEUX   123

him the job as his curate at Herstmonceux.[29] Hare left Bonn on 16 June, bound for England. A Rhine steamer took him to Cologne, and he went by barge through Belgium. On 20 June 1833 his "long and unpleasant voyage" ended with his safe arrival in England and return to Herstmonceux.[30]

The parish of Herstmonceux, where Hare was to spend the rest of his days, lies thirteen miles east of Lewes, county seat of East Sussex, and four miles inland from Pevensey Bay. Herstmonceux Castle and church overlook the Pevensey Marshes with a clear view of the English Channel beyond. In Hare's day the sight of ships' sails in the channel was commonplace. Herstmonceux is a sprawling, rural parish bordered on the east and west by the villages of Windmill Hill and Hellingly. The church lies two miles south of the village of Herstmonceux and its main thoroughfare, Gardner Street. In later years Hare established an auxiliary church at Cowbeech, one and one-half miles north of the village. Church services were held there for distant-dwelling villagers, and until the 1870s it also served as a primary school. The population of the parish was 1,358, engaged largely in agriculture.[31]

Hare had given instructions before he went to Italy for the addition of several rooms to the rectory. He therefore returned to Herstmonceux to find the house amply provided for his personal library, but also with a debt which stood at £2,000, at least twice the annual value of the living. At Cambridge he had managed with a single servant; he was now master of a modest rural establishment of servants, milk-cow, and dogs.[32]

Maria Hare's impression of the enlarged rectory was that "this house is quite perfect, not at all too grand for a parsonage-house, though outside it looks more like a small squire's than a rector's."[33] A.P. Stanley's recollections of the interior were vivid:

> The very first glance at the entrance-hall revealed the character of its master. It was not merely a house with a good library—the whole house was a library. The vast nucleus which he brought with him from Cambridge grew year by year. . . . At the time of his death it had reached the number of more than 12,000 volumes; and it must be further remembered that these volumes were of no ordinary kind. Of all libraries which it has been our lot to traverse, we never saw any equal to this in the combined excellence of quantity and quality; none in which there were

so few worthless, so many valuable books. Its original basis was classical and philological; but of later years the historical, philosophical, and theological elements outgrew all the rest. The peculiarity which distinguished the collection probably from any other, private or public, in the kingdom, was the preponderance of German literature. . . . And what perhaps was yet more remarkable was the manner in which the centre of this whole was himself. Without a catalogue, without assistance, he knew where every book was to be found, for what it was valuable, what relation it bore to the rest.[34]

Despite Lady Jones' desire to see them all burned, Hare had long been a collector of German books. In a letter to John Taylor in 1824 he boasted of owning three thousand volumes. In his later years at Cambridge, Hare gave his bibliomania free rein, and over the decades his collection grew to four or five times that number.[35] In 1825, when Hare renewed his boyhood acquaintance with Crabb Robinson, the older Germanist was amazed by the younger man's library: "I had great pleasure in looking over his collection of German books—the best collection of modern German authors I have ever seen in England."[36]

Hare's heroes were represented not only by books, but in more palpable form: "Busts also were there, . . . memorials of men whose names he honoured, or in whose friendship he rejoiced,— his brother Augustus, Schleiermacher, Niebuhr, Bunsen, Wordsworth. Seldom has any house been so in harmony with the mind and character of its occupant."[37] Hare's aesthetic taste was also manifest "in the few spaces left unoccupied [which] were hung [with] the noble pictures which he had brought with him from Italy. To him they were more than mere works of art: they were companions and guests."[38] A well-worn edition of Wordsworth's poetry lay ever at hand in the rectory. Hare never allowed it to be reshelved, and he read from it daily, after breakfast, when he also walked in his garden in his straw hat and doted on his plants.[39]

The size and splendour of Hare's house did not altogether compensate for its location. Hare was bothered by the absence of former friends and haunts. He had predicted that loneliness would be a problem, and in his letters to Whewell and other friends Hare was forever begging them to visit.[40] His nearest old friend was Henry Venn Elliott at Saint Mary's, Brighton, but many guests made their way to Herstmonceux, beginning with Thomas Worsley shortly after Hare's return in 1833.⁴¹ Moreover, during most of his tenure at Herstmonceux, Hare employed a curate to help him minister to his enormous parish. Several were quite remarkable young men, who reflected Hare's craving for intellectual company. The first three were former Cambridge Apostles.⁴²

John Sterling was the first curate, arriving in May 1834. He took deacon's orders, but his declining health and growing religious doubts caused him to leave after only nine months, and he was never ordained priest. Nonetheless, during his brief tenure Sterling was a constant joy to Hare. Sterling's interests were scholarly, not pastoral. In Germany he had learned German and developed his taste for theology. He wrote to Trench of wanting to write a treatise on ethics to raise Christianity from the level of Locke and Paley. Sterling's interest in Herstmonceux was in the company of Hare and access to his books.⁴³

Hare's attitude toward his ministry and the role of his curates is revealed in the correspondence which preceded his appointment of Edmund Venables. Hare sought not only personal testimonials, but pointedly asked for Venables' opinions on controversial questions as well as the nature of his party sympathies. This scrutiny was not, as he said, to raise fresh tests, but because

> in the peculiar intimate relation between a rector and his curate, preaching in the same church on the same day, visiting and admonishing, exhorting the same persons, it seems to be very desirable that their views of doctrine should not clash, and that there should be a considerable harmony between them . . . I will state that I should wish my curate not to be one of those who are now ascribing a paramount value to outward ordinances, but that he should regard it as his main business to preach Christ crucified for us, and to awaken a spiritual life in the souls of his flock; that he should hold the doctrine of Justification by Faith; that he should be a lover of the Reformation; that he should not be one of those who reject and revile the name of Protestant. . . . I believe many persons who differ from me on these points may be good and efficient ministers; but if a curate, holding the opposite opinions were to come into this parish, we should often jar, in a manner hurtful to our own friendly intercourse, and still more to the spiritual well-being of our parishioners.⁴⁴

Venables' sympathies were High Church, but Hare nevertheless offered him the post, and noted that while the Evangelicals, or Low Churchmen, proved best fitted for pastoral work, he also esteemed the greater learning in theology which High Churchmen brought to the cure of souls. Hare was even willing to overlook Venables' leaning to "Oxford views, . . . so long as you separate the truths which the promulgation of those views has been allowed to bring forward, from the extravagancies and very mischievous errors, into which they have been perverted."[45]

Indeed, Hare was not seeking slavish conformity, but rather a degree of toleration and diversity which characterized the Broad Church ideal of a National Church:

> That my curate's opinions should be in all things square with my own, I neither expect nor desire. Indeed, when so many peculiar circumstances have exercised so powerful an influence on the formations of my own mind—such as my acquaintance with German philosophy and theology, and my love for that which is good in both—my conviction that in both the Germans have made nearer approaches to speculative truth than any other nation, except some few persons whose tapers have been kindled at some German torch—it must be hopeless to find anyone in England whose frame of mind would coincide with my own. Nor is it to be wished, for the good of my parishioners. It is better for them that they should be supplied with different kinds of food, so long as we do not proclaim or imply that the food administered by the other is deleterious or unwholesome. In the Church at large I am anxious that the utmost range, compatible with the retention of the fundamental truths of Christianity, would be left open for diversities of opinion; and in my own parish I should rather wish, than object, that there should be as much diversity as can well co-exist with harmony and unity and hearty co-operation.[46]

Such a spirit of doctrinal conciliation was anathema to the militant factions in the English Church, but Broad Churchmen like Hare believed that only through unity, with a reconstructed National Church, could the way be prepared for the Kingdom of Christ.

Hare had not only his series of curates to lessen the intellectual and social isolation that he felt at Herstmonceux, but in the early years of his tenure there he also boarded young men preparing for matriculation at university. His motives were admittedly pecuniary "as I am two thousand pounds out of pocket by my living, I am not sure that I *ought* not, as a matter of duty, to take pupils, so long at least as that I may lift my head above water, and clear off my debts." Indeed, he only did it while finances required. Hare revealed doubts about his whole parochial undertaking when in regard to taking pupils he confessed himself "averse to it . . . both from taste and from principle; for I fear that even without them I shall have little time enough for anything beyond the work of the week, and I cannot help grieving at the thought that all I have been doing, all I have been labouring to acquire for the past five-and-twenty years, is to be utterly thrown away, and for what? In order to do, or rather to fail in doing, that which tens of thousands would have done quite as well, and thousands far better than I can do."[47]

The first such pupil was young Arthur Penrhyn Stanley, who spent two months at Herstmonceux in 1834 between his studies under Arnold at Rugby and his matriculation at Oxford. Stanley left vivid recollections of his stay at Herstmonceux, particularly of the strong impressions made upon him by the conversation and sermons of John Sterling and by discovering Coleridge. In addition to steering him through *Antigone,* Hare encouraged young Stanley to read Tennyson, Wordsworth, Digby's *Mores Catholici,* Thirlwall's preface to Schleiermacher, De Quincey's "Opium Eater," and Lamb's essays. With Hare and Sterling he argued over whether Wordsworth's or Coleridge's poetry was superior. Stanley was already a budding Broad Churchman in the liberality of his views, and so he found Hare and Sterling all the more delightful: "Conceive my delight on finding that both J[ulius] H[are] and Mr. Sterling agree with, or rather believe in, most fully, the advantage of comprehending all but Unitarians; indeed J.H. would make the Divinity of Christ the only Article." Stanley wrote to his mother: "Such an enlargement of my mind's horizon I seem to have had in these six weeks, and now I seem as if I were going to pass through . . . the consummation of my heterodoxical teaching, before I go to the place of supreme orthodoxy."[48]

In the following year, 1835, Hare had two pupils, George Wagner (1818–57), son of the squire of Hurstmonceux Place, and George Smythe (1818–57), son of the sixth Viscount Strangford. Smythe was sent to study with Hare although his father opposed the boy's desire to go to university.[49] He left Herstmonceux with a reverence for one of Hare's favourite books, *The Broadstone of Honour*. When Smythe entered Parliament he was associated with Disraeli in the movement known as Young England, which bore many marks of the *Broadstone*'s influence.[50]

With his other pupil, George Wagner, Hare had a longer and closer association. The Wagner family had occupied Hare's childhood home, Hurstmonceux Place, since 1819.[51] It is to Hare's tutorship and influence that Wagner's biographer attributes Wagner's love of learning. In sending him up to Trinity College, Hare certified Wagner "as neither genius nor thinker, but one who will do admirably," and asked Whewell that he be given "a good, attentive, painstaking tutor."[52] Wagner did have a gift for languages, and acquired French, German, and Italian in addition to Greek and Latin. He mastered German so completely that he was known to preach in that language. In this one sees Hare's influence. As a zealous clergyman, first at Dallington, Sussex, and later at Saint Stephen's, Brighton, he remained one of Hare's intimates.[53]

Family tragedy brought Hare a widowed sister-in-law as a long-term companion at Herstmonceux. In September 1833 Julius' younger brother Marcus was married to Maria Hare's friend, Lucy Stanley. Augustus, Maria's husband, had been in ill health for six months, so when Marcus and Lucy set off for Italy on their honeymoon, Augustus and Maria accompanied them in hope that the better climate would lead to Augustus' recovery. However, in Rome, Augustus William Hare died on 18 February 1834. Julius still lacked a curate at Herstmonceux, and was therefore prevented from rushing to his brother's side in Rome. Maria Hare returned to England and settled down in the Herstmonceux rectory, where "Julius's delight at my return was the nearest approach to that affection I so miss, of anything I have met with. I found him in great sorrow at the news of Coleridge's death."[54] Julius was a man of very different temperament from his brother Augustus, as Maria was already aware, but they delighted in each other's company. Maria resided in the rectory itself for a year, and then settled into a fine, white house in nearby Lime Park. For the next ten years she spent summers at Herstmonceux and winters visiting her father's rectory in the north of England. After the move to Lime Park,

Julius came every day for dinner, arriving at six "like clock-work," and walking back to the rectory after coffee at eight. He brought with him whomever might be visiting him, so that Maria was exposed to a most varied society.[55]

Maria occupied herself with reading, with the pious reflections with which she filled her letters and journals, and with works of charity among the villagers of Herstmonceux, who came to call her the "Lady o' Lime."[56] But for all the happiness she found at Herstmonceux, her bereavement was heavy, and her barrenness was a great source of grief. Before she left Rome, she had stood as Godmother for the fourth born child of Francis and Anna Hare. The infant had been christened Augustus John Cuthbert. Maria was aware that the birth of this new mouth to feed brought no joy to his parents. Therefore, shortly after her return to England, she wrote the Francis Hares to propose the unconditional adoption by her of their latest-born. The reply was unabashedly candid: "My dear Maria, how very kind of you! Yes, certainly, the baby shall be sent as soon as it is weaned; and, if any one else would like one, would you kindly recollect that we have others."[57] So in August 1835 A.J.C. Hare, or "baby-boy," as Maria and Julius called him, arrived with his nurse at Herstmonceux. A.J.C. Hare became the family chronicler, and also produced a narcissistic autobiography reputed to be the longest one in the English language. He thus provided an important account of the daily life of the Hares of Herstmonceux, as seen by a child, sometimes a maliciously inventive child who cannot be trusted. Julius Hare proved happy in the style of life he created for himself at Herstmonceux, which, if it lacked the intense intellectual stimulation of college life, compensated for that deficiency by the presence of his attentive sister-in-law and by a constant stream of visitors to the rectory.

Chapter 11

Parson and Archdeacon

John Sterling's presence at Herstmonceux revived Hare's connection with F.D. Maurice. Hare had discerned in Maurice unrivalled powers of metaphysical analysis, but as an undergraduate Maurice resisted Hare's proffered friendship and "the kindness which he was disposed to show me."[1] After converting to the Anglican faith from the Unitarianism in which he was raised, Maurice resolved to return to university and pursue a clerical career. But he chose to matriculate as an undergraduate at Oxford, and because of his age he required a personal recommendation from someone at Cambridge. He therefore wrote to Hare in 1829 and humbly requested a testimonial. Hare complied at once. Maurice explained his choice to Hare: "The subjection of an undergraduate's life . . . [will] be a useful discipline. . . . the same feeling makes me dread less than I should otherwise do the mere barren orthodoxy which, from all I can hear, is characteristic of Oxford. . . . If I could hope to combine in myself something of that freedom and courage for which the young men I knew at Cambridge were remarkable, with something more of solidity and reverence for what is established, I should begin to fancy that I had some useful qualities for a member of the English church."[2]

After leaving Oxford in 1833 Maurice served as a curate, and in 1836 became chaplain of Guy's Hospital in London. It was after Maurice moved to Guy's that his real intimacy with Hare developed, and he was often at Herstmonceux. Hare became Maurice's strong advocate, pushing him forward and nominating him for appointments which Maurice's own shyness and diffidence made him shun.[3] The Hares had other connections with the Maurice family. Maria Hare made friends with Maurice's younger sister Priscilla (1810–54), who came to visit Lime at Herstmonceux every summer. When Priscilla made her annual visit to Herstmonceux in 1837 she brought along her younger sister Esther (1814–64). This was the first time Hare met his future wife. Esther had been keeping a school in Reading, but suffered an illness that summer which required her to rest. That very summer Hare experienced a debilitating illness in his legs which laid him up for months. Their infirmities provided them with common ground for sympathy and interest. Hare once claimed to find chronically ill women most fascinating, and invalidism was rife in the Maurice family.[4]

Priscilla and Esther Maurice became frequent visitors to the parish, often for months on end, for Maria was closely attached to both. Maria said to Julius, "Priscilla is like silver, but Esther is like gold."[5] A.J.C. Hare had quite a different opinion of the Maurices, and in his autobiography, written long after their demise, he painted an unflattering portrait. He despised their self-conscious piety, their triviality, and the decidedly lower-class tone which he thought they brought to the society and conversation at Herstmonceux, both at Lime and at the rectory. Toward Esther, A.J.C. Hare was particularly vituperative, calling her "a fearful scourge to my childhood [who] completely poisoned my life at Hurstmonceux. . . . She had the inflexible cruelty of a Dominican."[6] A.J.C. Hare's portrait of Esther as a psycho-religious fanatic, and his catalogue of her barbarities against him make grim reading, and cannot be altogether dismissed. The strength of his language, however, and the outrageousness of Esther's alleged behaviour weaken the credibility of his story. At the other extreme Esther's twin sister, Lucilla Maurice Powell (1814–77) presented a picture of her in unpublished memoirs that is all sweetness and light. In July 1844 Esther accompanied Julius, Maria, and A.J.C. Hare on a trip to the Lake District, where they visited the Arnolds and the Wordsworths. On this trip Julius and Esther became engaged.[7]

A.J.C. Hare remembered "our pleasure was not unalloyed, for though Uncle Julius accompanied us, my mother took Esther Maurice with her . . . and never foreseeing what every one else foresaw, that Uncle Julius, who had always a passion for governesses, would certainly propose to her. Bitter were the tears that my mother shed when this result—to her alone unexpected—actually took place. It was the most dismal of betrothals: Esther sobbed and cried, my mother sobbed and cried, Uncle Julius sobbed and cried daily. I used to see them sitting holding each other's hands and crying."[8] This lugubrious scene had a sequel. John Sterling was succumbing to consumption at Ventnor in Wiltshire, where he was nursed by his sister-in-law, F.D. Maurice's wife. On 18 September 1844, after receiving news of his death, Julius and Esther went to Ventnor to the death-bed: "It was very solemn and awful, when I went with Esther into his room, and was locked in, and we gazed on his dear calm peaceful face, and on the heavenly quietness of his mouth, and then knelt and prayed beside his coffin. I had been anxiously wishing that, if his life had been spared so long, we might have gone to him after our marriage . . . to bless him and to seek his blessing. But it was differently ordered, and . . . I trust the memory of this solemn seal to our union will abide with us through life."[9]

On 12 November 1844 Julius and Esther were married by the bride's brother, F.D. Maurice, at Reading, home of the bride's aged parents. Not everyone was entirely pleased; Lucy Hare wrote, "I am too much overpowered by the unexpected tidings of Jule's engagement to say much. . . . I had so much considered him and Esther in the light of father and daughter that I can scarcely take it in."[10] Hare's friends were delighted at his belated marriage, though many must have been as surprised as Thirlwall, who said that a message from the "Lama of Thibet" could not have surprised him more.[11] Sterling had written before his death to confess that he had planned the match: "I never knew a man so formed for domestic happiness & I believe no woman is more capable of conferring it than Esther. I am most thankful to know that this is to be."[12] William Wordsworth wrote: "You both have *our* fervent wishes and dearest prayers for God's blessing upon a course so well begun. Be assured that the nearest approach that can be made to happiness upon earth is by a union such as you have in prospect."[13] Wordsworth passed the news of Hare's engagement to Whewell at Cambridge, and Whewell wrote to send Hare his hearty congratulations. Hare's reply to Whewell reveals his state of mind, when at the age of forty-nine he chose to marry: "Your letter has given me very great pleasure . . . from its expressions of friendly sympathy with my happiness. . . . Not however that I needed any such assurance to lull any fears in my own breast, or to strengthen my confident expectations, of the future, which expectations w[oul]d already be over-presumptuous, if they had not a ground mightier and more enduring than the mountains, among which our love . . . first overflowed its banks."[14] Hare was in the full bloom of romantic love, for the first time in years.

Maria Hare wrote of her continued happy life at Herstmonceux after the marriage of Julius and Esther; they gathered every morning for Bible reading, and usually all dined together at the rectory. But a few months later, in a letter to Lucy, Maria wrote: "I often think how unlike Julius and Esther's newly married life is to that of most people, even to what mine was—it is so chastened and solemn."[15] A.J.C. Hare observed that "the marriage . . . had brought with it much of a feeling, though not a reality, of separation between Lime and the Rectory; and the influx of new associations, new interests, and fresh guests . . . made my mother turn with greater warmth . . . to the friends of her earlier life, from whom the almost too-engrossing devotion of Julius had hither to comparatively separated her."[16] Later, in his autobiography, A.J.C. Hare wrote more openly, and complained that the rectory came to be filled up with Maurices, to the near-exclusion of other visitors.[17]

According to A.J.C. Hare his Aunt Esther dominated nearly everyone and everything around her, but to Julius' comfort and well-being she was totally devoted. A.J.C. Hare hated the hours spent at the rectory because they took him away from his happy home life at Lime. He always remembered Julius as one of the two great figures from his childhood, but he regretted "the excessive severity of Uncle Julius, who had the very sharpest possible way of speaking to children, even when he meant to be kind to them."[18] Julius "was never captivating to children," and was further made a bugbear to the young boy by being assigned the duty of administering corporal punishment whenever it was thought necessary. Not all the punishment was physical; young A.J.C. Hare was forced to sit quietly through his uncle's notoriously long sermons, twice each Sunday: "Uncle Julius' endless sermons were my detestation."[19] This lack of sympathy caused A.J.C. Hare to characterize his uncle as a model for the Reverend Theobald Pontifex in *The Way of All Flesh*. For his Aunt Esther he reserved a vituperation which requires special consideration.

A.J.C. Hare recorded how his Aunt Esther put him in unlighted rooms, made him sleep in unheated rooms with little bedding, and regularly locked him in the church vestry between Sunday services, an interval of three hours. Moreover, she openly reviled members of his family, mistook illnesses for "temper," forced him to eat sauerkraut because she knew it revolted him, gave him "rubbishy" and contemptible gifts, and sought to deprive him of all objects of affection including his cat, which he claims she ordered to be hanged. He did recognize some good qualities in his aunt, such as her devoted attention and heroic efforts during medical crises, to poor parishioners as well as to family members. Moreover, Esther was as exacting of herself as she was of others: "She was the Inquisition in person. She probed and analysed herself and the motive of her every action quite as bitterly and as mercilessly as she probed and analysed others. If any pleasure, any even which resulted from affection for others, had drawn her for an instant from what she believed to be the path—and it was always the thorniest path—of self-sacrifice, she would remorselessly denounce that pleasure, and even tear out that affection from her heart. She fasted and denied herself in everything." Esther Hare is a recognizable personality, the religious enthusiast whose religion enjoins pain and suffering, and proscribes all pleasures. Maria Hare was aware of what her son actually suffered at Esther's hands, but as he later explained, she truly believed in the Christian duty of turning the other cheek, and she grew to believe that Esther was a cross to be borne.[20]

As for Julius, so far from finding his wife's alleged behaviour neurotic, he believed she merely showed a high degree of spirituality: "Esther's spirit is assuredly one of the noblest and saintliest that ever dwelt even in a woman's breast. She is the only person I ever knew whose every word seems to be spoken, every action performed in the visible presence of God; and she has been so elevated by constant self-discipline, and so hallowed by divine grace, that self-denial and self-control seem with her to be not . . . efforts, but almost . . . the habits and impulses of her nature. How such an unspeakable blessing has been granted to me, I vainly strove to understand."[21]

Both before and after Hare's marriage the rectory was often filled with visitors. Marcus Hare and his family spent entire summers there, and indeed it was there that Marcus Hare died on 30 July 1845. Francis Hare, Julius' oldest brother, visited the rectory only once, briefly in 1838. After his death, however, his widow and children paid a visit in the autumn of 1842. A.J.C. Hare was taught to address his natural mother as "Italima" [Italian Mama]. A subsequent visit by Anna Hare in the summer of 1848 ended abruptly on the day after her arrival. She and Esther quarrelled, and Anna Hare left never to return to the rectory. The disagreement may have been religious, for soon afterwards Anna Hare became a convert to Roman Catholicism, "giving up her soul, such as it may be," said Julius, "to the Scarlet Woman on the Seven Hills."[22]

By far the most delightful long-term visitors at Herstmonceux were Bunsen and his family. In 1841 Bunsen was sent to England as Prussian Minister to the Court of Saint James. He sought a country residence, and at Hare's persuasion rented Hurstmonceux Place. Julius Hare was thrilled to have his dear friend resident in his own parish, but his nephew was also delighted. Young A.J.C. Hare felt the Bunsens brought to Herstmonceux a good deal of refinement, liberalism, and high-toned conversation. Unfortunately, the difficulty of getting from Herstmonceux to London caused Bunsen to give up his rural retreat after about two years of residence.[23]

Other guests at the Herstmonceux rectory included Whewell and Thirlwall, whom A.J.C. Hare remembered he disliked for their cold and formal manners, and Professor Sedgwick, to whom young Hare was devoted. He also recalled that he enjoyed the company of the poet George Darley (1795–1846), whom Julius often assisted in personal and financial crises. The "wonderfully varied society" at the rectory included "German philosophers, American philologists, English astronomers, politicians, poets."[24] Many of Hare's former pupils visited him. Everyone was made to feel comfortable at the rectory—at least this was true before Hare's marriage—even the irascible Thomas Carlyle, who visited in the summer of 1840.[25]

Carlyle met and befriended Sterling in London in the spring of 1835, and through Sterling became acquainted with Maurice and Hare. The following year when Carlyle read the *Guesses at Truth* he spoke of Hare as "a fresh, robust, light-loving man;—who ought to be a Bishop."[26] Hare was less generous in his opinion of Carlyle and his "monstrous doctrines."[27] But years later Carlyle recalled that he was immune to Hare's criticism: "Julius used to attack me for my heresies; always giving me due and grave notice. But when the attack came, it was really so mild that it made no impression on me one way or another."[28] In July 1840, as Hare prepared his sermon for the consecration of Thirlwall as Bishop of Saint David's, he received word from Carlyle that he intended to take up a longstanding invitation to visit Herstmonceux. As Hare explained to Whewell, "The consecration sermon is hardly worth reading. . . . Carlyle paid me a visit just two days before I came up to London, and thus the very two days which I had assigned to the sermon were spent in listening to him. . . . though I enjoyed his visit exceedingly, I sh[oul]d have done so more freely at another time."[29] Landor, too, was a guest at Herstmonceux rectory after he left his wife and returned to live at Bath. During his visits in 1847 and 1852 he thoroughly charmed Esther Hare. They continued to correspond, and Landor sent her verses, but his visits to Herstmonceux were rare.[30]

The widowed Mrs Alexander was the guest who probably spent the most time at Herstmonceux. In the late 1840s she appeared as a house guest. In A.J.C. Hare's words, she came to the rectory "for three days and stayed three weeks. The year after she came for three weeks and stayed five years."[31] At Herstmonceux she captivated everyone so that "from the first she was supreme at the Rectory, ruling even Aunt Esther with ever-increasing power; but on the whole her presence was an advantage. Her education and strong understanding enabled her to enter into all my uncle's pursuits and interests as his wife could never have done."[32] A.J.C. Hare found her far more appealing than his Aunt Esther, but still regarded her as a thoroughly scheming and egotistical woman. In his view "Mrs Alexander was now settled at the Rectory . . . , and she ruled as its queen. . . . And the odd thing was that Mrs Julius Hare . . . , instead of being jealous, worshipped with more enthusiasm than anyone else at the shrine of the domestic idol."[33] As for Julius Hare's behaviour in this bizarre domestic scene, after years of living in the all-male society of Cambridge, he enjoyed the devoted attention of several admiring women. The isolated rectory had become like a small seigniory, where Julius Hare was master, dispensing hospitality to his friends.

PARSON AND ARCHDEACON   137

For Hare the social life at Herstmonceux was very much secondary to his considerable clerical duties, which increased sharply after he became Archdeacon of Lewes in 1840. Though he found them distasteful, at least at first, he threw himself into parochial duties. His sermons were always much too long, and usually over the heads of his congregation. After a few years of pastoral experience, however, the subjects of his sermons became at least more interesting as he gradually foreswore philological analysis and biblical exegesis, and became more topical. Among his parishioners Hare was held to be "not a good winter parson" because his long evensong sermons kept people so late they could not reach home before dark.[34]

For those of some intellect Hare's sermons were usually substantive. For others there was still a joy and a power in his preaching which many remarked upon, and all could hear. A.J.C. Hare said, "Those who never heard Julius Hare read the Communion Service can have no idea of the depths of humility and passion in those sublime prayers."[35] Of Hare's preaching W.H. Thompson of Trinity College observed that "when Hare is to be lion[,] he roars well in the pulpit . . . though little better than a sucking dove when out of mahogany."[36] This comparison overlooks Hare's tendency to be abrupt and even loudly rude to those with whom he disagreed, whether they were friends or total strangers. At all events, Hare's effectiveness as a powerful, if long-winded, preacher was such that on two separate occasions he was invited to return to Cambridge to give a course of sermons as Select Preacher. For all his shortcomings as a parson, Hare was well regarded by his parishioners, partly because of the long association of the Hare family with the parish and manor of Herstmonceux.[37] The only thing that strained the happy relationship was the coming of the New Poor Law.

Before Hare settled at Herstmonceux he had no first-hand acquaintance with the relief of destitution. Nonetheless, he had formed definite ideas about poor relief, which reflected the fashionable view. Hare deplored the effects of the old poor law upon the character of the poor, and saw in the system of outdoor relief not only a burden upon the rest of society, but a moral trap for the pauper. In the 1820s he advocated a National Poor-Fund to serve both as unemployment insurance and pension-fund, and to be supported by workers' contributions, government grants, and voluntary charity.[38] Hare argued then for the very governmental interference that he deplored in the 1830s. However, he was eager to uphold the tradition of responsibility for the poor that dated from the Reformation and the dissolution of the monasteries. With the coming of the New Poor Law in 1834 Hare was elected to the Board of Guardians of the local Poor Law Union. His nephew said that "in spite of the habitual unpunctuality and irregularlity of his private life, he never failed in his attendance at . . . these meetings whatever the annoyance or inconvenience might be." The records of the Hailsham Union Board of Poor Law Guardians, though fragmentary, do not support that claim.[39]

His service on the Board of Guardians brought Hare a degree of unpopularity to which he was unaccustomed. After he visited the new workhouse in the neighbouring village of Hellingly, malicious rumours were spread about how Parson Hare planned to drown a boatload of paupers in Pevensey Bay. An elderly parishioner took Hare to task, asking how, when he had said "Those whom God hath joined together let no man put asunder," he could allow husbands and wives to be separated in the new union workhouse. Hare could only react to this question with tears; the harsh reality of the New Poor Law was not lost upon him.[40]

In 1840 Hare's clerical career took a new and important turn. The Archdeaconry of Lewes fell vacant, and William Otter (1768–1840), Bishop of Chichester, offered the post to Hare. Because of his views regarding certain parts of the creed and the liturgy, Hare hestitated to accept. He stated his reservations to his Bishop, and Otter replied, "I can allow these objections to have no weight, for my opinions on these points are just the same as your own. Therefore I again offer you the office and I hope you will take it."[41] Hare accepted and it was a happy decision, for during Otter's brief episcopate the diocese of Chichester began to take a lead in such activities as church building, enlargement, and restoration, in the augmentation of livings and the number of clergy, and in the building and provision of schools for all classes.[42] These efforts were carried on by Bishop Otter's two immediate successors, Philip Nicolas Shuttleworth (1782–1842) and Ashurst Turner Gilbert (1786–1870).

Hare's appointment as Archdeacon of Lewes did not make him hopeful of higher office. He assured his brother Marcus that he had no desire for promotion to a bishopric: "I can't concur in your wish that this dignity may prove a stepping-stone to a higher; at least if you mean to a mitre. For that, I feel sure, would be the greatest misfortune that could befall me. . . . Nor do I wish for any post that would take me away from Herstmonceux. May that, if it be God's will, be my home for life! . . . As Archdeacon, I think I may perhaps be of a little use in our part of the Diocese, especially in furthering the Bishop's plans for the improvement of education."[43] Maria Hare wrote, "It is an appointment that suits him well, as it will not take him away from Herstmonceux, and will yet give him an interest and influence over his brother clergy, that will benefit both him and them."[44]

The other archdeaconry in the Diocese of Chichester also fell vacant in 1840, but Bishop Otter died before he could fill it. His death was a great loss to his diocese. Otter's successor, Bishop Shuttleworth, chose Henry Edward Manning (1808–92), Rector of Graffham and Lavington, as Archdeacon of Chichester. Hare and Manning had already become friends, though some of their views were very dissimilar. When Manning announced his appointment as Hare's "yoke-fellow," Hare expressed his delight: "God be praised! I know of no event that could have given me so much joy as . . . that I might have you for my colleague."[45] Manning's appointment was in fact largely due to the influence of Hare and the Dean of Chichester, for the new bishop had been suspicious of Manning's orthodoxy. Hare told Manning that "it has been better ordained, that you should be appointed by the present Bishop, as he may be more willing to cooperate with you than if he had found you already installed. I hail it with delight and thankfulness, that he should have so overcome the prejudice he entertained against your opinions. It is a token that we may look for a continuance of God's blessing on the Diocese. . . . Meanwhile we will fight out our speculative differences at intervals by way of refreshment whether in penfights or tongue-fights."[46]

The "penfights" and "tongue-fights" were frequent, for though Manning became a regular guest at Herstmonceux and an intimate of the Hares, he and Julius were seldom in agreement doctrinally. Yet both men took delight in rehearsing their differences. For Hare this was an exercise in the toleration and comprehensiveness which he believed should characterize a National Church. He thought that differences should be made known and then accepted.

But Manning sought always to rationalize them away, for he could not really agree with Hare's ideas about tolerating differences. For Manning there could be only one acceptable truth: "I am too much of a Platonist to hold truth moderately. I should as soon think of holding the multiplication table in moderation."[47]

When Manning began to turn all argument in their letters to personalities, and attributed Hare's unwillingness to agree to some defect in his character, their cordial relations were strained. Hare wrote:

> In style I like plain words, and strong ones, if they are not exaggerated. . . . Of course I do not pretend to be free from prejudices; but I know of no one who is so anxious to pick out and hold by that which is good, not in one party, but in all, & to reject that which is erroneous & mischievous, not in one party, but in all, who is less anxious to uphold what is wrong in those with whom on the main I agree, or to do justice to that which is right in those with whom on the main I differ. It is irksome to talk about oneself; but if every objective discussion is to take a personal turn, I must do so once for all; & if my remonstrance be unavailing, my objective discussions must cease; and I must give over our writing about anything except our immediate official business.[48]

But this was quite an exceptional rift in their relationship, equalled only when Hare criticized J.H. Newman, and when Manning pressed upon Hare his ideas of how an Archdeacon should dress. On the latter occasion Hare expressed himself firmly, but gently:

> My rule will be to deviate as little as possible from the dress of the rest of the clergy. I will not be a party to introducing any distinction which has become at all obsolete; but where a practice has been universal down to this time I will not be the first to innovate. . . .
>
> Thus in these matters we shall not exactly coincide. This will not interfere in our concurrence in higher things, w[hi]ch I trust will be nearly complete: and you know I love *unity* without *uniformity,* which is the bane of unity. . . . I belong to a generation & a university that cares less about such matters, & the habits of my life & my own feelings have strengthened my indifference.[49]

No where does Hare's Broad Churchmanship shine more outstandingly than in his close association with Manning in the decade before Manning's conversion to the Church of Rome. Happily, Hare and Manning were in agreement upon many practical issues such as the building of schools and the suppression of box pews throughout the diocese. In these matters their collaboration was highly fruitful.

A.J.C. Hare recalled that after Julius Hare's appointment as Archdeacon of Lewes, clerical visitors, business, and conversation, dominated life at Herstmonceux. The principal function of an Archdeacon was to serve as a diocesan inspector-general, policing his parishes, swearing in churchwardens, and enforcing morality, sobriety, and good behaviour upon the occasionally unwilling clergymen. The diocesan records contain instances when Hare was called upon to handle drunken, promiscuous, or incompetent priests, to settle disputes involving clerics and vestrymen, and to deal with outsiders preaching without licenses.[50]

A great deal of trouble occurred in the diocese over the ritualism of clergymen with Tractarian sentiments. In one case the popular hysteria against Puseyism drove an innocent curate from his post when some women in the congregation denounced Tractarianism in his sermons, and deserted to the Methodist chapel.[51] The Rector of Shoreham was a long-standing problem in this regard. He was apparently a close friend of Dr Pusey's and a convinced Tractarian, and his sentiments set him at odds with his parishioners. Bishop Gilbert was forced to warn him repeatedly to temper his actions with moderation.[52] But these were quite exceptional cases, and the more routine problems which Hare faced as archdeacon involved disputes over box pews, rood-screens, cases of improper burial, the recalling of non-resident incumbents, and the provision of substitutes in cases of ill health.[53] On one occasion the routine matter of giving a character reference for a former clergyman proved vexatious. Hare's letter was published, and he was sued for libel as a result. Hare proved his charges in court and was acquitted, but the disappearance of the plaintiff, who should have borne the court costs, burdened Hare with the entire fee for his defence. He was aided by many of his clergy, who undertook a special subscription on his behalf.[54]

All of these duties were performed in addition to Hare's duties as the incumbent of his own parish. Moreover, Chichester was the first diocese in which rural deaneries were revived, another product of Bishop Otter's zealous programme. This activity involved Hare in regular meetings with rural deans and chapters, and required much arduous travel about a county notorious for its bad roads, which in wet weather were often impassable. Thirlwall claimed that Hare looked ten years younger after becoming an archdeacon. But seven toil-filled years later Caroline Fox described his appearance as "nervous" and "dragged-looking."[55] In addition to his other duties, Hare delivered an annual charge to his clergy. His charges dealt with the pressing needs of the Church as well as with the current controversies, and form a valuable source for the history of the Church during a stormy decade.[56]

While his pastoral duties prompted him to pronounce upon many social questions, no topic concerned Hare more, or commanded more of his attention, than education. He collaborated with Nathaniel Woodard of Shoreham in establishing new schools, and worked actively for the National Society for Promoting the Education of the Poor in the Principles of the Established Church in efforts to provide educational facilities for all children. Hare was active in fund raising for both the National Society and the Diocesan Association's fund for school building.[57] Hare felt that education was too often undervalued or overvalued; the poor could see no value, while the rich too often esteemed it for "outward wealth, personal distinction, & aggrandizement."[58] His own years as a teacher left him with decided opinions about the methods and aims of education. The end and indeed "perhaps the primary aim of education is to associate our moral duties with our affections, to harmonize the voices of Reason and Imagination." And once harmonized, both Reason and Imagination worked "to detect and apprehend the laws by which the almighty Lawgiver upholds and rules the world He has created."[59] Hare's views on the proper curriculum recall the argument in "The Children of Light." He thought scientific education was utterly "heartless," and maintained that "philosophy is the true centre of an university education, or at least that philosophy and religion are its two foci which ought ultimately to coincide." He would also permit the study of art, which he believed to be "next to . . . religion the most important part of the history of humanity."[60]

The pressing need, Hare argued, was to extend schooling to all orders of society. By the beginning of the nineteenth century the number of schools in England was at its lowest ebb since before the Reformation. The educational deficiencies of the new town-dwellers Hare condemned as "a plague-spot in the body of our Church."[61] He felt that "one of the first duties of the state [is] to provide means for the education of all those classes of its members that have no means of providing educations for themselves." Hare was not disturbed in this case by the spectre of state intervention, for he recognized that the size of the problem called for the capital resources and coercive powers of the government to help provide a solution. He also saw additional leverage for the established Church in state regulation of education; by this means some of the Dissenters might be reclaimed from "their blind, self-willed schism into a loving communion with the Church."[62] Voluntary efforts were still needed, and these would be religious efforts, for it was the Church's role to "purify" education and instil in everyone a love of knowledge for its own sake. Here was the great appeal of the Woodard schools, a voluntary effort to provide the middle classes with suitable education. This group had no need to study foreign languages, ancient or modern, but would, Hare urged, profitably pursue the study of the English language, English literature, English history, English laws, and the English constitution. As a result of this study, "They are to be bred up and trained to be good Englishmen, intelligent, loyal, patriotic members of the English Church."[63]

Hare felt there was a danger that if the state and its established Church did not provide for the children of all classes, other forces would. The Church's former neglect had driven many into religious Dissent, if not outright infidelity. To force children to work for wages, thus denying them education, was "moral and spiritual infanticide . . . one of the terrible sins of our age, which seems to be spreading throughout Europe, but in which England takes the shameful lead."[64] Only compulsory education could save children from "the cupidity of our manufacturers." To Hare it was clear that

> the need is so enormous and urgent, our exertions ought to be proportionate: nor is there any time for delay: every day thousands, and tens of thousands of children are left wallowing in all

manner of corruption, who might, with God's help, be reclaimed, if our manufacturing districts were supplied with an adequate number of efficient schools and teachers. . . . the necessity is vast: the misery is incalculable, and if it be not counteracted, will last forever: thousands of souls are perishing in the places from which England derives her wealth; and unless something be done to preserve them, they will perish utterly.[65]

This national crisis had manifold significance for Hare, who argued that "power and knowledge gravitate to Christian nations as a partial consequence of the knowledge of Christian truth." It was necessary to compete with the Dissenters, and to woo the people back into a semblance of religious unity. In addition to schools, therefore, Hare called for inland missions to the lower classes, which would serve as tools in the rebuilding of a National Church.[66]

As regards the education to be provided for girls, Hare was much less specific. They would, of course, be taught to read and write, the better to fulfil their Christian duties. The factory girls needed saving as much as their brothers. But Hare would have prescribed for all girls a domestic curriculum suitable to their station in life. His view of marriage reflected this: "The union between the husband and the wife should be like that between the brain and the heart."[67] Hare often exhibited the naïve, idealized view of womankind characteristic of his class. He appears to have held a low estimate of women's capabilities with his frequent references to "female reading." That Hare's views of women were so conventional is perhaps only surprising when one recalls that his mother was an accomplished blue-stocking, fluent in French, German, Italian, Latin, and Greek.

The educational deficiencies of the nation were only part of a larger national crisis involving the Church. Among both clergy and laity there was a fear of "the Church in danger," and this, like education, claimed a large share of Hare's attention. As Hare saw the problem it included both the struggle of the Church with its enemies for survival and the inadequacy of facilities for worship as well as education. Hare believed that the weakness of its enemies and not its own strength accounted for the Church's survival in the past, and he urged massive voluntary action to correct its woeful deficiencies.[68] But the Church's struggle brought in its train a more loathsome evil, as its partisans took up sides and committed ecclesiolatry. Hare could only lament that "religion, which ought to be the great bond of peace and unity, both between man and man, and nation and nation, is in these days, by a strange and monstrous perversion, become the main seat and focus of war, even among our own Church,—so that, while men are combining and cooperating zealously for every imaginable worldly object, the moment a religious work is taken in hand, it becomes a signal for all manner of jealousies and suspicions, if not for discord and contention."[69]

It was their disgust with factiousness within the Church which gave the Broad Churchmen their abhorrence of party. At the very time that the Tractarian Movement was forming at Oxford, Hare, also agitated by the government's dissolution of several Irish bishoprics, wrote that "it is an evil case to be born at a time when the shadow of coming events almost forces one to join a party. For what party can one join? When . . . there is so much of absurdity, & so little of charity."[70] The following year, 1834, Thirlwall was forced to leave Cambridge by the wrath of Christopher Wordsworth, Master of Trinity, in response to a pair of pamphlets in which Thirlwall urged the removal of compulsory chapel and religious tests.[71] Hare vented his anger in a letter to Whewell: "Surely this is a most outrageous step. The high church party seems all gone stark-mad, and to have been all seized with a fanatical desire of martyrdom at all costs and risks. Else I should be utterly unable to comprehend how the Master could be guilty of such a piece of insolence and folly."[72] Six years later the Church's polarization into factions had increased, and Hare wrote:

> It is very sad to see how the Church is divided by parties, and how, hardly anybody can see any good except in those who belong to his own party. For my part I love all good and pious men, from Pusey to . . . Manning. . . .
> The opinions that reach me . . . furnish sad evidence of the same narrow party-spirit. We in England read, not to learn, but to find confirmation of the opinions we already entertain, and like no voice so well as our echo, no picture as well as a looking-glass. That all our numberless insulated societies, though they have been the instruments of much good during the lethargy and torpor of the Church, are still attended with much mischief; and that, if the Church were full of organic life and energy, they would be superceded by much better institutions, I am convinced.[73]

As Archdeacon of Lewes, Hare took a lead in directing clergy and laity in the large task of making good the Church's deficiencies. The population of the Chichester diocese had increased eighty per cent between 1801 and 1831. In the towns, the centres of greatest growth, church facilities could not cope with numbers. In Lewes, population 9,227, the established Church provided only 732 free sittings, all others being rented pews. The bulk of the urban population, if it sought any religious services, had to do so in the chapels of the Dissenters or the Roman Catholics. Hare was active in church building and restoration throughout the diocese, and Herstmonceux church was a model of what a concerned rector and congregation could achieve. Maria Hare donated the profits of Augustus' posthumously published sermons to build a school and restore the church at Herstmonceux.[74]

As Archdeacon, Hare suggested that greater seating capacity could be achieved by building galleries, as he had done at Herstmonceux, or—even better still—by abolishing the box pews which all but drove the poor out of Church. This was a practical reform that could also help restore some unity to the congregation, and rid the churches of their ugly "pens and styes," which Hare compared to the cattle market at Smithfield. Allied with Henry Manning, Hare waged war against box pews all over the Diocese of Chichester. Both men had good reason to oppose them, not least because over half the church disputes requiring archidiaconal settlement involved pews and their owners.[75] A.J.C. Hare recalled that "Uncle Julius, as soon as he became Archdeacon, used to preach a perfect crusade against pews, and often went, saw and hammer in hand, to begin the work in the village churches with his own hands."[76] Hare was also opposed to rood-screens and altar rails. The former created a division between priest and worshippers, while the latter were no better than "semi-Romish fences."[77] In less urgent tones Hare also inveighed against the ugly iron stoves that had become prominent features in most churches. He saw the stoves to be an admission of spiritual as well as physical laxness, as if the word of God were not sufficient to warm the hearer.[78]

Hare's efforts to eliminate the impure and anti-spiritual accretions in modern Church life also extended to the liturgy. He sought to restore the baptismal ceremony to its rightful place in the middle of the service. He also urged more frequent communion services, the abolition of baptismal fees, and an end to the distinction between fee payers and non-payers at burial services. In these matters Hare was an active reformer, but he stopped short of anything that could suggest Puseyite or Tractarian sentiments.[79] In addition Hare pressed for administrative changes in the Church at all levels. He was actively involved in the restoration of Convocation, and some years earlier had rejoiced to secure restoration of rural deaneries in the Diocese of Chichester. Moreover, Hare sought to establish small circulating libraries within each deanery, to facilitate continuing education among clergymen.[80]

Such reforms in the Church, both proposed and achieved, were desirable in themselves. But Hare saw greater issues at stake. Throughout his work and writings runs a strong vein of nationalism.[81] Successful reform was necessary for England's preservation. Writing to a friend in 1848, Hare argued that "we must fight the battle of truth & order ag[ain]st falsehood & lawlessness, so as to win mens minds for the truth; or the glory of England will pass away."[82] Hare believed that saving the masses from sin, ignorance, falsehood, strife, and idolatry was not merely a good work, but a necessity to prevent God from withdrawing favour from England, "whom He has chosen above all other countries, to manifest His truth in her.[83]

To the duty of supporting domestic or inland missions, Hare added that of supporting foreign missions, and lamented "that eighteen hundred years have passed away, and yet so little progress has been made towards the bringing of the nations into the Kingdom of Christ."[84] The empire and wealth vouchsafed England were not for the service of Mammon, but for "casting across the wide world a highway for our God."[85] Hare believed that England had a special role to play because "we in England are especially called. For to us, in a temporal sense, may it be said, to us, above all other nations, has God given the heathen to us for an inheritance and the uttermost parts of the earth for our possession."[86] In contemplating England's national glory and world leadership Hare slipped unwittingly into the same authoritarian righteousness that he condemned in "The Children of Light," and became an exponent of the White Man's Burden. Near the end of his life, in a sanguinary sermon on war, this spirit of righteousness enabled him to justify the Crimean War. Maurice later claimed that Hare shared the general enthusiasm and hope that the war would mean the end of Mammon-worship and of Church parties.[87] Hare's conception of the English nation and National Church stopped short of the Coleridgean system. In his writings Hare also drew back from the exalted status granted to educators and transmitters of culture, the "clerisy" in Coleridge's model. Nonetheless, Hare shared Coleridge's notion of a National Church and universal education binding all classes to the state through dutiful citizenship.[88]

If Julius Hare was clumsy in performing some of his less-cherished duties in the cure of souls, he was far more adept and happily employed in his administrative role as an archdeacon. But his life and attentions did not remain parochial. His central position amid a friendly circle of liberal or Broad Churchmen meant that he was called upon not only for advice, counsel, and the loan of German books, but also to defend his friends when they came under attack. Hare came to fill this role with such regularity and fidelity that he is chiefly remembered as a liberal polemicist. In this capacity he became the most articulate spokesman of his generation for the ideals of the Broad Church.

Chapter 12

Friend and Partisan

Julius Hare's heavy archidiaconal duties left him with little time for literary pursuits. The increasing division of the Church into antagonistic parties, and the hostility with which those parties treated each other, prompted Hare to write a series of polemics. He wrote vindications of people and positions which he believed had been unjustly attacked, but he did not write to promote those people or positions. Hare had a reactive intellect, content to translate books that inspired him, rather than to create new ones. Only a man with this temperament could have endured the job of playing midwife to Landor's *Imaginary Conversations*.

Hare's reactive nature and lack of ambition were reflected in his disorganized work habits. Ever prone to the distractions provided by other people—family members, friends, parishioners, and fellow clergymen—he had difficulty organizing and controlling his day. Thus while he managed to write pamphlets with some facility, he produced few more substantial works in his later life. Some minor literary productions did flow from his pen, for example a new translation of the Psalms, designed for singing by congregations, and an edition of his late brother Augustus' sermons.[1] Hare also produced the revised editions of the *Guesses at Truth* that appeared in the 1830s and 1840s. But he believed that his discipline had weakened. As he confessed in a letter to his brother Marcus: "Though I once had the faculty of getting through some work, that was in olden times and seems entirely to have passed away. At present were I set . . . to piece-work, and paid only according to what I did, I am afraid, when Saturday night came, my week's wages would stand only just above Zero. Nor can I plead guilty to the charge of being the 'laziest,' unless a horse in a mill, because he does not get on, is lazier than a horse in the stable or field. For, though I do nothing, I am mostly trying to do something from nine in the morning till two the next morning."[2] Hare's sermons and charges took a long time to appear partly because of the lengthy notes which he appended to them, and because he felt "that no author is justified in saying that which he has not taken such means as lie within his power of ascertaining to be true. I extend this even to little things; & this is one of the reasons why my books linger so long in the press."[3] There is, of course, a note of self-congratulation in this comment, but there is no denying that integrity and commitment to the truth, as he saw it, were among the qualities that made Hare attractive to his friends and helped to keep him close to the centre of the growing Broad Church network.

In addition to his other tasks Hare was a member of the Sussex Archaeological Society, and served a term as a Vice-President.[4] He also made himself available to the many people who sought his advice and counsel, whether they were old friends or total strangers. The young oriental scholar, Friedrich Max Müller (1823–1900), who came to England in 1846 and became the protégé of Baron Bunsen, recorded the kindness which Hare showed him on numerous occasions, including receiving him as a guest at Herstmonceux, and helping him find a teaching position.[5] Susanna Winkworth (1820–84), a Germanist who had served as Bunsen's personal secretary, also met Hare through Bunsen. Just weeks before Hare's death she sought his advice regarding her edition of *Tauler's Life and Sermons* (1857). He gave her the support and encouragement that she needed. In his last illness Hare wrote to Longman, the publisher, for whom he had undertaken to write captions for a series of illustrations of Luther's life, and recommended that, inasmuch as he was unable to complete the task, Miss Winkworth be commissioned to finish it. She accepted the commission and the work appeared that same year as *The Life of Luther in 48 Historical Engravings by Gustav König*, With Explanations by Archdeacon Hare, Continued by S. Winkworth (1855).[6]

One old friend who sought Hare's advice was William Whewell, who wrote in 1840 that his scholarly labours were completed, and that he feared to grow old in the solitude of his college rooms. He was therefore considering whether to accept a college living and become a country parson. But he feared he could not sympathize with the common people. Torn between a desire for change and a real reluctance to leave the University, Whewell turned to Hare for advice.[7] Hare replied in a very long and self-revealing letter:

> Most fully do I agree with you that college rooms are not a home for ones later years. . . . And yet I have never been able to think with satisfaction of your taking a parochial cure. I can neither fancy that you would suit it, nor that it would suit you. . . . not merely in your regular Sunday ministrations, but in the schools, in visiting the sick, in talking to the poor about the petty concerns of their daily life, your life w[oul]d be a very unsatisfactory one. Many blessings attend on these labours, when one does take a hearty interest in them: but when one does not, they become an intolerable weariness, until by degrees one grows to neglect them. . . . All are not meant to be *pastors:* some are to be apostles, some *doctors.* . . . Your ministry in this world seems to me to be that of a doctor, rather than a pastor. . . . I would have you pursue your work in moral philosophy . . . it would be an evil thing for England that you should abandon it.[8]

Hare perceived correctly that Whewell was merely suffering a momentary dissatisfaction with his life at Cambridge, and that his was not a personality to fit into a pastoral mould.

Whewell had expressed reluctance to give up all his literary and scholarly work, and Hare raised this issue with reference to his own experience:

> True, you would not have to give up literature & philosophy as I have done. . . . I believe there is a narrowness in me that disqualifies me from taking a deep interest in more than one thing at once. Besides, as you know from my etymological vagaries, I can never rest satisfied until a thing is done as thoroughly as my faculties & means will enable me. This is almost a disease; and hence I have been forced to leave so many things incomplete. But you are not so hyperscrupulous about petty details, nor do you allow yourself so easily to be monopolized. Therefore I doubt

not that you might be able to pursue your speculative studies amid the cares of your parish. . . . I doubt not you would find time. But I do doubt whether you could ever refashion your mind according to your new calling, whether you could unravel the whole network of your thoughts, to weave them anew, whether you could descend like Apollo, to become a shepherd.

I am the more urgent upon this point, because I myself felt the misery of the distractions occasioned by an uncongenial calling during the two years I was in the Temple. And many a hard struggle have I had, many a long fit of despondency, since I came to Herstmonceux, from the reluctance to forsake my old pursuits, from the difficulty of adapting myself to my new ones, and from the impossibility of reconciling the two. From my misery in the Temple you rescued me, and so were one of the greatest benefactors of my life. Out of my struggles here I have gradually been freed, by God's grace, and by the infinite blessing he has given me in my sister-in-law. . . . And now, in my new office, I find myself again engaged in work for which it seems to me that the habits & frame of my mind qualify me better than for pastoral ministrations. Hence my happiness in these last years has greatly increast.[9]

Hare's advice was well taken by Whewell, who announced two months later that he was giving up the idea of a parish, for he had decided that he still had much to do in the University. Indeed, he did, for at the end of 1841 Christopher Wordsworth resigned the mastership of Trinity College, and Whewell was chosen by Sir Robert Peel's government to succeed him. In a long letter Hare poured out his supreme joy at seeing Whewell's talents at last so well utilized.[10]

Another one of the people who sought Hare's help and advice was a stranger, but his overtures led to an important and long-term relationship. Daniel Macmillan (1813–57), a young Scot who worked as a bookseller's assistant in London, happened to read the Hares' *Guesses at Truth* in 1840, and was spell-bound by it. He sent an admiring letter to Hare, and urged him to write a book for the guidance of young "commerical men who have a taste for reading without anything like extensive culture."[11] Macmillan soon read Hare's other works, including *The Victory of Faith,* which prompted him to write again. In successive letters Macmillan reiterated his concern for the lack of spiritual guidance which young men of his own class faced. Hare was impressed by Macmillan's plea but feared that he himself could do little to help. He suggested that Macmillan contact F.D. Maurice. Macmillan soon fell under Maurice's spell, and was as moved by reading Maurice's *Kingdom of Christ* as he had been by the *Guesses at Truth*. Under the combined influence of Hare and Maurice, Macmillan withdrew from the Dissenting chapel which he had attended in London, and became a member of the established Church.[12]

In 1843 Daniel Macmillan and his younger brother Alexander opened their own bookshop in London, and Hare was soon giving them all of his not inconsiderable custom. Macmillan explored the possibility of establishing his business in Cambridge, but he concluded that he could not afford to buy an established business which was for sale, Mr Newby's at 17 Trinity Street. Hare expressed an interest in the venture, and came to Macmillan's aid with a loan of £500 at four per cent interest. Hare also promised to provide Macmillan with the patronage of his Cambridge friends. The business prospered in Cambridge until its move back to London in the 1860s.[13]

Macmillan lamented that Hare had allowed the *Guesses at Truth* and *The Victory of Faith* to go out of print; he had sold his own copies to a friend emigrating to New Zealand. When a new printing of the *Guesses at Truth* was undertaken in 1844, Macmillan asked to have his name appear on the title-page. By 1847 Macmillan alone had sold one hundred copies of the new printing, and begged Hare to keep the book in print. After Hare's death in 1855 the Macmillans purchased the rights to all of his theological books from John William Parker (1792–1870), Hare's theological publisher of many years. The *Guesses at Truth* had a special significance for the Macmillans, and they kept the book in print into the twentieth century. In 1867 Alexander wrote, "It is a pet book of mine, and I owe both to it and to its chief author, Julius Hare, more than I can tell. Five and twenty years ago it was the book my brother and myself were reading together most constantly, and was the fruitful source of much profitable and pleasant discussion to us."[14]

Once the Macmillans had moved in earnest into publishing as well as bookselling, the connections which Hare provided them proved extremely beneficial. Hare's friendship with a young man who came to him seeking help for others led to the founding of a business which grew into a publishing empire. Daniel acknowledged this valuable assistance in a letter written less than two years before Hare's death: "I have seldom ventured, when writing or speaking to you, to do more than allude to how much I feel that I owe to your great kindness. . . . If it had not been for your kindness & encouragement & friendly recommendations I sh[oul]d not have been here—I sh[oul]d never have been in a position to marry, nor w[oul]d my brother. When I see so many blessings showered down on my brother & myself & more who are dearest to us[,] I cannot but feel God has sent them to us in a great measure through you."[15]

In addition to making and helping new friends, Hare was called upon to render service to old ones. In Coleridge's case, the service rendered was posthumous. In July 1834 Coleridge died. Sterling proposed that a Coleridge Memorial Prize be established at Cambridge, to be awarded annually for "an English essay on some question, speculative or historical, of metaphysical philosophy, more especially on such as bear on . . . religion, as set forth in the Canonical Scriptures, and in the articles of our National Church."[16] The prize competition was to be open to all graduates within seven years post-baccalaureate, and £300 would be sought to endow the prize. Hare forwarded a prospectus to Whewell at Cambridge, and urged that such a memorial prize would associate Coleridge's name with Christian philosophy, and would make "it openly recognized that philosophy might do much toward an emancipation of our theology. Besides it would be a good thing to do anything to encourage the trad[ition] of thinking divines."[17]

Whewell replied pessimistically to the plan, for he felt that "philosophy of Christianity" was a subject beyond the ken of those unfamiliar with modern German theology, and—worse—likely to frighten Cambridge dignitaries, who might "see it nothing but a trumpet call to heresy and extravagance."[18] Hare and Sterling revised their prospectus and urged that it would be a more fitting memorial than a monument in Westminster Abbey. Whewell was swayed by this, and said he hoped it would answer to call attention to Coleridge as a Christian philosopher. But the matter died the following February, when the heads of houses at Cambridge met and quashed the proposal. According to Christopher Wordsworth's report to Whewell, the heads remembered Coleridge not as a religious philosopher, but only for "the vagaries of his earlier times."[19]

Coleridge's literary executor, Dr Joseph Henry Green (1791–1863) placed all of Coleridge's unpublished theological manuscripts in Hare's hands in the summer of 1834, with directions that Hare and Sterling begin editing them for publication.[20] Hare began by transcribing a number of Coleridge's letters on inspiration, and submitting them to Thomas Arnold for his opinion. Arnold replied eagerly: "My Opinion is decidedly in Favour of their Publication; they seem to me to be a very mild Dose of what must and will come ere long in a more violent Form, if the Gentle Alternative be not timely administered. . . . I think they want an Editor, and, if you will pardon the Heresy, an Interpreter in sundry Passages. . . . I talked with Wordsworth about the Subject, and we both agreed in wishing *you* to be Coleridge's *Biographer*."[21] As it turned out, Hare, so far from writing Coleridge's biography, was allowed to edit none of the theological works. Sara Coleridge, the poet's daughter, decided to withhold the theological works from publication until she could widen the audience for Coleridge's works by first publishing things likely to be less controversial.[22]

In September 1834, before Coleridge had been dead two months, a scurrilous article appeared in *Tait's Edinburgh Magazine* by Hare's old adversary, Thomas De Quincey. This was the first of a series of four articles by De Quincey that contained recollections of Coleridge, which he wrote ostensibly as a friend and admirer of the late poet. In these articles, however, De Quincey castigated Coleridge on many points, including procrastination, opium addiction, being unhappily married, being unable to earn a living, being ungrateful for De Quincey's financial benefactions, and alleged plagiarism from the work of the German philosopher Schelling (1775–1854).[23] After the first three of De Quincey's articles had appeared in September, October, and November 1834, Hare wrote and published a counter-attack entitled "Samuel Taylor Coleridge and the English Opium-Eater." Hare rebuked De Quincey for his bad taste and bad faith in embarrassing Coleridge's family by publicly revealing things which had been learned in the confidence of friendship. He made no attempt to discuss or excuse Coleridge's addiction, procrastination, or marital failures, but turned instead to De Quincey's charges of plagiarism. Hare reviewed Coleridge's *Biographia Literaria* (1817), and turned up a number of examples of borrowings from Schelling, including several which De Quincey had missed. He then argued convincingly that Schelling had been acknowledged—elsewhere in the book—and that Coleridge had merely been a careless note taker, not a plagiarist with malicious intent. Hare denied, furthermore, that Coleridge's powers had declined in his later years, for he still wrote verse, and had turned his attention to "forwarding the great atonement of philosophy and religion."[24]

Sara Coleridge showed her gratitude to Hare by profuse thanks in the correspondence which she later maintained with him, by dedicating her edition of *Essays of His Own Times* (1850) to him, and by incorporating many of Hare's arguments in her own editions of the *Table-Talk* (1835) and the *Biographia Literaria* (1847). For many years Hare supplied Sara Coleridge with advice and the loan of German books. She later wrote to Hare of his tendency to take up pen in the defence of others: "You have had the satisfaction in your literary life on so many occasions of especially serving individuals while you were doing service to the public by throwing light on truth in which private character was concerned, that you must feel, I think, as if to act the part of the champion was a part of your vocation; it is one which is by no means out of harmony with 'theological studies' & pastoral cares."[25]

In defending Coleridge against De Quincey's calumnies, Hare was behaving completely in character. He was always careful to qualify his acceptance of Coleridge's ideas, though he expressed his admiration for the man in what sounded like exaggerated terms. He was aware of Coleridge's personal shortcomings, and keenly aware of the German sources of much of Coleridge's thought.[26] Yet he could not allow De Quincey to traduce the memory of one unable to defend himself. Moreover, in this particular "vindication" Hare expressed his sense of personal obligation to Coleridge, and also discharged any lingering animosity which he may have felt from De Quincey's attack upon Goethe several years earlier.[27] Hare's mood at the time of Coleridge's death predisposed him to respond vigourously to De Quincey's assault. In the course of only a few years Hare had seen the death of nearly all of the great men whom he admired—Niebuhr, Goethe, Schleiermacher, and then

Coleridge. Only Wordsworth remained. With misgivings Hare contemplated the world with "one more great man gone: soon there will be nothing but little ones left."[28]

Hare's defence of Coleridge was not a vindication of his religious principles or orthodoxy, which were among the few things De Quincey did not impugn. However, Hare's vindications of other people were defences of their religious orthodoxy, and they give the impression of Hare as a partisan, a polemicist writing to defend members of his own religious faction. That faction has popularly been known as the "Broad Church," a phrase that has often been used vaguely and indiscriminately. In this work it denotes a group of colleagues and friends with whom Julius Hare shared a liberal theological and ecclesiastical perspective. Before proceeding to an examination of Hare's later vindications, the phrase "Broad Church" warrants closer scrutiny, for it denotes a position that is difficult to define.

According to the *Oxford English Dictionary* "Broad Church" was "a designation popularly applied to members of the Church of England who take its formularies and doctrines in a broad or liberal sense, and hold that the Church should be comprehensive and tolerant so as to admit of more or less variety of opinion in matters of dogma and ritual." As a general definition of position this admirably fits Hare, Thomas Arnold, A.P. Stanley, and others, and describes the comprehension which they sought in a National Church, the "unity without uniformity" of which Hare so often spoke. The *OED* continues by tracing the etymology of "Broad Church." Benjamin Jowett (1817–93) first heard the expression used at Oxford in the years just preceding 1850. The first appearance of the phrase in print was in that same year in an article by A.P. Stanley in which he remarked that in view of its history of comprehension "the Church . . . is, by the very condition of its being, not High or Low, but Broad."[29] Three years later, in an article on Church parties, William John Conybeare (1815–57) used the expression "Broad Church Party" as if it were accepted usage. His own sympathies were enthusiastically Broad Church: "Side by side with . . . High and Low Church, another party of a different character . . . is called by different names; Moderate, Catholic or Broad by its friends; Latitudinarian or Indifferent by its enemies. Its distinctive character is the desire of comprehension. Its watchwords are Charity and Toleration. . . . the Broad Church are . . . the originators of ecclesiastical reform, and the pioneers of moral progress." Conybeare's too-simple description of the divisions of the Church created a new semantic category which has ever after persisted. In its partisan sense the phrase "Broad Church" came into wide use only at the time of the controversy over *Essays and Reviews* (1860), after Hare's death. Indeed, Conybeare had been forced to admit that while he numbered many of the most eminent Churchmen of his day as members of the Broad Church, they "have so little organisation or mutual concert of any kind, that they can scarcely be called a party at all. They are even destitute of that instrument, which every fractional subdivision of the smallest sects possesses, an organ in the periodical press."[30]

Julius Hare may have been acquainted with the phrase "Broad Church," but he does not appear to have expressed an opinion about it. However, Thirlwall and Maurice did give their opinions, and included Hare in their remarks. Thirlwall, writing in 1874, the year before his death, denied that he was a Broad Churchman, though he said he considered it to be no term of reproach. But he did not feel that it described any existing "school" or "party" within the Church:

> I understand it as signifying a certain stamp of individual character, which I would describe as a disposition to recognize and appreciate that which is true and good under all varieties of forms, and in persons separated from one another by the most conflicting opinions. . . . He has no quarrel with High Church or Low Church, though he could not consent to attach himself to either. He claims the right of taking up a position of his own, which he may be prepared to maintain without disturbing the convictions of others. . . .
>
> No doubt it also implies an intellectual peculiarity, which parts it alike from the High and Low school. What this is I would rather illustrate by example than attempt exactly to define. I would name among those of . . . my own generation, Archdeacon Hare, as furnishing a sufficient illustration of my meaning. . . . To hold a prominent place in such a brotherhood as answers to my conception of the Broad Church would to me appear a most enviable distinction. I can only lament that I can lay no claim whatever to such an honour.[31]

Here Thirlwall was entirely too modest, for in 1834 he had been at the very centre of the first great controversy involving Broad Church principles, namely the admission of Dissenters to the universities by the removal of religious tests and compulsory chapel. Thirlwall's "martyrdom" in this cause served to define for that period the limits to heterodox opinion and its free expression within the universities. It also demonstrated the way in which religious partisanship was becoming tripartite, dividing among groups of High Churchman, Low Churchmen, and those who were later called "Broad" Churchmen. For F.D. Maurice, who is popularly thought to have been the leader of the Broad Church, the very idea of belonging to any party or faction was anathema. Maurice grew up in a home bitterly divided by religious differences, and accomplished a painful transition from Unitarianism to Anglicanism.[32] This experience left him with a craving for religious unity which bordered on an obsession. Hare often spoke and preached of the need for unity; for Maurice it was the object of his religious strivings, and he admitted that "the desire for Unity and the search after Unity both in the nation and the Church has haunted me all my days."[33] Maurice would countenance no partisan activity, and went to great lengths to dissociate himself from what came to be known popularly as the Broad Church. He had a low opinion of those who professed a Broad Church affiliation, and on one occasion in 1860 he wrote: "I do not know what the Broad Church is. I always took it to be a fiction of Conybeare's." Maurice perceived the paradox of joining a party in order to accomplish the abolition of parties; he said he would not fall into the snare of faction even if a group inscribed "No Party" on its flag.[34]

Some allowance must be made for Maurice's strong prejudice in considering his statements regarding Hare's abhorrence of party:

> To be an aider and abettor in setting up a new party in the land, with whatever specious name it might be adorned, whatever pretensions of largeness and liberality it might put on, he would have regarded as an act of treason against the sovereign of England, and against the King of kings. To aid and abet, even within the narrowest sphere, in making England a united country under its Queen, in making the Church feel its own union in Christ, he regarded as the highest honour which could be bestowed upon a clergyman, as the highest duty which he could

fulfil. All the polemics he engaged in had reference to this end.
... he felt himself called to bear a continual witness against those who confound the crushing of opponents with the assertion of principles; he believed that every party triumph is an injury to the whole Church, and an especial injury to the party which wins the triumph.[35]

Crabb Robinson had written of Hare, "It is his misfortune to satisfy no party."[36] In addition to sharing views on the perniciousness of Church parties, Hare and Maurice shared a personal sympathy and understanding which marked their friendship from its beginnings. Yet, as if to emphasize the non-partisan nature of the Broad Church, it is noteworthy that these two men, whom virtually all critics of the Broad Church were unanimous in branding as its ringleaders, stood apart upon most issues of Church doctrines and institutions. In Church politics Hare was a liberal and reformer, who supported the revival of Convocation and the inclusion within it of laymen. On matters of Church order and institutions Maurice was very conservative, and not at all sanguine about the benefits of a revived Convocation. Maurice's basic conservatism is something which his reputation as a theological rebel and his association with Christian Socialism have done much to obscure.[37]

In a letter to his future wife, Georgiana Hare, Maurice attempted to account for his differences with her half-brother: "I have always felt the differences you speak of between my views of the position of the English Church, and Julius's. . . . I am content to be strictly national, and so make the best of our national treasures; he has been nourished on German food. . . . I often feel bitterly the want of his gifts, but I believe there are some to whom I could not speak as well if I had them, or at all events if my mind were not cast in a more English mould."[38] A.R. Vidler thinks that the explanation of their differences on Church organization might be more simply explained by the fact that Maurice, unlike Hare, did not have any direct responsibility for administering the Church establishment, and therefore did not experience at first-hand the need for administrative reforms.[39]

In their theology Hare and Maurice were frequently divided in opinion. Maurice himself testified, "My theological convictions had already been formed by a discipline very different, I should imagine, from any to which he was subjected; they were not altered in substance, nor, so far as I know, even in colour, by any intercourse I had with him. But to his lectures on Sophocles and Plato, I can trace the most permanent effect upon my character, and on all my modes of contemplating subjects, natural, human, and divine."[40] To the extent then that Hare opened Maurice's mind to Plato, and that Hare shared with Maurice a respect for Coleridge's thought, Hare can be said to have influenced Maurice theologically. In a letter written in 1849 Maurice summed up his fundamental difference from Hare who "wishes to make everyone comfortable [while] I want no one to be comfortable in it, so cross grained am I. Yet I seek for unity in my own wild way."[41]

That two men so different in many respects as Hare and Maurice could have been accused of being the chieftains of a Church party reflects the nature of the Broad Church bond. It was a shared point of view on the National Church and the status of the Bible, not a rigid commitment to specific articles of belief. The accusation against Hare and Maurice also reflects the strength of the tendency toward factionalism in the mid-century Church. The convictions of High and Low Church factions that the Broad Church constituted a formal party, set out to oppose them, was unfortunately reinforced by Hare's efforts as a polemicist. Hare became, against his inclinations and in spite of his frequent protestations of impartiality, a party man.

Chapter 13

The Broad Church Vindicator

In 1841 the prime subject of religious controversy was the creation of a Protestant Bishop of Jerusalem. When Baron Bunsen paid Hare a brief visit in August of the previous year, he revealed that his royal master, Friedrich Wilhelm IV of Prussia, had sent him to England with the plan to promote the creation of a joint Anglo-Prussian Bishopric of Jerusalem, with the authority to protect Protestants in the Turkish Empire, and to direct missionary efforts, principally among the Jews, in the Levant. Hare was at once enthusiastic, for he was naïvely unaware of the diplomatic pragmatism behind the plan, as the governments of Britain and Prussia sought to gain leverage in Turkey by a religious subterfuge. France and Russia had obtained recognition from the Porte for their claims to act as protectors of Catholic and Orthodox Christians, so Britain and Prussia sought the same recognition of Protestantism, even though the number of Protestants in the Turkish Empire was negligible. The English Bishops were to consecrate the Bishop of Jerusalem, who would alternately be nominated by the British and Prussian Crowns. The British government accepted the plan in July 1841, and the following month produced legislation to empower the Archbishops to consecrate for foreign countries Bishops with jurisdiction over Anglicans as well as other willing Protestants.[1]

Clerical opinion in England divided along predictable lines. Maurice joined Hare and Bunsen enthusiastically. Arnold saw the new bishopric as a vindication of his own writings on Church

THE BROAD CHURCH VINDICATOR 163

reform.² Lord Ashley (later seventh Earl of Shaftesbury) and the Evangelical party were delighted by this first step toward union with continental Protestants, and by the assertion of Protestantism in the east. Ashley had the honour of selecting the appointee to the new see, Michael Solomon Alexander (1799–1845), a converted Jew of Prussian birth, who was a professor of Hebrew and Arabic at King's College, London.³ The reaction of the Tractarians was mixed at first, but they soon closed ranks behind Newman's opposition. Insisting upon the importance of Apostolic succession, they could hardly condone even this small act of union with the "heretical" Protestants of the continent. Gladstone, however, proved a waverer. He cautiously watched Newman's position, offered Manning meaningless assurances, and drank the new Bishop's health with Ashley.⁴

Manning set forth his reaction in a letter to Hare: "I do not think we may lawfully consecrate a Bishop as Bishop of Jerusalem or of Palestine, or by any fiction treat as void, or under our jurisdiction sees which if they belong to any[,] certainly do not belong to us. . . . What man can foretell the strife among Christian men & Churches which one such act may bring on? We are now opening friendly relations with the Eastern Churches. . . . One act of intrusion, & they will turn their hearts from us as obstinately as they have turned them from Rome."⁵ But Hare was not persuaded. Bishop Alexander was consecrated at Lambeth Palace on 7 November 1841 in robes provided by Esther Maurice and the Churchwomen of Reading.⁶

Newman, whose days as an Anglican were numbered, reacted violently and against the better judgement of his friends. He sent a public protest to the Bishop of Oxford in which he declared that Lutheranism and Calvinism "are heresies, repugnant to scripture."⁷ This denunciation of fellow Protestants was too much for Hare, who wrote to Manning:

> I must retract what I said about Newman's being free from party-spirit. Have you heard of his sending a protest to the Archb[isho]p & the B[isho]p of Ox[ford?] This seems to me an awful act: few things have ever pained me more, or made me more indignant. Such is the hateful fruit of episcopolatry: & then the consistency & the presumption in a single individual, of no authority in the Church, to protest ag[ain]st the act of its rulers

& his audacity to call those doctrines *heretical,* which almost all the great divines of our Church have been accustomed to regard . . . among the best expositions of the truth. . . . how does he, John Newman, dare to call them *heresies?* Unless he means thoroughly to doom his adhesion to the Council of Trent.[8]

Manning made his annoyance at Hare's words known, and Hare replied, "The calmest reflection I can exercise in no way diminishes the awful sin of Newman's protest. . . . I have always considered the anathematizing spirit of Popery one of its most hateful and sinful features, so, when I see the same spirit manifesting itself . . . in a calm soberminded man, who weighs his words, and acts deliberately, I cannot regard it in any other light than as most hateful and sinful."[9] This dispute was patched over like all the others between the two archdeacons.

Newman's public protest was not the first occasion when he gave offence to Hare. At a gathering in Rome in 1833, at which Hare was present, someone questioned Niebuhr's orthodoxy, whereupon Arnold's word was invoked as evidence that Niebuhr was a true Christian. Newman interjected, "But who speaks for Dr Arnold?" Hare recalled this occasion in his correspondence with Manning, and said, "The very first thing I ever heard of him, when I was at Rome, taught me that this portion of the spirit of Anti-Christ dwelt in him; and alas! it seems to be still with him, and to have gained strength with years."[10] Nor was the protest the first occasion upon which Newman attacked Luther. In his *Lectures on Justification* (1838) Newman criticized Luther for basing all of Christianity upon the single doctrine of justification by faith, which Newman claimed lacked all precedent in the Scriptures and in the writings of the fathers.[11] In the sermons which Hare delivered at Cambridge as Select Preacher in 1839, later published as *The Victory of Faith* (1840), he expounded his views of justification by faith, linked the doctrine to Pauline teaching, and showed that contrary to Newman's claims, it was no neologism, but a venerable part of Christian doctrine.[12]

In 1846, when Hare published his second series of university sermons, *The Mission of the Comforter,* the extensive notes included a defence of Luther which ran to over two hundred pages. This is reputed to be the longest footnote ever written, and was subsequently republished as *Vindication of Luther against His Recent*

English Assailants (1855).¹³ Hare was well qualified to act as Luther's champion. His veneration for Luther, which Coleridge had reinforced, led him to collect and read nearly every book and pamphlet of Luther's.¹⁴ To Hare's contemporaries Luther represented many things. To the Tractarians he was an upstart heretic, an early neologian; To the Evangelicals he was a larger-than-life hero. Often Luther was misrepresented or misunderstood because few took the trouble to read his works. Hare was abrupt with the ignorance of Evangelical admirers of Luther who failed to consider him historically as a man of his age: "Luther, apart from the Reformation, would cease to be Luther."¹⁵ In his *Vindication of Luther* Hare tackled four critics at once, the historian Henry Hallam (1777–1859) and the Scots philosopher Sir William Hamilton (1788–1856), who criticized Luther for preaching antinomianism and immorality, and Newman and his friend William George Ward (1812–82), who criticized Luther doctrinally. Hare claimed to seek only to clear Luther's name from "unmerited stigmas," and found the best defence to be in examining and quoting from the works of Luther himself.¹⁶

Hallam's remarks against Luther were, Hare admitted, trivial, but the author's "reputation for learning, accuracy, judgement, and impartiality gave weight to his testimony." So Hare marshalled dozens of specific quotations, ransacked scores of Luther's works, and argued forcefully for many pages to refute the charge of immorality and antinomianism. The counter-attack was a success, but out of all proportion to the seriousness of the threat. In the process Hare revealed so intimate a knowledge of Luther's life and writings that one regrets that such vast erudition was never turned to writing a life of the great German reformer. Sir William Hamilton had also attacked Luther for his destructive criticism of Scripture, and so Hare was called upon to defend German *Bibelkritik*, and in the process show that Luther was not the founder of rationalist theology. Hare argued forcefully in defence of biblical criticism that "the very freedom of Biblical Criticism, that practice of trying and proving every part of the Scriptures by the severest tests, fearlessly and unshrinkingly, which the Protestant Churches have derived from the Reformation, is itself a proof of their reverence for the Bible. For we know it to be of gold, and feel assured that it will only come out the purer, thought it be tried . . . in the fire."¹⁷

Regarding the Tractarians' assaults upon Luther, Hare was bellicose:

> By our modern Romanizers the mightiest enemy of the Romish corruptions is naturally regarded with dislike, with aversion, almost with hatred. His intense love of truth revolts those who dally with truth, and play tricks with it, until they cease to discern the distinction between truth and falsehood. His straightforwardness finds no sympathy among those who walk in crooked ways. His hunger and thirst after that which is spiritual, and his comparative indifference about outward forms, are mortal offences to those with whom forms, institutions, rites, ordinances are the main thing, and almost everything. Hence the contest about Luther's character now has a peculiar interest and importance. It is a part of the great contest by which our Church is so dismally torn.[18]

After this outburst Hare set about refuting the charges of Newman and Ward with the same vigour he applied to the other "assailants." Professor W.J. Baker has called attention to Hare's commendable and scholarly willingness to give a fair hearing to Luther when others condemned him unheard. Hare stood in a liberal minority during what Baker has labelled "a Victorian Dark Age of Luther studies."[19]

Hare was always reluctant to give a clear exposition of his own views on the inspiration of Scripture. Like Thomas Arnold he believed that the orthodox view that everything in the Bible was divinely inspired was untenable, and that it was best to make this known gradually. To reject the orthodox position all at once would create a shock that might cause many to lose their faith altogether.[20] In 1849, in replying to a criticism of his reticence in speaking of inspiration, Hare said that he also had fears about the immature and imperfect nature of his own views on the subject. Hare's fears of the shocking effect of advanced views on inspiration were realized with the publication of David Friedrich Strauss' *Leben Jesu* (1835) in an English translation (1846). Strauss (1808–74) took a relentlessly historical view of the Bible, and argued that its stories were not literally true but historically functional and in the past had been useful in propagating the faith. Strauss' book was widely read in

England, and gave great offence, although his view of Scripture was not designed to attack Christian faith.[21]

Hare was bitterly opposed to Strauss' rejection of a divinely inspired Bible. As he explained in a letter to his brother Francis: "Nothing can be more fallacious than his fundamental principle, that everything must be progressive. In whatever is at all akin to inspiration, it is just the contrary, as Homer, Dante, Shakespeare, Raphael, Phidias show."[22] Hare said that he could not himself accept the "popular view" that the whole of Scripture was divinely inspired. Although he was evasive about his own view, he obviously stood between Coleridge and Strauss and was most likely quite close to Coleridge's position, which was that those passages of Scripture which present the word of God must be considered divinely inspired, while the rest need not be.[23] Hare's oft-expressed contempt for the idea that inspiration must extend to such petty details as dates and chronology in the Scriptures, his regard for Coleridge as a religious philosopher, and the repugnance he felt for Strauss indicate that he believed selectively in the divine inspiration of Scripture.

When *The Mission of the Comforter,* with its fiery defence of Luther, appeared in 1846, Hare sent a copy through Bunsen to the Prussian King. The result was an unexpected honour for Hare, as Bunsen wrote: "His Majesty writes me to tell you . . . that He has found *great comfort* in seeing you come forward as a champion of Christian and Evangelical truth and spiritual liberty, and in particular as a triumphant vindicator of the great German Reformer. . . . In token of these feelings the King has sent me the *Golden Medal of Science* to be transmitted to you in His name, as a sign of His particular regard and affection."[24] Hare's letter of thanks to the King of Prussia survives in a draft:

> I would crave your Majesty's permission to express my deep and humble gratitude for the generous marks of favour with which Your Majesty has been pleased to honour me in sending me the gold medal of science. . . . Such a reward would be a rich compensation for years of hard and painful toil; but they have been bestowed upon me when the labour itself has been its own reward, and when it has been a quickening delight to endeavour in some measure to pay off the incalculable debt which I owe to the literature, philosophy, & theology of Germany, by vindicating

the character of her great Reformer, and by striving to awaken our Church to a livelier consciousness of her unity with the other Protestant Churches.[25]

Though Hare and his admirers were delighted by this unexpected honour, such a link with continental Protestantism served as further damning evidence to convince the Tractarians of Hare's irreconcilable hostility to their position.[26] But in the meanwhile the ranks of the Tractarians themselves had been reduced by conversions to the Church of Rome, with Newman in the vanguard. Those Tractarians who remained in the Anglican Church were demoralized, but their hostility was undiminished, and Hare was next called upon to produce a vindication of his friend Bunsen.

In 1845 the first volume of Bunsen's *Ägyptens Stelle in der Weltgeschichte* was published, in which Bunsen gave the Old Testament critical analysis as a source of historical chronology. As Hare wrote to a friend, "Bunsen's work on Egypt . . . seems to me destined to form an epoch in the science of Primeval History. . . . I do not know how to controvert the evidence w[hi]ch Bunsen's book collects to prove the great antiquity of the world, & I look forward with anxious interest to the publication of his next two [volumes], w[hi]ch will enter into the general discussions on the subject."[27] Dr Edward Bouverie Pusey, Regius Professor of Hebrew at Oxford, became the *de facto* leader of the Tractarians upon Newman's conversion to Romanism. Since the death of H.J. Rose in 1838, Pusey was also the only eminent Tractarian with a good knowledge of German. In the July 1846 issue of the High Church journal the *Christian Remembrancer* a letter appeared criticizing Bunsen's orthodoxy, and an unsigned article indicated Bunsen as a rationalist.[28] This article was unsigned, but the letter bore the initials "E.B.P." Hare set about writing his "Vindication of the Chevalier Bunsen," which appeared in the September 1846 issue of the *British Magazine and Monthly Register*.

Hare sent extra copies to Whewell and explained: "I have been forced to engage in another battle to defend Bunsen ag[ain]st a shameful attack of Pusey's. . . . It was a most difficult and painful letter to write, from the temptation to transgress both on the side of praise & of blame, & from the necessity of touching upon the question of inspiration. But I have done this as delicately as I could; &

what I have said is no less necessary for the establishment of scientific than of historical truth."²⁹ This vindication was in one sense easier for Hare to compose than some of the others insofar as Pusey's earlier published statements in his mildly pro-German *An Historical Enquiry into the Probable Causes of the Rationalist Character Lately Predominant in the Theology of Germany* (1827) were neatly turned against him on the question of inspiration. Hare felt that the attack was inspired by lingering rancour over the Jerusalem Bishopric, and might have been ignored altogether. "But E.B.P.'s letter derives an importance from the character of him, who, we may fairly suppose, intended by those initials to avow his authorship; and as the bulk of English readers know little about German literature, except that there is a great deal of evil in it, especially in its theology, the assertions of a person known to be conversant with that literature . . . will naturally find credit, if uncontradicted." Hare denied that Pusey was "a detractor and calumniator," but said only that "the terrible curse of party-spirit" had led him to employ "the base weapons and stratagems which properly belong only to the unprincipled and reprobate."³⁰

The most absurd part of the attack upon Bunsen was the suggestion that those parts of the Old Testament narrative not discussed in *Ägyptens Stelle* were totally disbelieved by him. Dispatching the attempt to damn Bunsen by what he left unmentioned in his book, Hare moved to the question of Bunsen's upsetting biblical chronology. He explained that Bunsen's

> direct object is to show that the book of Genesis does not contain sufficient information on which to construct a chronology for the early history of mankind. . . . a person may believe that the Scriptures are inspired, that they are a revelation of Divine truth, and yet may conceive it possible that the inspiration does not extend to such things as dates; and it is the most unjustifiable to assert that he who questions the correctness of the chronological statements, does not believe the facts; and that too when his argument itself shows that he does believe them, one of his reasons for questioning the chronological statements being their apparent inconsistency with these facts.

This was a work of historical, not religious inquiry, Hare argued, but nonetheless involves the whole of that most weighty, but most difficult and troublous question concerning the nature, the mode, and the extent of inspiration in the composition of the Scriptures; and in connexion therewith, on the oppositions which are continually supposed to exist between Scripture and the ever-advancing discoveries of science. On this subject I would not presume to speak publicly . . . unless I could see the way clearly to a satisfactory solution of the various great difficulties . . . and could hope to set it forth calmly and fully, without needlessly disturbing and shocking the minds of simple believers.

Hare ended on a conciliatory note, saying that he hoped Pusey would be led to retract his baseless charges, so that Hare might throw down his arms, and "embrace his adversary . . . joyfully."[31]

Hare was not only grieved by the hostility of the Tractarians, he was also truly saddened by the defection of Newman and so many others to the Roman Church. He devoted his charges in 1845 and 1846 to the seductive trap which the Roman Church offered to many fellow Churchmen. Hare's concern with the Romanizing of some of his contemporaries was not the product of intolerance, but stemmed from the doubts raised in the minds of others about the tenets of the Anglican Church: "It is from the character of the converts, I say, in part from the intellectual eminence of a few, but in a far greater degree from the piety and Christian activity of many amongst them, that the recent schism derives its importance."[32] Hare believed that the converts simply had insufficient knowledge of the true nature of the Church of Rome, else they could not so readily have embraced it. When it came to a contest between the Roman and the English Churches, Hare's nationalism was elicited; the English Church must needs have truth on its side. Hare was thus led to contribute to the publicly voiced anti-Catholic sentiments which reached fever pitch at mid-century.

Popular Protestantism and anti-Catholicism were fuelled by the rash of conversions to Romanism. But in the process the partisan tendency within the English Church was also accelerated.[33] The attack upon Bunsen was evidence of the continued hostility of the Tractarians. Two years later, the nomination of Renn Dickson Hampden (1793–1868) to the see of Hereford elicited a bitter attack in which many Churchmen participated, a large number of

THE BROAD CHURCH VINDICATOR 171

them ignorant of Hampden's offences, real or imagined. Hare, asked to join in the condemnation of Hampden, declined and produced instead a stirring defence directed against Hampden's assailants.

Hampden's troubles dated from the year 1836, when Lord Melbourne, the Whig Prime Minister, made him Regius Professor of Divinity at Oxford, instead of the men recommended by the Archbishop of Canterbury. A tremendous protest erupted at Oxford. Hampden was personally blameless and was well regarded by many. His character was beyond reproach—almost. Newman, Pusey, and their adherents suspected Hampden's orthodoxy, because of his willingness, in his theological writings, to deal with Christian and non-Christian positions on equal terms. Turning therefore to Hampden's Bampton Lectures, *The Scholastic Philosophy Considered in Its Relation to Christian Theology* (1833), Newman in one night's effort produced a pamphlet to denounce its heretical tendencies, *Elucidations of Dr Hampden's Theological Statements*. Pusey also issued a pamphlet against Hampden. Melbourne stood his ground, and the appointment was implemented.[34]

For eleven years Hampden quietly and conscientiously performed his duties, and the controversy over his appointment was forgotten. In 1846 the Whigs were returned to office under the leadership of Lord John Russell. The Archbishop of Canterbury assured Russell that Hampden was a worthy and unobjectionable candidate for a bishopric. When the appointment was officially announced, in the words of Professor Chadwick, "It was 1836 all over again."[35] The Provost of Oriel College and most of the other heads of houses stood behind Hampden. Two hundred and fifty members of the University petitioned the Crown on his behalf. But this time the revived fear of the Whigs on the part of many Churchmen led to a more general dispute over the royal supremacy and the abuse of the Crown's right of episcopal patronage. The dispute was exacerbated when the Dean of Hereford denounced Hampden, and it appeared that the cathedral chapter might refuse to elect the appointee of the Crown. Such refusal would have precipitated a disastrous confrontation between Church and State, as Russell's government threatened to resort to practices unused since the sixteenth century, to create Hampden a Bishop by letters patent, and prosecute all who refused to recognize him for *Praemunire*. But the Dean of Hereford was outvoted, and the Hereford chapter elected Hampden.[36]

Unlike the controversy over Hampden in 1836, which had been largely an Oxford affair, the 1847–48 dispute involved many of the clergy of the established Church. Numerous petitions were drafted to protest Hampden's appointment, or rather what was seen as a tyrannical exercise of the royal supremacy. In the midst of this national uproar Hare received a letter from the Dean of Chichester asking him to help obtain support for a petition. Hare described his reaction in a letter to Whewell:

> When I was called upon by divers of my clergy to draw up some kind of remonstrance ag[ain]st Hampden's appointment, as I had never read a word of his writings, I of course replied that before I took any step, I must read them, especially the Bampton Lectures carefully: whereat they marvelled, esteeming it, I suppose, a rationalistic work of supererogation, & a heresy almost as dangerous as any of Hampden's. However, I was obstinate, & thus was led to read the B[ampton] L[ectures] & was quite amazed to find the utter groundlessness of the charges brought ag[ain]st him, and how they had all risen mainly from an incapacity to enter into his philosophical habits of thought, & his love for etymological speculations. . . . as the only way of allaying this miserable & disgraceful agitation seemed to be to set the true state of the matter plainly & simply before mens minds, whereby one might hope at least to disabuse some, & to withdraw them from this shameful persecution, I set to work at a pamphlet . . . & it was a great comfort a morning or two afterwards to get your letters, & thereby to gain an assurance that I was right. . . . I have had another awful series of lies to expose, not mere misunderstandings, but gross & malignant misrepresentations. It is dismal to see how this faculty of lying is cultivated by this new Oxford religionism. They really seem to have an incapacity of speaking the truth. . . . May God preserve us from the taint of all lying-religiousity.[37]

In 1847, however, Hare was not the only one to take the trouble to examine Hampden's writings. Parker, the Oxford bookseller, had 850 copies remaining of his earlier order of 1,000 copies of Hampden's Bampton Lectures, and, when the 1847 controversy erupted, he promptly sold them all. For many like Manning, who had read the lectures during the first Hampden controversy, Hampden's heresy was that he was willing to explore philosophically matters which his critics believed should be articles of faith.[38]

In his vindication of Hampden, Hare deplored the thousands of clergy who had been led to condemn a brother in ignorance of his crimes. He dismissed the excuse that the petitioning was merely to call for an inquiry into Hampden's views, because the spirit of the protest presupposed a condemnation of Hampden. If Hampden were a heretic, how, asked Hare, had he been allowed to teach error for eleven years as Professor of Divinity without being properly charged in an ecclesiastical court? Hare made it quite clear that in defending the man, unfairly accused and persecuted, he was not attempting to justify his appointment. As a result of close examination of Hampden's book Hare was forced to conclude that those who condemned Hampden were unacquainted with the book, or could not understand it, or, worse, maliciously misrepresented it.[39]

F.J.A. Hort wrote to a friend, "Hare's pamphlet seems to me to be quite a floorer for all those who babbled about Hampden's 'heresy.' "[40] Whewell expressed his hearty agreement with Hare.[41] Charles Cavendish Greville wrote: "The Hampden war has been turned greatly to the advantage of the Doctor; his enemies have exposed themselves in a most flagrant manner, and Archdeacon Hare has written a very able pamphlet also exposing the rascality (for that is the proper word) of his accusers, and affording his own valuable testimony to Hampden's orthodoxy."[42] But these were people who needed no converting. Newman, whose attack in 1836 had started the whole thing, took a strong interest in the controversy of 1847–48.[43]

In taking an unpopular stand amid the clamour of a witch hunt, Hare was behaving in characteristic fashion.[44] Once again he made enemies, and the following year he was writing a vindication of himself, as well as others, after becoming the object of yet another heresy hunt. On that occasion Hare himself provided his opponents with all the ammunition which they felt they needed. The accusations that were flung at Hare were in large measure transcribed from his memoir of his beloved friend, John Sterling.

Chapter 14

John Sterling and the Subversion of Faith

Upon the death of John Sterling at the end of 1844, Hare and Carlyle found they had been designated his literary co-executors. It was an unhappy combination, for although the two men were on friendly terms, two more opposite mentalities can hardly be imagined. Carlyle was preoccupied by work upon his monumental *Oliver Cromwell's Letters and Speeches* (1845), and so showed little interest in Sterling's literary remains. Sterling had desired a collected edition of his many periodical writings, as a memorial to leave to his children, so Hare set to work collecting his *Essays and Tales* (1848). The preface was a two-hundred page biography of Sterling. Hare felt compelled to present a biographical portrait of his late friend, but Sterling's religious scepticism pained him. He shared his anxieties with Sterling's good friend, Caroline Fox, who wrote in her diary: "He seems almost forced to publish more than he would wish in order to leave [John Stuart] Mill and Carlyle no pretext for an opposition portrait."[1]

The revelations of modern scholarship, biblical criticism, geology, and then biology, fostered a growing tendency for otherwise socially respectable people to become doubters. That John Sterling had become a doubter after pursuing, albeit briefly, a career in the Church, suggested to many that the rot of disbelief was present in the very fabric of the Church.[2]

In his memoir Hare wrote that when Sterling left the ministry, he fell prey to increasing religious doubts. He read the notorious *Leben Jesu* by Strauss,

> a book which a person can hardly read without being more or less hurt by it. If we walk through mire, some of it will stick to us, even when we have no other aim than to make our way through it, much more when we dabble about in it and sift it. . . . The only security for such persons is, when their purpose is, with God's help, to purify the mire. . . . Of Sterling's opinions during the latter part of his life, I cannot give so full an account as during the period of our greater intimacy and sympathy. For after some painful controversial letters on the subject of Strauss . . . our correspondence became much less frequent; and though his love of truth and his frankness would not allow him to suppress or disguise his convictions, he did not dwell on what he knew would so deeply distress me.[3]

This admission of ignorance of Sterling's later views led hostile critics to suspect even worse of Sterling. Hare did not specify the extent of Sterling's disbelief, but critics were not reassured to learn that in 1839 Sterling formed a close friendship with J.H. Newman's free-thinking younger brother, Francis Newman (1805-97). Sterling's desire to "shake off the articles" as a fetter to belief, settled the matter of Sterling's character in the minds of most critics.[4]

Why did Hare reveal so much? Was he not, as he had accused De Quincey, guilty of lack of taste and tact by revealing publicly what had been learned in the confidence of friendship? As Hare saw it:

> I have felt it a solemn duty to speak of my Friend's errors as well as of that in him which was noblest and wisest, and which I could most heartily sympathize with and admire. Had I omitted the former, the representation would have been false,—a procedure unjustifiable in all cases, above all, in the portraiture of one who hated every kind of falsehood with an intense hatred, and whose spirit burnt with a consuming love of truth. . . . The representation of his life is unsatisfactory, because the problem of his life was incomplete. . . . to reconcile faith with knowledge, philosophy with religion, the subjective world of human speculation with the objective world in which God has manifested Himself. . . . It may be thought that the story of Ster-

ling's life is a warning to refrain from all speculation. But this would be to misread and pervert it. . . . If there is any man, who, having exerted himself laboriously and perseveringly to pry into the hidden recesses of our nature, to pierce through the unfathomable abyss of evil, and to catch a glimpse of the light and glory beyond and behind, can say he has never been shaken or troubled in the calm composure of his faith, let him cast a stone at Sterling; I cannot.[5]

For Hare, whose whole bent of mind was analytical, and for whom reason and faith were not incompatible, Sterling's lapse from the fold was only the lamentable casualty of innocent intellectual endeavour. Sterling's dearness as a friend, and the tragedy of his early death, rendered it personally more painful to Hare. But for others, insecure in their religious faith, and unaccustomed to subjecting such things to intellectual inquiry, Sterling was another dangerous defector, and arms were not wanting to cast stones.

In the December 1848 issue of the *English Review* William Palmer (1803–85), an Oxford High Churchman who was associated with the Tractarians, published a review article covering sundry liberal publications, including Hare's edition of Sterling's *Essays and Tales* and Hare's *Mission of the Comforter*. The article was entitled "On Tendencies towards the Subversion of Faith." Hare was the chief target of Palmer's criticism because he had held Sterling, an "infidel," up to public admiration, and also because he had helped to create a climate of interest in England for the products of German theology.[6]

Palmer's tone was mild and restrained throughout, and only displayed emotion when he described the subversive circle that revolved around Sterling:

> It was, doubtless, the boldness and speculativeness of his views which gathered around him the friendship of a host of congenial minds, sympathizing in the general complexion of their philosophical and theological tendencies, though separated by strongly marked differences in points of detail. . . . the names of Hare, Bunsen, Carlyle, Coleridge, Emerson, Thirlwall, Maurice, Francis Newman, John Mill, Samuel Wilberforce, Arnold, and Trench are familiar to all the readers of this work, as the friends and associates of Mr. Sterling. . . . His life reveals a link between writings and doctrines, which we mentally class to-

gether almost involuntarily, notwithstanding their differences in many points, but which we could hitherto only connect by their tendencies. In Sterling's life, however, these various systems are brought together as parts and offshoots of one great movement, each playing its part, and allied by secret ties of sympathy with the rest.

In this mixed group of men Palmer discerned a threat within the Church itself from Germanizers and revolutionaries. "In this day we have nothing to fear from either Heresy or Infidelity if they willingly show themselves. It is when they lurk under the guise of Christianity, and are sapping and undermining the edifice of faith without disclosing their ultimate objects" that they pose a real threat.[7]

Such sympathies as may have been shared by Sterling and his admirers, whether they were inspired by wicked or benign motives, could only increase the spread of unbelief, such as that which engulfed Sterling. Palmer raised this point most cogently in his demand for a more open statement of opinion on the sensitive question of biblical inspiration:

> Mr. Hare intimates, that he did not himself concur in Sterling's view on the subject of inspiration, and yet it is evident that he differs widely from the prevalent belief on the subject.... We really cannot but wish that these men would more fully and frankly state their opinions on the subject of inspiration. They are continually assuring their disciples that all our existing views are wrong, and that there certainly will be an awful explosion which will subvert the authority of the Scriptures. We think that more mischief is done by such anticipations, than could be done by an open avowal of sentiments, even if they were erroneous.[8]

Here was a serious and well-articulated challenge, which called forth Hare's least successful vindication.

With a pained and heavy heart Hare took up his pen, and wrote a reply to Palmer. His displeasure is reflected in the title: *Thou Shalt Not Bear False Witness against Thy Neighbour*. Hare began with a candid explanation of his action in writing a life of Sterling:

> I did not undertake it without counting the cost, nor without much hesitation and reluctance. No other work I ever engaged in caused me a hundredth part of the painful anxiety. Not that I anticipated any evil consequences to the faith of anyone from it. On the contrary, I thought that Sterling's life might be so represented, with all faithfulness, and with all tenderness, as to be a useful lesson and warning to the many young men of our age, whose minds are in a state of perplexity more or less resembling his. . . . I have reason to know that my anticipations were not erroneous. But I did fear lest I should be the instrument of holding up my dear friend to severe reproach and condemnation, which if I did, I should violate the duties of friendship, as well as the first duty of a biographer. . . . Why then did I undertake the work? For a long time I shrank from it. . . . Now I felt a deep conviction that, if such a monument was to be erected to Sterling, I was the person whom he would have wisht to erect it.

As for the much-repeated charge that Hare held Sterling, an "infidel," up to admiration, Hare asked, "Having undertaken to write his life, how could I do otherwise than exhibit the beautiful and noble features of his character?"[9] Hare remarked that he had received a good deal of private censure for publishing the life of Sterling. He did not mention names, but John Sterling's brother Anthony was displeased by the memoir, and Maurice was so pained by the whole subject of Sterling's loss of faith, that he could not bring himself to read it.

As for the heterogeneous group of people whom the reviewer had gathered to indict for subversion of the faith, this was no infidel conspiracy, inspired by Sterling, but merely a trick to damn several people of diverse views by mutual association, and to tar them all with the brush of rationalism. Many of these people were not Sterling's friends, and were barely, if at all, acquainted with him. The reviewer demanded a clear statement of views on the inspiration of Scripture, to which Hare replied:

> I shall not be tempted by the reviewer's defiance to enter into a discussion on the inspiration of the Scriptures. He fancies that the only reason why those who cannot adopt the popular view of the subject, do not straight-away promulgate another view, is personal fear. Having his own opinions ready cut and dried, as he received them from his teachers, he cannot conceive why others

should find any difficulty in the formation and exposition of theirs on this mysterious and delicate subject. He does not understand how they should hesitate to bring forward what they feel to be immature and imperfect, nor how they should shrink from the shock it would be to many pious persons, if they were led to doubt the correctness of their notions concerning the plenary inspiration of every word in the Bible.

Hare also took up the charge that he had promoted a taste for German theology. Pointing to the notes of *The Mission of the Comforter* as his only substantial contribution on the subject, Hare denied that he had done as much as H.J. Rose or E.B. Pusey, with their analyses of German theology published in the 1820s, to "draw men's minds in that direction."[10] Here is a denial which, given Hare's considerable personal influence, does not ring true.

The violence and length of Hare's reply were out of all proportion to the charges that he refuted. His antagonist had struck upon open nerves. Hare's pamphlet reflected his pain and sensitivity in dealing with Sterling's life, as well as his despair at the continual need to engage in polemics:

> It has so often fallen my lot of late years to have to expose a series of gross misrepresentations in matters pertaining to theology. The multitude of such misrepresentations in these days . . . tempts one to fear that the faculty, either of perceiving the truth, or of speaking it, must be passing away from England, at least from our theological writers. . . . There is a want of candour toward those who differ from us, a rash haste snatching at anything that seems to flatter our prejudices, a carelessness and sluggishness in the pursuit of truth, an indifference about truth, except so far as it is subservient to our preconceived notions, or to the interests of our party.[11]

Hare's earlier vindications showed a zest, which marked them as labours of love. In this vindication the feeling of zest is nowhere evident, only grief and pain at the obliquy heaped upon Sterling's memory and at being personally indicted and forced to defend himself. For Hare the fear and hostility in Palmer's article represented the irreconcilable nature of party spirit within the Church. Hare's vindication was well received by those who were not initially hostile. F.J.A. Hort wrote, "Hare's pamphlet . . . is very good, tho' certainly abusive and once or twice unfair; he speaks excellently on Inspiration."[12]

Palmer's assault in the *English Review* offended some of the other partisan religious journals, not all of which had been unsympathetic to Hare's memoir of Sterling.[13] The fiercely partisan organ of the Evangelical party, the *Record*, entered the controversy by chastising both Hare and his High Church antagonist:

> Archdeacon Hare was betrayed into the error or fault, some months since, of becoming the biographer and eulogist of a former curate of his, a Mr. Sterling, who . . . fell into scepticism and retired from the ministry. . . . It is lamentable to see the noble defender of Luther sink into the apologist of Sterling.
>
> But the *English Review* has done its best to put Archdeacon Hare in the right, by making a very unjust attack upon him. The occasion is taken to represent him as one of a large group of conspirators against the faith. . . .
>
> Archdeacon Hare seems to us, in his *Reply to the English Review*, just published, to have the best of the argument, so far as the *Review* is concerned. But we are sorry to add, that he does not leave the mind in a satisfied and tranquil state, *as to himself*.[14]

Hare was still a champion of Protestantism for the Evangelicals, if somewhat tainted by his intimacy with German neologians. During the following week, however, the editors of the *Record* got wind of a story which convinced them that the *English Review*'s charges of a conspiracy to subvert the faith may have been well founded. This revelation was of the existence in London of a club named after the "infidel" Sterling.

In 1838 John Sterling founded a dining society which met monthly. The club was originally christened the "Anonymous Club," and over the years its membership grew to include nearly four score men of the most diverse views. The only purpose of the society was to bring men together "over a frugal dinner . . . to talk together."[15] The deterioration of Sterling's lungs compelled him to remove himself soon afterward from London society, but the monthly dinners continued, and the members soon renamed their club "The Sterling."

The *Record* announced its discovery of this infamous coven in terms of outrage:

> What has been our surprise to learn . . . that seven out of ten of the surviving members of the Reviewer's list, including Mr. Carlyle and Mr. Mill, have united with Mr. Hare to form a club in honour of Sterling. . . .
> It is time that we should know how we stand. Who then are the leading members of this Sterling Club? Infidels, Papists, Tractarians, Trimmers, Benthamites, speculators, of every class, painters, poets, and humourists, are in the Sterling Club, all intermingled with Bishops, Archdeacons, College Fellows, and College Tutors. With shame we read the names of all *three* Wilberforces in a club whose common bond of union seems to consist in reverence for Sterling as a bold speculator.[16]

The club was proof positive of infidel tendencies within the very bosom of the Church. Having the ingredients for creating a scandal where none existed, the *Record* launched a crusade against the members of the Sterling Club which lasted for a year. Later Hare came in for special reprobation: "We acquit Mr. Hare of the crimes of treason and perjury; but we do so at the expense of his character as a man of sense and judgement. He is numbered with those of whom it is said, 'Professing themselves wise, they became fools.' What man of common sense in Mr. Hare's position would ever have sat down to write and publish such a life as that of Sterling, or to reprint the essays and remains of an Infidel and Pantheist?"[17] Although Hare did not dignify them by a formal reply, these savage attacks caused him great pain.

Within the ranks of the Sterling Club fear filled some of the clerical members, who had to give thought to their professional image. Archdeacon John Allen was the first to resign when he failed to carry a motion to change the name of the club. Samuel Wilberforce and Henry Manning also resigned after careful deliberation. The name "Sterling" was subsequently dropped "to suit weak brethren," and the club survived "happily once more in a private condition."[18] The *Record* kept up its attacks sporadically for a year, but it had begun to look ridiculous for its obsessive interest in such weighty matters of heresy as whether or not grace had been said when the members of the Sterling Club sat down to dine. Indeed, some younger members of the Evangelical party were themselves offended by the *Record*'s campaign. In later years it became a badge of honour among some Broad Churchmen to be attacked in the pages of the *Record*, as Thirlwall observed: "The hostility of the 'Record' . . . I consider is a proof of excellence in every one who is its object."[19]

After all the furor had died down, and Sterling's name had again been allowed to lapse into obscurity, Carlyle took up his pen and did precisely what Hare had hoped to avoid. Carlyle's *Life of John Sterling* (1851) was written in two months of feverish inspiration. Carlyle claimed that Hare's biography had portrayed their friend only as a clergyman, not at all like the Sterling of Carlyle's own recollections.[20] Indeed, Carlyle poured out his anticlerical spleen in the marginal notes which he made in his own copy of Hare's life of Sterling.[21] Nonetheless Carlyle's delay of three years before sitting down to write is not easy to reconcile with his claim that anger with Hare's treatment was his motivation. Sterling's brother was said to have asked Carlyle to undertake the work, having himself collected manuscript materials. In 1849 Jane Carlyle told Caroline Fox that her husband wanted no part of Anthony Sterling's request, for "he would, by doing so, get into a controversy which he would sooner avoid; had he undertaken the matter at the beginning, he would have been very short and avoided religious questions altogether."[22] John Mill thought to begin a life of Sterling to contend with Hare's but was dissuaded by Miss Fox, who feared that Mill's reputation as a non-believer would only revive the controversy over their late friend.[23] One highly plausible explanation of Carlyle's behaviour is that his increasing jealousy over the influence which Coleridge had upon Sterling, and which Hare carefully delineated in his memoir, led him, after several years of resisting, to compose his book.[24] This explanation is borne out in Carlyle's treatment of his subject, whom—in the words of Mill's biographer—"he depicted . . . as a saintly, affectionate but effete young man, successively misguided first by Coleridge and then by Hare, until eventually rescued by himself."[25]

Hare explained in a letter to Archdeacon John Allen: "Carlyle's biography my wife read, I merely glanced over, of course with deep pain and sorrow. But I was glad to find that there did not seem to be anything requiring an answer from me, as, I think, you will agree, if my Memoir falls in your way. . . . The saddest part of the whole is the picture of Carlyle himself, who seems to have been sinking lower & lower into a moral and intellectual chaos."[26] Caroline Fox was so distressed at Carlyle's portrait of Sterling that she refused to see Carlyle ever again. The book was, however, a tremendous popular success, surprising Carlyle himself, who refused to take it seriously.[27]

Chapter 15

The Church Divided

In the spring of 1848 F.D. Maurice became involved in a project to counteract the Chartist threat of revolution by striking at the spirit of commercial competition. On the day of the great Chartist demonstration on Kennington Common, 10 April 1848, he was approached by Charles Kingsley, who was agitated about the Chartist threat. Maurice introduced him to a young man, John Malcolm Forbes Ludlow (1821–1911), who had just returned from France, where he had witnessed the late revolution. Ludlow went to Maurice to convince him of the need to Christianize socialism before it engulfed all society. These three men discovered a common sympathy from which the Christian Socialist movement was born.[1]

The history of the Christian Socialists between 1848 and 1854 is well documented, and Hare played only a minor role in it, so no more than a brief discussion is warranted here.[2] Yet some reassessment of Hare's influence in the movement is required. Ludlow, Kingsley, and Maurice discussed the possibility of issuing a series of penny tracts, addressed to the workers of England. Maurice and Daniel Macmillan had talked of a similar project in 1842 as a means of providing guidance for young commercial clerks, but nothing had come of that. On 13 April 1848 Maurice met with Hare, and reported to Ludlow: "I did not mention our tracts to my brother-in-law. . . . He proposed of himself . . . that there should be something of a paper set up, not like our present, but more like

THE CHURCH DIVIDED 185

Cobbett's 'Political Register,' for short, pithy weekly comments on the great questions of the day in a religious spirit. He said he would speak to [John W.] Parker on the subject. I assented, thinking such an organ might be very useful . . . as we could be sure of having our articles inserted. Hare thought of you as editor if it was consistent with your plans."[3]

So Hare, too, had been concerned about the Chartist agitation. He was not thinking in formal ideological terms, as Ludlow was, of Christianizing socialism. Hare saw instead an opportunity to attack the Mammon-worship against which he so often inveighed. By ending the spirit of commercial competition, selfish individualism could be replaced by Christian co-operation, and this is what Hare understood by the word "socialism." To achieve these ends Hare believed that a religious channel of communication must be opened to the working class, to offer an alternative to the physical-force Chartists.

J.W. Parker was enthusiastic about Hare's idea, and called a meeting in his offices which was attended by Hare, Maurice, Kingsley, and Ludlow. At this meeting *Politics for the People* was born, a penny weekly journal for the Christian working-man. The new effort was carried forth amid high hopes.[4] While Hare did not contribute to the new journal, he was eager to promote it. To his friend Daniel Macmillan he wrote: "I know you will take a most lively interest in the Politics for the People. I hope that it will be the means of very great good, & that, in turn, it will have a very large circulation. . . . It will be a fine scandal, if every vulgar, immoral, anti-religious paper can maintain itself for year after year, and when a paper at last publisht to maintain political, moral, & religious principles, it sh[oul]d be let die away."[5]

The first divisive note arose from Hare a month after the journal had begun. Under the pen name "Parson Lot," Kingsley had contributed an open letter to the Chartists. Hare took offence and wrote to Kingsley:

> I had been much pained by part of your second Letter to the Chartists. . . . it will almost compel me to abandon all efforts to promote the circulation of the Journal.
>
> The objectionable matter . . . lies in what you say of the manner in which the Clergy have mis-represented the Bible. That they have by no means fulfilled their political duties in

England, I allow. Indeed, I myself have said so more than once. . . . But the rule w[hi]ch seems to be imposed on us by Christian wisdom . . . has been to tell people of their own faults, & not of the faults of their neighbours, least of all those whom they regard as opponents. . . . Now, I believe, from all I have heard, that if there be any feeling universal among the Chartists, it is an almost intense dislike or distrust of the Clergy. . . . Now it seems to me that your Letter will grievously encourage this feeling, that the Chartists will say, Here is a parson himself confessing that all his brother parsons are cheating and juggling us: and the mischief thus effected will be more than Politics for the People will remedy in a twelvemonth.

Hare ended his letter on a conciliatory note, with praise for Kingsley's work in general, and with some patronizing remarks about how "genial, enthusiastic young men" were especially prone to behave like the children of light.[6] Maurice's reply to Hare's demand that he censor Kingsley's article was mildly indignant.[7]

Before any further controversy over the contents of *Politics for the People* could arise, the journal died, or rather, was killed, for Parker was unwilling to continue it after the first three months. Ludlow strongly suspected that Parker had undertaken the journal only out of jealousy of Charles Knight's success with the *Voice of the People,* so that when Knight discontinued his paper, Parker followed suit, although the circulation of *Politics for the People* was steadily rising. But Ludlow, although an honest and goodhearted man, was given to lurking suspicions. He could not understand Hare's motives:

I am not sure that I ever met Archdeacon Hare at Parker's after the first conference when the starting of "Politics" was decided on, but I used to meet him at Mr. Maurice's or Mr. Powell's. . . . He was still a delightful talker, and was always to me all that is kind and friendly. But it must be said that he was now past his prime. I heard him in Lincoln's Inn, and it would have been difficult to recognize in him the preacher of the "Victory of Faith". An old Cambridge pupil of his . . . heard him on the same occasion as myself, and told me that Hare was but the shadow of his former self. *It was always my impression that he acted rather as a drag on Mr. Maurice,* and I suspect that even "Politics for the People", which he had so powerfully helped to found, though falling far short of its original purpose, was too advanced for him. Hence probably the fact that he never contributed to it, although he certainly had intended to do so.

Ludlow could never overcome his lingering resentment of the Hares, Julius Hare and Maurice's wife, Georgiana Hare: "I may now say . . . that I consider one powerful influence towards withdrawing Mr. Maurice from any active part in the co-operative movement was the Hare influence."[8] To Ludlow in his singlemindedness the Hares' interference was simply obstructionism against the cause of co-operation.

Julius Hare and Ludlow were at one, however, in recognizing a common enemy in *laissez-faire* capitalism. While Ludlow dreamed of Christianizing socialism, Hare dreamed of killing Mammonworship by eliminating competition and individualism. In his dispute with Kingsley over the letter to the Chartists, Hare revealed that he placed the safety of the Church ahead of the Christian Socialist programme, but in his clerical position it would have been more surprising had he not done so. These priorities in no way detract from Hare's genuine and sincere interest in the aims of Christian Socialism, as he conceived them. Hare was concerned for the cause of co-operation, but after 1851 his deteriorating health prevented him from doing more than showing his support financially.[9] He does not even appear to have become disheartened with co-operation after 1853, when Maurice was dismissed from his professorship at King's College, London. This was precisely the outcome against which Hare, Bunsen, and others had sought to protect Maurice. In the event the immediate excuse for the dismissal was not Maurice's political and social activities, but his theology.

In June 1853 Maurice published his *Theological Essays* in which he analysed the principal doctrines of the Christian faith, and defended orthodoxy in speculative terms which rationalists would accept. The book was addressed to Unitarians, and Maurice was well aware of the revulsion which the sect felt toward the Christian doctrine of hell and damnation. Therefore in dealing with these eschatological dogmas Maurice appeared to waver from orthodoxy by suggesting that "eternal punishment" need not be construed as "everlasting," but that damnation might be seen as a special state of the soul in which it stood outside of time and apart from God. With such a logical distinction a liberal theologian found it possible to reconcile the biblical threat of hell and damnation with the idea of a loving God.[10] The orthodox view was that the threat of hell and damnation was not only ordained by Scripture, but was also essential to maintain morality and the social order. Maurice's effort to explain certain Christian doctrines in rational terms was misunderstood, and he was branded a crypto-rationalist.

Dr Richard William Jelf (1798–1871), Maurice's principal at King's College, London, was puzzled by Maurice's views, as well he might have been. Maurice at his most lucid is not very clear.[11] Jelf was already ill-disposed toward Maurice, who had become an object of attack in much of the sectarian religious press for being a neologian, a friend of Sterling and Hare, and a member of the notorious Sterling Club. Maurice's public association with Christian Socialism and his political reputation brought him into conflict with Jelf as early as 1848, and Maurice had been given repeated warnings to show more concern for the reputation of King's College.[12] Jelf delved deeply into the *Theological Essays,* and read them with scrupulous care. In correspondence Jelf questioned Maurice about specifics, and sought to pin him down in his vagueness, and commit him to specific interpretations. Maurice consulted with Hare constantly before sending his replies to Dr Jelf, and in August 1853 Hare saw clearly what was coming when he wrote to Thirlwall:

> A good deal of trouble, I am afraid, awaits [Maurice] in consequence of his last volume of Theological Essays. To me it seems a most noble book, worthy of Luther in its dauntless bravery, and fitted to deliver the Church from divers notions, offensive to reason & conscience, w[hi]ch have become attacht to some of the primary doctrines of the faith. I cannot doubt that it will do a . . . great good among the thoughtful[,] reconciling many to what they now reject: but the rabble have been setting up a fierce cry against it; and he is even threatened with an attempt to remove him from his Professorship. May God frustrate it: for its success w[oul]d be very disastrous.[13]

Jelf tired of Maurice's logical and semantic evasions, and put to him flatly the question of whether or not he believed in hell and everlasting punishment. Jelf rejected Maurice's non-horological definition of "eternal," and countered it with fifty-seven passages in the New Testament where "eternal" entailed time-passing in its obvious meaning.[14] In a letter to Hare, Maurice explained his decision to fight Jelf, rather than bend to his notions of the orthodoxy suitable for professors.[15]

Hare's sympathies were with Maurice, but he tried to maintain an impartial outlook:

> Of course I cannot but feel a strong personal interest in the question. For it is impossible to know Maurice . . . without admiring and loving him. . . . Still I have not the slightest wish that the decision in this matter should be influenced by any motive but a strict regard to truth and justice, and to the good of the Church; nay, if the laws of our Church require that Maurice should be expelled from his professorship, let him be so, although I can anticipate nothing but the most disastrous consequences from this condemnation.

Hare then elaborated upon these disastrous consequences:

> a terrible shock . . . such a condemnation would give to that large portion of the intelligent minds of all classes whom [Maurice] has powerfully influenced by his teaching and writings. . . . I believe it is in great measure owing to him that the intellect of the rising generation is with us rather than against us. . . . Now it will grievously disturb all these men if they find that the Church rejects him whom they revere as her wisest teacher. Many of them will probably fall away from her, some, it is to be feared, into some of the forms of rationalism.[16]

Maurice and the principal were on a collision course from which neither would deviate. Jelf urged Maurice to resign, but Maurice held out for a hearing before the college council, and certain dismissal. On 27 October 1853 the council obligingly made Maurice a martyr to theological intolerance.[17]

Much sympathy lay on Maurice's side. Many thoughtful Churchmen abhorred the measure. Maurice's supporters did not accept his dismissal without protest, as Kingsley wrote to Maurice: "I have been writing to various people about it all; & shall see the Bishop of Oxford tonight. I have had two letters from Hare & I think we have hit on a plan: but he begs me to do something in a hurry."[18] But the formal plans for protest did not live up to expectations, as Hare revealed in a letter to Derwent Coleridge:

> I hear you have expresst indignation at the King's College proceedings: and well you may. The mode in w[hi]ch the act has been done is no less disgraceful than the act; and both are disastrous to the Church. We have been trying to get up a Protest in opposition to it, of w[hi]ch I send you a copy. I have invited a good number of Clergymen, from whom we lookt for support, to meet . . . in order to consider the matter. But the answers I have received lead me to fear we shall do nothing, & that our meeting will be very thinly attended. If you can come however to join in our Dirge, if in nothing else, we shall rejoice to see you.[19]

In this crisis Hare produced no vindication. In addition to the breakdown of his health, he realized from the clamour of the *Record* after the appearance of *Thou Shalt Not Bear False Witness* that he would be preaching to deaf ears.

Maurice's dismissal was a turning-point in the history of the Broad Church, a diminishing of the hopes, aspirations, and ideals which had been cherished by Hare, Maurice and their friends for the achievement of a truly comprehensive and tolerant National Church. The action of the King's College Council served notice that theological liberalism was an unwelcome element within the Church, that they, who sought to comprehend as many as possible within the establishment, might not be tolerated themselves.[20]

Disappointments were Hare's frequent companions in his last years, though his spirits remained high, and Crabb Robinson could record that "he is consistent, to a degree I envy, in his faith that all will end well."[21] In 1849 the Regius Professorship of Divinity at Cambridge fell vacant. At the persuasion of his womankind, as he called them, Hare fancied that this post would be a suitable climax to his theological career, as he explained in a letter to Whewell:

> I . . . wish that I might myself be allowed to take part in helping to work out the new system in my beloved University. . . . though still fitter to learn than to teach in theology, my

own views have become much firmer of late years, and I have a securer knowledge of the foundations on w[hi]ch my doctrines rest. The many testimonials of gratitude & affection w[hi]ch I have received from students of divinity at Cambridge encourage me to think that, if I were living amongst them & opening my heart and mind to them, I might render them service in helping them to steer among the quicksands by w[hi]ch theological speculation in these days is beset. And it might be of some use to show them that one may admit and recognize whatever is true and valuable in German Theology, and yet retain a strong conviction of all the positive truths of the Gospel. Many signs show that this is one of the main perils of our days; & we cannot escape it by turning away from it. We must face it dauntlessly, & overcome it.[22]

Both Whewell and Sedgwick voiced encouragement for Hare's "weighty claims," along with some counsel of warning about the "jealous fears of German Theology, Rationalism, & what not" that his candidacy might elicit.[23] Such a possibility found Hare dauntless, but in the end he was prevented from standing for the election by a simple geographical dilemma. He was unwilling to relinquish his Herstmonceux living, giving as his excuse his unreliable health, which might at any time compel him to resign the professorship, and therefore he must have his living to fall back upon. Whewell informed him that it was deemed unacceptable for him to hold both the living and the professorship, because they were so far distant. Although Hare dropped his plan to stand in the election, he took some comfort from learning that three of the candidates were his former pupils and old Apostles.[24]

In the spring of the following year, 1850, William Wordsworth died. Hare served with Crabb Robinson, Thirlwall, and others on the monument committee which sought to do honour to his old friend by instituting a public subscription for monuments in Westminster Abbey and at the church at Grasmere, Westmoreland.[25] Only a month after this sad task was undertaken Hare learned that his old schoolmate Henry Havelock had returned from India and was living at Plymouth. Havelock had spent twenty-six uninterrupted years in India, and he and Hare had not met in thirty-eight years, or corresponded in nearly as long. Joyful letters as well as reunion visits were exchanged by the old Carthusians, and something of their friendship revived during the course of Havelock's two-year leave of absence in England.[26]

The reunion with Havelock, however, was not entirely a source of happiness for Hare, for he learned that his long-lost friend had become a devout Baptist. While he embraced Havelock with fervour, Hare did not shrink from touching upon this one source of disappointment: "There was one thing w[hi]ch of course I sh[ou]ld have wisht otherwise: I sh[oul]d have wisht to see you still a member of our Church. But it was easy to discern the train of causes w[hi]ch led you to separate from us; and there was much in the aspect of our Church, as you had seen her, w[hi]ch might not unreasonably repel you from her."[27] Hare was probably referring to the indolent state of the Anglican Church in India, where Dissenting groups, like the Baptists, were far more active. He felt that the Church had made real and visible progress in England itself in the previous four decades. To Havelock he might have pointed with pride to the tremendous increase in the number of churches and schools, the removal of disabilities from Catholics and Dissenters, and the commutation of tithes. But Hare could not have concealed the fact that spiritually the Church was ailing from the partisanship which divided it, and the ugly schism in which many of her most devout members entered the Church of Rome. In 1851 the urgency of this problem was brought home sharply to Hare by the unexpected conversion to Rome of his friend and brother Archdeacon, Henry Manning. According to Hare's nephew, Manning's conversion provided Hare with a painful shock from which he never recovered.[28]

Before Manning's conversion Hare wrote to him:

> Of the difference in our opinions on the constitution of the Church, perhaps I was more distinctly conscious than you were. At least I used to bring forward mine almost obtrusively . . . when you lovingly turned away from them, & sought out the points where we agreed. In doing the latter I joined you most gladly, & thought it a precious blessing that we c[oul]d work together so harmoniously, notwithstanding our differences. It exemplified what I have ever desired to see in the Church, practical union & zealous cooperation, along with wide intellectual differences. Were it not for the evil in ourselves, & in the world, this w[oul]d not only be practicable, but easy. For some

years we were able to continue thus. . . . Unhappily the plot thickened; the breaches in the Church became wider. Necessity seemed laid upon me to speak out more strongly in opposition to what seemed to me very destructive errors. . . . In these troublous, contentious times, I much fear, other points of difference will start up. The desire of my heart is after the peace of the Church; but it is still more strongly after Truth and Righteousness, without w[hi]ch there can be no peace.[29]

In March 1851, when Hare was bedridden, he received a sympathetic letter from Manning: "All these things are working together for our good. Anything which loosens us from this world and unites our heart as well as our intelligence with the eternal world is an unspeakable gift of God's grace & love."[30] Hare replied to report on his recovery: "Yes for us all it is a blessed prospect that the time will come when the darkness of doubt, & the clouds of distracting opinions, shall pass away forever, & we shall see Him, who is the Truth, as he is. May this comfort abide with you continually: & when God so wills, may you enter into His light."[31]

At the beginning of April 1851 Manning called at Herstmonceux upon what Hare feared "was meant as a farewell visit, and so it proved, though he said not a word which could imply that it was so."[32] In the words of Shane Leslie, one of Manning's biographers, "The end had come. Break followed break. He parted from Archdeacon Hare in silence, each reading the truth in the other's eyes."[33] Manning's endurance as an Anglican was exhausted when the Judicial Committee of the Privy Council overturned the decision of the Court of Arches in the case of G.C. Gorham *versus* the Bishop of Exeter, and upheld the right of Mr Gorham, an Evangelical clergyman of thirty-nine years' experience, to his private opinion on the efficacy of baptismal regeneration while also holding a living in the Church. Manning and ten others issued a declaration against the decision, and claimed that by failing to enforce "the essential meaning of the article of the creed," the English Church was separated from the Catholic doctrine of the Church Universal, and forfeited the assurance of grace in its sacraments.

Hare responded with a pamphlet addressed to Richard Cavendish, one of Manning's co-signers in which he lauded the decision of the Judicial Committee for preserving to the Church the many Evangelical clergymen who might have been driven out, at least from the ministry, by their consciences over this matter. Although Hare believed in the efficacy of baptism for the remission of sins, he felt that the Articles of the Church allowed ample scope for individual conscience: "We have no warrant for demanding assent to any particular explanation of an Article in the Creed, or to any particular consequences deduced from it, except insofar as the Church has defined or expounded the Article in her Formularies."[34] Hare was contemptuous of the notion that to allow broad comprehension of views within the Church would cause it to be severed from the body of Christ's Church. The need for comprehension and unity in the Church was clear; Broad Churchmen were not the only victims of intolerance.

Hare's letter made little impression upon those to whom it was directed. Richard Cavendish replied to charge that Hare was compromising truth by interpreting the Articles of the Creed on the basis of expediency. As for Hare's fear for the consciences of Evangelical clergymen, Cavendish dismissed it as "morbid sentimentality." Other critics replied to Hare's pamphlet to scoff at his notion that Evangelicals would desert the Church.[35] Hare was inconsistent in arguing for theological comprehension to maintain unity in the Church. When Samuel Wilberforce used a similar argument on behalf of High Churchmen during debates in Parliament on the Episcopal Bill of 1850, Hare rejected as an exaggeration the plea that many might secede from the Church.[36]

Anxiety over the divisions and dissensions in the Church taxed Hare both mentally and physically. His health had never been robust. Throughout his life he suffered from bouts of illness, serious enough to require long convalescences. In the winter and spring of 1851 he was taken ill to such a degree that all parish duties were beyond his powers, and his friend and former pupil George Wagner joined with Hare's curate, Edmund Venables, in taking services at Herstmonceux. Hare's convalescence was prolonged, but as he observed in a letter to Manning, the ministrations of "so many dear loving nurses" was like "feeding upon the richest, sweetest cream of life."[37]

From this illness Hare never thoroughly recovered, but merely proceeded to others. In the late summer of 1852 Hare and his wife travelled to Tunbridge Wells for the sake of his health. At the end of 1852, while visiting his sister-in-law, Lucilla Powell, in London,

Hare was taken seriously ill with acute erysipelas, and was confined to bed for three months. Mrs Powell recalled, "It was a delight to have him with us, though it was sad to see his sufferings. But his patience and cheerfulness made it always a pleasure to be with him, and minister to him, and he had such wonderful fortitude in bearing pain, that it was difficult to imagine how much he was enduring."[38] The Hares were unable to return to Herstmonceux from London until Easter 1853, when his parishioners met them with a public demonstration of rejoicing at their homecoming.[39]

The following June brought an unexpected honour from court. The Lord Chamberlain wrote to announce that "the Queen has been pleased to express Her intention to confer upon you the appointment of one of Her Majesty's Chaplains in Ordinary."[40] The nomination probably originated with Prince Albert, who was an admirer of Bunsen and a supporter of the Jerusalem Bishopric, and was unlikely to be put off by the criticism of Hare as a Germanizer and a neologian. Indeed, here was a palpable reward for years of diligent service to the Church, to scholarship, to international understanding, and above all to the service of truth.

Unfortunately, Hare's deteriorated health limited his capacity to perform the duties of a Royal Chaplain, as he confessed in his letter of acceptance:

> May I request your Lordship to express my deep gratitude to the Queen for the mark of her favour with which her Majesty has been so generously pleased to honour me?
>
> I should feel proud of serving her Majesty in any capacity in which she may vouchsafe to command my services.
>
> At the same time I feel bound to state that the condition of my health during the last two years has been so precarious . . . that this may justly be thought to disqualify me from any office, the duties of which I might be unable to discharge at the very moment when they were required of me.
>
> Should this not be deemed a reason for selecting a more efficient Chaplain, I should most gratefully obey her Majesty's gracious command.[41]

In the summer of 1854 Hare again fell ill, and his frequent and severe attacks of illness were unrelieved by a holiday and the sea air at Brighton in September. He thought to resign his archdeaconry, but his old friend Henry Venn Elliott persuaded him not to, for Hare's influence in the diocese was highly valued. In October he was able to deliver a very brief charge at the annual visitation. The winter of 1854–55 was intensely severe, with hard frosts and heavy snows even on the Sussex coast. Shortly before Christmas Hare was confined to his bed, and he scarcely left it again. His sister-in-law, Lucilla Powell, recalled that

> his weakness was extreme, but he was always full of thankfulness for all that was done for him, and when he could not speak, he would look at us, with loving eyes and gestures. Once when Esther had raised him, and I was giving him his medicine, he looked from one to the other saying "My two dear nurses!" and on another occasion, when unable to articulate, from the dryness of his throat, he looked long and lovingly at his wife, and then at me, with a wistful beseeching look, which conveyed as clearly as words could have done, that he left her in my care.[42]

On 22 January 1855 Hare's physician noted a lessening of all symptoms and an improved pulse. But Esther told her twin-sister, Lucilla, "If all the doctors in the world told me he was better today, I would not believe them, for I *know* he is worse," and Lucilla added, "Alas, she was but too right. . . . In the early dawn a figure entered my room and the words rang in my ears—'He is gone'—and then I knew my sister was indeed desolate."[43]

Hare's friend Elliott, in his eulogy, recounted a version of his last words:

> When it was said to him . . . later in that night, that he was going to his heavenly Father's home; he faintly answered, "I think I may be;" and after a short pause added, "Bless the Lord for all his mercies to me." But his last clear words were remarkable; for they were in a voice more distinct and strong than he had reached for several days past, and in answer to the question how would he be moved. With his eyes raised towards heaven, and a look of indescribable brightness, he said, "Upwards, upwards!" Soon after which he passed from earth to heaven.[44]

On 30 January 1855, "a cold and piercing day," a large number of clergy and laymen gathered at Herstmonceux for the funeral. H.V.

Elliott and J.N. Simpkinson took the service jointly, and both delivered funeral sermons in the Herstmonceux Church the following Sunday. The pall bearers included Connop Thirlwall, Arthur Penrhyn Stanley, and George Wagner; they carried Hare's earthly body and laid it to rest beneath the large yew tree in his own windswept churchyard.[45]

Notes

Abbreviations Used in the Notes

BL	=	British Library.
B-PP	=	Bayne-Powell Papers, private collection.
CHEL	=	*Cambridge History of English Literature.*
CUL	=	Cambridge University Library.
DNB	=	*Dictionary of National Biography.*
FP/V.&A.	=	Forster Papers, Victoria and Albert Museum Library, South Kensington, London.
Guesses	=	J.C. and A.W. Hare, *Guesses at Truth by Two Brothers.* New ed. London: Macmillan, 1866.
MA/SMA	=	Manning Archive, St Mary of the Angels, Bayswater, London.
Maurice	=	F.D. Maurice, *Life of Frederick Denison Maurice Chiefly Told in His Own Letters,* ed. F. Maurice. 3rd ed. 2 vols. London: Macmillan, 1884.
McF/A	=	G.F. McFarland, "The Early Literary Career of Julius Charles Hare." *Bulletin of the John Rylands Library,* XLVI, no. 1 (Sept. 1963), 42–83.
McF/B	=	G.F. McFarland, "Julius Charles Hare, Coleridge, De Quincey, and German Literature." *Bulletin of the John Rylands Library,* XLVII, no. 1 (Sept. 1964), 165–97.
Memorials	=	A.J.C. Hare, *Memorials of a Quiet Life.* 13th ed. 3 vols. London: Daldy, Isbister, 1876.
NCBEL	=	*New Cambridge Bibliography of English Literature.*
OED	=	*Oxford English Dictionary.*
Plumptre	=	E.H. Plumptre, "Preface." In J.C. and A.W. Hare, *Guesses at Truth.* London: Macmillan, 1866.
RLEMS	=	Rylands Library English Manuscripts, Manchester.
Stanley	=	[A.P. Stanley], "Archdeacon Hare." *Quarterly Review,* XCVII, no. 2 (June 1855), 1–28.
Story	=	A.J.C. Hare, *The Story of My Life.* 6 vols. London: George Allen, 1896–1900.
TCL	=	Trinity College Library, Cambridge.
Thirlwall	=	J.C. Thirlwall, *Connop Thirlwall: Historian and Theologian.* London: S.P.C.K., 1936.
WP/TCL	=	Whewell Papers, Trinity College Library.

Chapter 1

1. A.J.C. Hare, "Francis Hare (1671–1740)," *DNB;* Essex County Record Office, Q/SR 342/36, 345/48, 349/75, D/DBg 12, 24 April 1694.
2. CUL Cholmondeley MSS., nos. 72, 78, 2326a, 2641, 39; W.S. Churchill, *Marlborough: His Life and Times* (London, 1967), II, p. 153; N. Sykes, *Church and State in England in the XVIIIth Century* (Cambridge, 1934), pp. 163–64; *Memorials,* I, p. 73.
3. *Memorials,* I, pp. 73–74; W. Coxe, *Memoirs of the Duke of Marlborough* (London, 1848), I, p. 156; Churchill, *Marlborough,* II, pp. 7, 23, I, pp. 99, 398; Sykes, *Church and State,* p. 164; G.S. Holmes, *British Politics in the Age of Anne* (London, 1967), p. 54; Francis Hare to Provost Roderick, 2 May 1707, resigning his fellowship, King's College, Cambridge, MS. Coll. 1.82.
4. E. Venables, "The Castle of Herstmonceux and Its Lords," *Sussex Archaeological Collections,* IV (1851), 163–64; *Memorials,* I, p. 76; J.H. Monk, *Life of Dr Richard Bentley,* 2nd ed. (London, 1833), II, pp. 218–19, 233–36. The etymology and proper spelling of "Herstmonceux" are subjects of some controversy. "Herstmonceux" remains the most widely accepted spelling, with "Hurst-" used in some local variants like "Hurstmonceux Place." Even the Ordnance Survey maps are confused upon this point. A. Mawer and F.M. Stenton, *The Place-Names of Sussex,* pt. II (Cambridge, 1930), pp. 479–80. For the history of the castle and parish, see Venables, "Castle of Herstmonceux," *passim; Victoria County History of Sussex,* vol. IX: *Rape of Hastings* (London, 1937), pp. 131–34; T.W. Horsfield, *History of the County of Sussex* (Lewes, 1870), pp. 254–56.
5. Venables, "Castle of Herstmonceux," pp. 165–66; *Memorials,* I, pp. 76–84.
6. *Memorials,* I, pp. 77 and n., 83–86; *Story,* I, pp. 3–5.
7. *Memorials,* I, pp. 86–87; *Story,* I, pp. 5–6; W. Jones, *Letters of Sir William Jones,* ed. G. Cannon (Oxford, 1970), I, p. 65 n. 3, II, p. 594 n. 2.
8. *Story,* I, pp. 5–6; *Memorials,* I, pp. 93–94; Jones to Franklin, 15 Nov. 1782, in Jones, *Letters,* II, p. 594.
9. J.M. Stifler, ed., *"My Dear Girl": The Correspondence of Benjamin Franklin with . . . Georgiana and Catherine Shipley* (New York, 1927), pp. 226–27; C. Van Doren, *Benjamin Franklin* (New York, 1964), pp. 413–420; B. Franklin, *The Papers of Benjamin Franklin,* ed. W.B. Willcox, XVIII (New Haven, 1974), *passim; Memorials,* I, p. 92.
10. Georgiana Hare to Franklin, Aix-la-Chapelle, 12 Jan. 1784, in Stifler, ed., *My Dear Girl,* pp. 244–46, cf. pp. 243–44; Van Doren, *Franklin,* pp. 573–74.
11. Franklin to Georgiana Hare, Passy, 25 Jan. 1784, in Stifler, ed., *My Dear Girl,* pp. 246–48.

NOTES TO CHAPTER 1

12. Georgiana Hare to Franklin, Vicenza, 20 Aug. 1785, in *ibid.*, pp. 254–56.
13. *Memorials,* I, pp. 94–100, 166; *Story,* I, pp. 15–16.
14. J. Ridley, *Lord Palmerston* (London, 1970), p. 12; *Memorials,* I, p. 98; W.G. Constable, *John Flaxman* (London, 1927), pp. 45, 98.
15. Georgiana Hare to Lady Jones, Valdagno, 10 Oct. 1795, in *Memorials,* I, p. 100
16. Francis Hare to Flaxman, Bologna, 9 Feb. 1796, BL Add. MS. 39781, f. 23.
17. Georgiana Hare to Mrs Flaxman, 20 Feb. 1797, *ibid.*, f. 409.
18. Georgiana Hare to her son Francis, 10 Oct. 1797, in *Memorials,* I, pp. 122–27, *cf.* pp. 101–02; *Story,* I, p. 13.
19. *Memorials,* I, pp. 128–33.
20. Father Aponte to the Hare-Naylors, 16 Sept. 1797, in *ibid.*, I, p. 105.
21. Tambroni to Georgiana Hare-Naylor, 28 Oct. 1797, in *ibid.*, I, p. 106.
22. Father Aponte to Georgiana Hare-Naylor, n.d., in *ibid.*, I, p. 107.
23. Francis to his parents, n.d., in *ibid.*, I, pp. 102–04.
24. Father Aponte to the Hare-Naylors, 17 March, 24 March, and 12 May 1798, in *ibid.*, I, pp. 110–12, 113–14.
25. Hare to William Whewell, London [1819], WP/TCL MS. 0.18. M6.24; *Memorials,* I, pp. 116–19, 133.
26. Georgiana Hare-Naylor to Lady Jones, Padua, 16 March 1799, in *Memorials,* I, pp. 134–35.
27. Georgiana Hare-Naylor to Lady Jones, Hurstmonceux Place, 31 Dec. 1799, in *ibid.*, I, pp. 137–40.
28. Georgiana Hare-Naylor to Lady Jones, 1 and 27 Feb. 1800, in *ibid.*, I, pp. 138–39, 147.
29. Georgiana Hare-Naylor to Lady Jones, 31 Dec. 1799, in *ibid.*, I, p. 137, *cf.* pp. 147–48.
30. Hare to Whewell, 2 July [1843], WP/TCL Add. MS. a77.134. See D.C. Somervell, *History of Tonbridge School* (London, 1947), pp. 37–38.
31. H.C. Robinson, *Diary, Reminiscences, and Correspondence of Henry Crabb Robinson,* ed. T. Sadler (London, 1869), I, p. 212; *cf. Memorials,* I, pp. 144, 148–50; Plumptre, p. xix.
32. Georgiana Hare-Naylor to Lady Jones, 12 Nov. 1804, in *Memorials,* I, pp. 150–51; *cf.* [F.D. Maurice], "Introduction Explanatory of [Hare's] Position in the Church," in Hare, *Charges to the Clergy of the Archdeaconry of Lewes* (Cambridge, 1856), pp. x–xi; Plumptre, pp. xix–xx.
33. Hare to Maria Hare, 4 Feb. 1842, in *Memorials,* II, p. 235; *cf.* Hare to Francis Hare, 6 March 1834, in *ibid.*, II, pp. 54–55. See also *ibid.*, I, pp. 151, 153–54, 166.
34. CUL Add. MS. 3905(14), f. 4, is a copybook prepared by Francis for Julius' instruction.

35. [Maurice], "Introduction," pp. xi–xii; *cf.* Stanley, p. 3.
36. Georgiana Hare-Naylor to Mrs Flaxman, Weimar, 30 March 1805, BL Add. MS. 39781, f. 419; *cf.* John Flaxman to the Hare-Naylors, London, 17 Nov. 1804, BL Add. MS. 39780, f. 86.
37. *Memorials,* I, pp. 149, 151; *cf.* Plumptre, p. xx; Stanley, p. 3.
38. *Memorials,* I, pp. 154–55.
39. Georgiana, b. 11 Nov. 1809 (F.D. Maurice's second wife); Gustavus, b. 15 Sept. 1811; and Reginald, b. 29 Dec. 1812. *Ibid.,* I, p. 157.
40. *Ibid.,* I, pp. 155, 159; Plumptre, p. xx; [Maurice], "Introduction," p. xii. With the sale of the Herstmonceux estate—which did not include the sale of the advowson—the name "Naylor" was dropped.
41. *Memorials,* I, p. 160.
42. Hare, MS. Itinerary, 1806–29, B-PP. Hare dated many letters from South Audley Street.
43. Quoted in [Maurice], "Introduction," p. xiii.
44. Hare to Lady Jones, Jan. 1820, in *Memorials,* I, p. 195, *cf.* p. 191.
45. Quoted in *ibid.,* I, pp. 166–67.
46. Quoted in *ibid.,* I, p. 167.
47. Georgiana Hare-Naylor to Mrs Flaxman, 30 March 1805, BL Add. MS. 39781, f. 419; *cf. Memorials,* I, pp. 163 *et passim.*
48. E.P. Eardley Wilmot and E.C. Streatfield, *Charterhouse Old and New* (London, 1895), pp. 38–39; W.F. Taylor, *The Charterhouse of London* (London, 1912), pp. xiii–xiv, 251; A.H. Tod, *The Charterhouse* (London, 1900), chap. 1; N. Carlisle, *A Concise Description of the Endowed Grammar Schools of England and Wales* (London, 1818), II, pp. 2–19; M. Seaborne, *The English School: Its Architecture and Organisation* (Toronto, 1971), I, pp. 45–47.
49. Quoted in J.C. Marshman, *Memoirs of Major-General Sir Henry Havelock* (London, 1891), p. 6; *cf.* J.L. Smith-Dampier, *Carthusian Worthies* (Oxford, 1940), pp. 153–54.
50. *Thirlwall,* p. 9; *cf.* C. Thirlwall, *Letters Literary and Theological of Connop Thirlwall,* ed. J.J.S. Perowne and L. Stokes (London, 1881), p. 2.
51. Sir William Norris, *On the Meeting of Three Schoolfellows and Friends, After a Separation of Forty Years* (Np. 1850), p. 14 n. 1. See M.L. Clarke, *Richard Porson* (Cambridge, 1937), pp. 11, 34, 54.
52. Marshman, *Havelock,* p. 6, *cf.* p. 3. Note the precocity of Thirlwall, three years younger than the others. Thirlwall, *Letters,* p. 2.
53. Carlisle, *Endowed Grammer Schools,* II, p. 13.
54. M.L. Clarke, *George Grote: A Biography* (London, 1962), pp. 5–6.
55. *Idem., Greek Studies in England, 1700–1830* (Cambridge, 1945), p. 14, citing William Field's *Memoirs . . . of the Rev. Samuel Parr* (London, 1828), II, p. 82.
56. G.S. Davies, *Charterhouse in London* (London, 1921), p. 263; Clarke, *George Grote,* p. 5.
57. T.W. Bamford, "Public Schools and Social Class, 1801–1850," *British Journal of Sociology,* XII, no. 3 (Sept. 1961), 229 ff.

58. Hare, MS. Commonplace Book, 1816–18, ff. 58–59, B-PP.
59. Davies, *Charterhouse in London,* pp. 264 ff.; Carlisle, *Endowed Grammar Schools,* II, p. 8; Wilmot and Streatfield, *Charterhouse,* p. 167; Seaborne, *English School,* I, pp. 166–67, 192 n. 13.
60. G.N. Ray, *The Buried Life: A Study of the Relation between Thackeray's Fiction and His Personal History* (London, 1952), pp. 14–15 *et passim;* Clarke, *George Grote,* p. 7.
61. Marshman, *Havelock,* pp. 3, 6; M. Edgeworth, *Maria Edgeworth: Letters from England, 1813–1844,* ed. C. Colvin (Oxford, 1971), pp. 136–37, xxxv, describes her meeting with Hare and his enthusiasm for the Charterhouse.

Chapter 2

1. J. and J.A. Venn, eds., *Alumni Cantabrigiensis* (Cambridge, 1922–54), pt. II, vol. III, p. 241. For "pensioner," see *OED.* On the enrolment, see V.A. Huber, *The English Universities* (London, 1843), vol. II, pt. 2, p. 505.
2. Francis Hare to Augustus Hare, Nov. 1812, in *Memorials,* I. p. 190. On student credit and debt, see S. Rothblatt, "The Student Sub-culture and the Examination System in Early 19th Century Oxbridge," in *The University and Society,* vol. I: *Oxford and Cambridge,* ed. L. Stone (Princeton, 1974), pp. 249–50, 273–76.
3. N.G. Annan, "The Intellectual Aristocracy," in *Studies in Social History,* ed. J.H. Plumb (London, 1955), pp. 243, 284–86; *cf.* J. Barzun, *The House of Intellect* (New York, 1959), pp. 10–11; W.F. Cannon, "Scientists and Broad Churchmen: An Early Victorian Intellectual Network," *Journal of British Studies,* IV, no. 1 (Nov. 1964), 69–76 ff.; *idem.,* "The Role of the Cambridge Movement in Early 19th Century Science," in *Acts of the 10th International Congress of the History of Science* (Ithaca, 1962), 317–20; S. Rothblatt, *Tradition and Change in English Liberal Education* (London, 1976), p. 119; R. Robson, "Trinity College in the Age of Peel," in *Ideas and Institutions of Victorian Britain,* ed. R. Robson (London, 1967), 312–16; W.W. Rowse Ball, *Trinity College, Cambridge* (London, 1906), pp. 89–90 ff.; G.M. Trevelyan, *Trinity College: An Historical Sketch* (Cambridge, 1946), pp. 76–82, 86–89.
4. R. Robson and W.F. Cannon, "William Whewell, F.R.S. (1794–1866)," *Notes and Records of the Royal Society of London,* XIX, no. 2 (Dec. 1964), 168; Mrs J.M. Stair Douglas, *Life and Selections from the Correspondence of William Whewell* (London, 1881), pp. 8–9 *et passim;* J.W. Clark, *Old Friends at Cambridge* (London, 1900), pp. 20–21; A.G. Clark, "William Whewell," *Macmillans Magazine,* XIII (April 1866), 546; *Memorials,* I, p. 190.
5. W.W. Rowse Ball, *A History of Mathematics at Cambridge* (Cambridge, 1889), chap. 7, pp. 117–28; D.S.L. Cardwell, *Organisation of Science in England,* 2nd ed. (London, 1972), pp. 53–56; C. Babbage,

NOTES TO CHAPTER 2

Passages from the Life of a Philosopher (London, 1864), pp. 28–29; G.B. Airy, *Autobiography of George Biddle Airy* (Cambridge, 1896), pp. 45–48.

6. J. Bateman, *Life of Henry Venn Elliott*, 3rd ed. (London, 1872), pp. 24–25, 86, 259–62; J.W. Burgon, *Lives of Twelve Good Men* (London, 1888), I, pp. 124–25; M.A. Lower, *Worthies of Sussex* (Lewes, 1865), pp. 181–83; W.S. Walker, *Poetical Remains of William Sidney Walker . . . with a Memoir*, ed. J. Moultrie (London, 1852), pp. viii *et passim;* B.H. Holland, *Memoir of Kenelm Henry Digby* (London, 1919), pp. 11, 81–82; [Maurice], "Introduction," p. xvii; Stanley, p. 5; *Memorials*, I, p. 190; Digby to Whewell, on the death of Hare [Jan. 1855], WP/TCL Add. MS. a203.14.

7. Quoted in J.W. Clark and T. McK. Hughes, *Life and Letters of the Reverend Adam Sedgwick* (Cambridge, 1890), II, p. 496, *cf.* I, p. 280; *Memorials*, I, p. 190; [J.M.F. Wright], *Alma Mater* (London, 1827), I, pp. 125–27.

8. Whewell to his father, 17 Feb. 1813, in Stair Douglas, *Whewell*, pp. 8–10.

9. Hare, MS. Commonplace Book, ff. 9, 18, 41, B-PP; *cf.* J. Clive, *Scotch Reviewers: The* Edinburgh Review, *1802–15* (London, 1957), pp. 156–60, 162–64.

10. Hare, MS. Commonplace Book, ff. 121, 16–17, B-PP.

11. *Ibid.*, f. 161.

12. *Ibid.*, f. 117 [emphasis added], *cf.* ff. 38, 116 *verso*.

13. Quoted in V.H.H. Green, *Religion at Oxford and Cambridge* (London, 1964), p. 253; *cf.* Hare, MS. Commonplace Book, f. 99, B-PP; J. Roach, ed., *Victoria County History of Cambridge*, vol. III: *The City and University of Cambridge* (London, 1959), pp. 257–58; C. Smyth, *Simeon and Church Order* (Cambridge, 1940), p. 109; C.A. Bristed, *Five Years in an English University* (New York, 1852), II, pp. 36, 44, 55–56.

14. Hare, MS. Commonplace Book, ff. 22–25, B-PP.

15. *Ibid.* The "curses" were slavery and civil disabilities for Roman Catholics.

16. *Ibid.*, ff. 111, 10–11, 129, 162.

17. Quoted in P. Cradock, *Recollections of the Cambridge Union, 1815–1939* (Cambridge, 1953), pp. 7–10, 169; *cf.* D.A. Winstanley, *Early Victorian Cambridge* (Cambridge, 1940), pp. 25–28; Rothblatt, "Student Subculture," pp. 266–68; E.P. Thompson, *Making of the English Working Class* (New York, 1963), pp. 639–42; O. Teichman, *The Cambridge Undergraduate 100 Years Ago* (Cambridge, 1926), pp. 85–90; *Thirlwall*, p. 16.

18. B.Q. Morgan and A.R. Hohlfeld, *German Literature in English Magazines, 1750–1860* (Madison, 1949), p, 37; V. Stockley, *German Literature as Known in England, 1750–1830* (London, 1929), pp. 2–3.

19. F. Ewen, *The Prestige of Schiller in England, 1788–1859* (New York, 1952), pp. 129, 168.

20. Lady Blennerhassett, *Madame De Staël* (London, 1889), III, pp.

435–36; Morgan and Hohlfeld, *German Literature*, pp. 50, 52, 115, 119; F.W. Stokoe, *German Influence in the English Romantic Period, 1788–1818* (Cambridge, 1926), pp. 18, 33 ff., 89 ff.; Stockley, *German Literature*, pp. 7–13; E. Jaeck, *Madame De Staël and the Spread of German Literature* (New York, 1915), pp. 141–62; Ewen, *Prestige of Schiller*, pp. 168–69; *Thirlwall*, p. 28.

21. C.H. Firth, *Modern Languages at Oxford, 1724–1929* (London, 1929), pp. 1–19; H.P. Liddon, *Life of Edward Bouverie Pusey* (London, 1894–98), I, p. 72.

22. Winstanley, *Early Victorian Cambridge*, p. 175; *Thirlwall*, p. 29; H. Gunning, *Reminiscences of the University, Town, and County of Cambridge*, 2nd ed. (London, 1855), II, pp. 270–72; G. Pryme, *Autobiographical Recollections of George Pryme* (Cambridge, 1870), p. 89.

23. *Memorials*, I, pp. 190–92; [Maurice], "Introduction," pp. xi–xiv.

24. Thirlwall, *Letters*, pp. 47–48.

25. Clark, *Old Friends*, pp. 92–93.

26. *Thirlwall*, p. 16.

27. McF/B, p. 165; Burgon, *Twelve Good Men*, I, pp. 133, 173; R.W. Church, *The Oxford Movement: Twelve Years, 1833–45*, 3rd ed. (London, 1892), pp. 96–97.

28. Stair Douglas, *Whewell*, pp. 20, 56; Bristed, *Five Years*, II, p. 26; Rowse Ball, *Mathematics at Cambridge*, pp. 181–82, 190–93, 209; W. Whewell, *Of a Liberal Education in General*, 2nd ed. (London, 1850), pp. 169–97; Pryme, *Autobiographical Recollections*, p. 90; Rothblatt, "Student Sub-culture," pp. 283–88; *idem., Revolution of the Dons: Cambridge and Society* (New York, 1968), pp. 184–89.

29. Hare, MS. Commonplace Book, ff. 16–17, 121, B-PP; *Memorials*, I, p. 192; Plumptre, p. xxi.

30. Thirlwall, *Letters*, p. 22; Clark, *Old Friends*, p. 95.

31. Maria Edgeworth, 3 Nov. 1818, in Edgeworth, *Letters*, p. 136.

32. Hare to Whewell, 12 Aug. 1818, WP/TCL MS. 0.18.M6.23.

33. Hare, MS. Itinerary, B-PP; Whewell to Hare, 25 Feb. 1819, WP/TCL MS. 0.18.W2.2; Sheepshanks to Whewell [1819], WP/TCL Add. MS. a213.61.

34. Plumptre, p. xxiii; *cf. Memorials*, I, pp. 185, 194 ff.; Thirlwall, *Letters*, pp. 52–53; Whewell to Hare, 26 July 1818, WP/TCL MS. 0.18.W2.1.

Chapter 3

1. Hare, MS. Itinerary, B-PP; Whewell to Hare, 29 Nov. 1820, WP/TCL MS. 0.18.W2.5.

2. [Hare, trans.], introd. to *Sintram and His Companions: A Romance*, by Baron de la Motte Fouqué (London, 1820), pp. i–iii.

3. Whewell to Hare [postmarked 1 July 1820], WP/TCL MS. 0.18.W2.4.

NOTES TO CHAPTER 3

4. Soane in *Minstrel Love*, quoted in Stockley, *German Literature*, pp. 231–32.

5. [Hare], introd. to *Sintram*, by Fouqué, p. xiii.

6. McF/A, pp. 48–50; *cf.* Stockley, *German Literature*, pp. 231–32.

7. Stockley, *German Literature*, p. 231.

8. B.Q. Morgan, *A Critical Bibliography of German Literature in English Translation, 1481–1927*, 2nd ed. (Palo Alto, 1938), p. 119.

9. *Guesses*, pp. 215, 522–23, 366.

10. Stockley, *German Literature*, pp. 227–29; McF/A, p. 48.

11. Thirlwall to Hare, 30 Nov. 1824, in Thirlwall, *Letters* p. 83.

12. Fouqué said the inspiration for *Sintram* was Dürer's woodcut "The Knight and Death." See J.W. MacKail, *Life of William Morris* (London, 1899), I, p. 41.

13. McF/A, pp. 50–51.

14. Hare to Charles Ollier [postmarked 1819], Boston, Mass., Public Library MSS.

15. *Olliers Literary Miscellany*, no. 1 (London, 1820), 1–39, 90–153, 54–61. Hare's own marked copy is in the TCL. Translations by Hare of two other idylls by Fouqué survive in manuscript in B-PP and Beinecke Library, Yale University, MS. Lloyd (Tinker) 1501.

16. Hare to Charles Ollier [1820], Boston, Mass., Public Library MSS.

17. McF/A, pp. 52–53; MS. shelflist of the Hare Collection, ff. 34/116–46, TCL.

18. Quoted in McF/A, p. 53.

19. MCF/A, pp. 45, 47, 52; *cf. Memorials* II, p. 85; C.R. Sanders, *Coleridge and the Broad Church Movement* (Durham, N.C., 1942), p. 126.

20. L.E. Watson, *Coleridge at Highgate* (London, 1925), pp. 83–84 ff.; R.W. Armour and R.F. Howes, *Coleridge the Talker* (New York, 1969), pp. 235–37, 339–45; McF/A, pp. 55–56; T. Carlyle, *Life of John Sterling* (London, 1904), pp. 52–62; F.D. Maurice to unknown correspondent, 3 Aug. 1855, University of Kansas Library MS.; B. Willey, *S.T. Coleridge* (London, 1972), p. 256.

21. Sanders, *Coleridge and the Broad Church Movement*, p. 123; *cf. Memorials*, I, p. 194; [Maurice], "Introduction," p. xviii; Plumptre, p. xxi.

22. *Guesses*, pp. ix–xi; Plumptre, p. xxii; Wordsworth to Landor, 21 Jan. 1824, FP/V.&A. MS. 48.E.2.52, and printed in part in W. and D. Wordsworth, *Letters of William and Dorothy Wordsworth, 1821–50*, ed. E. de Selincourt (Oxford, 1939), I, p. 136.

23. E. Blunden, *Keats' Publisher: A Memoir of John Taylor* (London, 1936), pp. 123–31; McF/A, p. 56; McF/B, p. 167; see also T. Chilcott, *A Publisher and His Circle: The Life and Work of John Taylor* (London, 1972), pp. 129–35 ff.; T. Hood, *Letters of Thomas Hood*, ed. P.F. Morgan (Toronto, 1973), pp. 65 nn. 2, 6; J. Bauer, *The London Magazine, 1820–29* (Copenhagen, 1953), p. 334; J.L. Cherry, *Life and Remains of John Clare* (London, 1873), p. 43.

24. H.J. Rose to Whewell, 10 Dec. 1820, WP/TCL Add. MS. a211.230;

Hare, MS. Itinerary, B-PP; *Memorials,* I, p. 192 ff., misdates this journey as 1819–20; Hare, MS. Travel Diary, 1832–33, p. 201, B-PP.

25. Thorp to Whewell, Genoa, 27 April 1822, WP/TCL MS. 0.18.T1.37; Whewell to Hare, 12 May 1822, *ibid.,* 0.18.W2.6; Hare, MS. Intinerary, B-PP.

26. Hare to Whewell, 30 April [1822], WP/TCL Add. MS. a77.126 [emphasis added]; *cf. Thirlwall,* pp. 38–40. Thirlwall underwent the same disenchantment with the law, and poured it out in letters. Thirlwall to Bunsen, 20 Jan. 1823, TCL MS. 0.15.44.3; Thirlwall to Hare, 29 May and 28 Oct. 1823, *ibid.,* 0.15.44.13–14, the last printed in Thirlwall, *Letters,* p. 70.

27. Whewell to Hare, 12 May 1822, WP/TCL MS. 0.18.W2.6.

28. Hare to Whewell [postmarked 13 May 1822], *ibid.,* Add. MS. a77.127.

29. Hare to Whewell [postmarked 16 July 1822], *ibid.,* Add. MS. a77.128.

30. Thirlwall to Hare, 8 Nov. 1822, in Thirlwall, *Letters,* pp. 61–62; *cf.* Whewell to Hare, 17 July 1822, WP/TCL MS. 0.18.W2. 7.

Chapter 4

1. [Maurice], "Introduction," p. v; Stanley, pp. 4–6. On "sides," see Bristed, *Five Years,* I, pp. 14–15.

2. [Maurice], "Introduction," pp. vi–x. Maurice's memoir (pp. vi–x) was reprinted in *Maurice,* I, pp. 52–55.

3. [Maurice], "Introduction," pp. vii–viii.

4. Maurice to his mother, Oct. 1823, in *Maurice,* I, p. 48.

5. H.J. Rose to Whewell, 25 Oct. 1822, WP/TCL Add. MS. a211.135.

6. Quoted in Earl of Lytton, *Life of Edward Bulwer, First Lord Lytton* (London, 1913), I, p. 74.

7. Thackeray attended Hare's lectures. W.M. Thackeray, *Letters and Papers of W.M. Thackeray,* ed. G.N. Ray (Cambridge, Mass., 1945), I, p. 43 and n. 41; Ray, *Thackeray: The Uses of Adversity, 1811–46* (New York, 1955), pp. 115–38.

8. H. Tennyson, *Alfred Tennyson: A Memoir,* new ed. (London, 1906), p. 59.

9. F.M. Brookfield, *Cambridge "Apostles"* (London, 1906), p. 4. See, for preference, P.R. Allen, *The Cambridge Apostles: The Early Years* (Cambridge, forthcoming).

10. Brookfield, *Apostles,* pp. 204–05; *Maurice,* I, pp. 56, 176; H. Tennyson, *Tennyson,* pp. 36–37; C. Tennyson, *Alfred Tennyson,* 2nd ed. (London, 1968), pp. 68–74; A. and E.M. Sidgwick, *Henry Sidgwick: A Memoir* (London, 1906), pp. 29–31, 34–35, 403.

11. Marginal MS. note quoted in J.W. Adamson, *English Education, 1789–1902,* 2nd ed. (Cambridge, 1964), pp. 72–73.

12. C. Merivale, *Autobiography and Letters* (Oxford, 1898), pp. 97–99, *cf.* pp. 301–02; Brookfield, *Apostles,* pp. 8, 13–14; *Thirlwall,* pp. 54–59.

13. *Maurice*, I, pp. 176, 56; Hare, MS. Commonplace Book, f. 41, B-PP; *Guesses*, pp. 416–18; Hare, MS. Travel Diary, p. 219, B-PP; Carlyle, *Life of Sterling*, pp. 32–33.
14. *Guesses*, p. 519, *cf.* pp. 147–49.
15. Hare, "The Children of Light," in *Sermons Preacht on Particular Occasions* (London, 1858), pp. 3–7, 12–13; *cf.* Plumptre, pp. xxvii–xxviii.
16. Plumptre, p. xxvii. Joseph Romilly, Bursar of Trinity College, recorded his praise for the sermon in his diary. Romilly's diary, 30 Nov. 1828, CUL Add. MS. 6809. Romilly's diary runs from 1818 to 1864, CUL. Add. MS. 6804–42. For excerpts, see *Romilly's Cambridge Diary, 1832–42*, ed. J.P.T. Bury (Cambridge, 1967).
17. M.L. Clarke, *Paley: Evidences for the Man* (London, 1974), pp. 128 ff.
18. [F.D. Maurice], "The children of Light," *Athenaeum*, II, no. 62 (31 Dec. 1828), 977–78.
19. Hare, "The Law of Self Sacrifice," in *Sermons Preacht*, pp. 49, 79–80, 81; *cf.* Hare, MS. Commonplace Book, f. 99, B-PP.
20. Hare to Whewell, 30 April 1822, WP/TCL Add. MS. a77.126.
21. Hare, "Education the Necessity of Mankind," in *Miscellaneous Pamphlets on Some of the Leading Questions Agitated in the Church during the Last Ten Years* (Cambridge, 1855), p. 6.
22. *Guesses*, p. 236.
23. *Thirlwall*, pp. 57–58.
24. A. Momigliano, *Studies in Historiography* (London, 1966), p. 62.
25. CUL Archives and Registry MSS. 39.4, ff. 30.1–4.
26. *Ibid.*, 39.4, f. 30.3a.
27. Walker, *Poetical Remains*, pp. lxxx–lxxxii.
28. John Croft to Joseph Romilly, 2 May 1853, CUL Archives and Registrary MS. 39.4, f. 31. Credit for discovering this document is due Professor McFarland. McF/A, p. 74 n. 1.
29. For more on Hare's politics, see my "Julius Charles Hare and the 'Broad Church' Ideal," in *The View from the Pulpit: Victorian Ministers and Society*, ed. P.T. Phillips (Toronto, 1978), pp. 45–65. For university politics, see Winstanley, *Early Victorian Cambridge*; Pryme, *Autobiographical Recollections*; and Clark and Hughes, *Life of Sedgwick*.
30. Burgon, *Twelve Good Men*, I, p. 129; *cf.* Thirlwall, p. 75.
31. J.H. Newman, *Apologia Pro Vita Sua* (Garden City, N.Y., 1956), pp. 153–56; *cf.* Burgon, *Twelve Good Men*, I, p. 133.
32. Clarke, *Greek Studies in England*, p. 101.
33. Clark and Hughes, *Life of Sedgwick*, I, p. 280; *cf.* Bateman, *Life of Elliott*, pp. 86–87; Holland, *Digby*, p. 11.
34. *Guesses*, pp. 163–64. See Holland, *Digby*, pp. 10, 12, 43, 60–61 ff., 81–82; Lytton, *Life of Edward Bulwer*, I, pp. 73, 78–79; D. Coleridge, *Poems of W.M. Praed, with a Memoir* (London, 1864), I, pp. xv–xviii; D. Hudson, *Poet in Parliament: The Life of W.M. Praed* (London, 1939), pp. 86–90; J. Clive, *Macaulay: The Shaping of the Historian* (New York, 1974), pp. 46–47.

35. Hare to Lady Malcolm, n.d. WP/TCL Add. MS. a57.8+2; *cf.* Holland, *Digby,* p. 43.
36. Holland, *Digby,* pp. 46–47; Burgon, *Twelve Good Men,* I, pp. 174–76; G. Faber, *Oxford Apostles* (London, 1974), pp. 348–49; Y. Brilioth, *Anglican Revival: Studies in the Oxford Movement* (London, 1925), pp. 27–28; Newman, *Apologia,* pp. 153–56.
37. Quoted in R.E. Prothero, *Life and Correspondence of Arthur Penrhyn Stanley* (London, 1893), I, pp. 135–37.
38. R.H. Froude, *Remains of the Late Reverend Richard Hurrell Froude* [ed. J.H. Newman and J. Keble] (London, 1838–39), I, p. 310. Initials identified in L.I. Guiney, *Hurrell Froude* (London, 1904), p. 103 and n. 5; *cf. Memorials,* III, p. 224.
39. Romilly's dirary, CUL Add. MS. 6805, *passim;* Clark, *Old Friends,* pp. 41–43.
40. Walker, *Poetical Remains,* pp. civ–cvi.
41. J.W. Kaye, *Life and Correspondence of Major-General Sir John Malcolm* (London, 1856), II, pp. 415–18; Clark and Hughes, *Life of Sedgwick,* II, p. 327.
42. *Guesses,* p. 528; *cf. Memorials,* I, p. 203; Kaye, *Life of Malcolm,* II, pp. 417–22; Clark and Hughes, *Life of Sedgwick,* I, p. 283; Hare, MS. Travel Diary, pp. 215–17, B–PP; Thirlwall, *Letters,* pp. 251–52; Plumptre, p. xxvi.
43. Quoted in Stair Douglas, *Whewell,* pp. 86–87.
44. Sheepshanks to Whewell, n.d., WP/TCL Add. MS. a213.80.
45. *Story,* I, pp. 248–49, *cf.* pp. 249–50; *Memorials,* I, p. 204.
46. *Memorials,* I, p. 205; *cf. Story,* I. p. 158. III, pp. 127–28; Hare, MS. Itinerary, B-PP.
47. *Memorials,* I, pp. 321, 410, 432.
48. Quoted in Hudson, *Praed,* p. 137; *cf.* Hare, MS. Itinerary, B-PP.
49. Hudson, *Praed,* pp. 137–39; Plumptre, p. xxvii; *Memorials,* III, p. 228.
50. *Story,* I, pp. 16–17, 18, 28–33, 158–59, IV, p. 18; *Memorials,* I, pp. 261–65.
51. *Story,* I, p. 484; *Memorials,* II, pp. 363–64; TCL MS. Conclusions Book, pt. II, 1811–86; Winstanley, *Early Victorian Cambridge,* p. 426.
52. Hare to Charles Ollier [1820], Beinecke Library, Yale University, MS. Lloyd (Tinker) 1501.

Chapter 5

1. J. Forster, *Walter Savage Landor: A Biography* (London, 1869), II, pp. 2–3; *cf.* R. Super, *Walter Savage Landor: A Biography* (London, 1957), p. 131.
2. Quoted in Forster, *Landor,* II, p. 2. See also *Story,* II, p. 407; Super, *Landor,* pp. 490, 505–06.

NOTES TO CHAPTER 5

3. A.L. Prasher, "The Censorship of Landor's *Imaginary Conversations*," *Bulletin of the John Rylands Library*, XLIX, no. 2 (spring 1967), 427 n. 2; *cf.* Forster, *Landor*, II, p. 11.

4. Forster, *Landor*, II, pp. 11–12, 14–15; Super, *Landor*, pp. 159–60; Prasher, "Censorship," p. 427; McF/A, p. 61; McF/B, p. 166; R. Super, *The Publication of Landor's Works*, Supplement to the Bibliographical Society's *Transactions*, no. 18 (London, 1954), pp. 31–40 ff.

5. Super, *Landor*, pp. 160, 184; Prasher, "Censorship," pp. 428, 463; McF/A, p. 61.

6. Hare to Taylor, 3 March [1823], RLEMS 1238:1; full transcription in Prasher, "Censorship," pp. 428–29; *cf.* Forster, *Landor*, II, p. 19.

7. Hare to Taylor, 4 March [postmarked 1823], RLEMS 1238:2. Hare misdated this and the previous letter. Taylor's reply, dated 4 March, is given in Blunden, *Keats' Publisher*, p. 157; *cf.* Hare to Whewell, 21 Jan. [1823], WP/TCL MS. 0.18.M6.27.

8. Hare to Taylor, 15 April [1823], RLEMS 1238:3.

9. Prasher, "Censorship," pp. 429–30, misdates this as 1 April. Blunden, *Keats' Publisher*, pp. 157–58, gives 16 April 1823, a more plausible dating.

10. Hare to Taylor, 19 April 1823, RLEMS 1238:5.

11. Prasher, "Censorship," pp. 430–34; Blunden, *Keats' Publisher*, pp. 158–59.

12. Hare to Taylor, 27 April [1823], RLEMS 1238:8.

13. Taylor to Hare, 2 May 1823, *ibid.*, 1238:62; Hare to Taylor [5 May 1823], *ibid.*, 1238:9; Super, *Landor*, pp. 46, 162–64 ff.; Prasher, "Censorship," pp. 435–36; Forster, *Landor*, II, pp. 20 ff.; McF/A, pp. 61–63; *cf.* R. Southey, *Selections from the Letters of Robert Southey*, ed. J.W. Warter (London, 1856), III, pp. 388–89.

14. Hare to Southey, 5 June [1823], RLEMS 1238:59; *cf.* Hare to Taylor [?1 June 1823], *ibid.*, 1238:15.

15. Hare to Taylor [postmarked 30 June 1823], *ibid.*, 1238:16.

16. Hare to Taylor [summer 1823], [autumn 1823], [Oct. 1823], and [late 1824], *ibid.*, 1238:58, 38, 14, 6; Hare to John Hessey [postmarked 29 Oct. 1823], *ibid.*, 1238:4; Super, *Landor*, p. 163; Prasher, "Censorship," pp. 445–46.

17. Hare to Taylor [summer 1823], RLEMS 1238:46; *cf.* Taylor to Southey, 4 July 1823, *ibid.*, 1238:69; Forster, *Landor*, II, p. 19; Prasher, "Censorship," pp. 438–39.

18. *London Magazine*, VIII, no. 1 (July 1823), 5–9, 109; Bauer, *The London Magazine*, pp. 161–62 and n. 7; Wordsworth to Landor, 1824–25, FP/V.&A. MSS. 48.E.2:50–52; Forster, *Landor*, II, pp. 23–24.

19. Hare to Taylor [postmarked 21 July 1824], RLEMS 1238:11; *cf.* Forster, *Landor*, II, p. 23.

20. Wordsworth to Landor, 21 Jan. 1824, FP/V.&A. MS. 48.E.2:52; *cf.* Thirlwall to Hare, 29 May 1823, TCL MS. 0.15.44.13.

21. Hare to Taylor, 3 March [1823], RLEMS 1238:1; Forster, *Landor*, II, p. 86; *cf. Guesses*, p. 11 n. 1.

NOTES TO CHAPTER 5

22. Forster, *Landor*, II, pp. 87–88; Super, *Landor*, p. 168; Prasher, "Censorship," pp. 448 and n. 1, 449; McF/A, p. 64.
23. [Hare], "On Walter Savage Landor's *Imaginary Conversations*," *London Magazine*, IX, no. 5 (May 1824), 523–41. See Robinson, *Henry Crabb Robinson on Books and Their Writers*, ed. E.J. Morley (London, 1938), I, p. 305; Forster, *Landor*, II, pp. 89–90; Super, *Landor*, pp. 168–69; Prasher, "Censorship," p. 449; McF/A, pp. 64–66; R.B. Clark, *William Gifford: Tory Satirist, Critic, and Editor* (New York, 1930), p. 235; H. Taylor, *Autobiography of Henry Taylor* (London, 1885), I, pp. 95–96; H. Taylor, *Correspondence of Henry Taylor*, ed. E. Dowden (London, 1888), pp. 292–93; Hare to Taylor [postmarked 16 April 1824], RLEMS 1238:18.
24. Taylor to Hare, 12 July 1824, in Blunden, *Keats' Publisher*, pp. 160–61; Forster, *Landor*, II, pp. 144–46; Super, *Landor*, p. 181; Prasher, "Censorship," pp. 450–51.
25. Hare to Taylor, 26 Nov. [1824], RLEMS 1238:12.
26. Hare to Taylor [Nov. or Dec. 1824], *ibid.*, 1238:6. Prasher, "Censorship," p. 451, has extracts from Taylor's intervening letter.
27. Taylor to Hare, 19 April 1825, RLEMS 1238:64; Prasher, "Censorship," pp. 454–56; Forster, *Landor*, II, pp. 150–51; Super, *Landor*, pp. 181–82; McF/A, pp. 66–67; Blunden, *Keats' Publisher*, p. 162.
28. Landor to Southey, 11 April 1825, in Forster, *Landor*, II, p. 152.
29. Forster, *Landor*, II, pp. 150–53; Super, *Landor*, pp. 182–84; Prasher, "Censorship," pp. 453–54; Blunden, *Keats' Publisher*, pp. 161–64.
30. Hare to Taylor [April 1825], RLEMS 1238:48.
31. Taylor to Hare, 19 April 1825, *ibid.*, 1238:64.
32. Hare to Taylor, 20 April [postmarked 21 April 1825], *ibid.*, 1238:24; *cf.* McF/A, pp. 67–68; Prasher, "Censorship," pp. 457–58.
33. Hare to Landor, 21 April 1825, in Forster, *Landor*, II, pp. 156–57; *cf.* Prasher, "Censorship," pp. 457–58; Taylor to and from Landor of Rugeley [1825], RLEMS 1238:63, 66–68.
34. Hare to Taylor [21 April 1825], RLEMS 1238:55; *cf.* Landor to Hare [1825], B-PP.
35. Hare to Taylor [postmarked 26 April 1825], RLEMS 1238:25; *cf.* Taylor to Hare [23/4 April 1825], in Forster, *Landor*, II, p. 159.
36. Prasher, "Censorship," p. 463; McF/A, pp. 68–69.
37. Hare to Landor [1825], in Forster, *Landor*, II, p. 160; *cf.* Landor to Hare, 7 April 1825, B-PP; Super, *Landor*, p. 184.
38. Landor to Hare [1825], B-PP.
39. Super, *Publication of Landor's Works*, pp. 41–44; Forster, *Landor*, II, pp. 161–66.
40. Hare to Taylor [postmarked 28 Nov. 1828], RLEMS 1238:28.
41. Hare to Landor, July 1829, in Forster, *Landor*, II, pp. 166–67; *cf.* Super, *Publication of Landor's Works*, pp. 44–45; Hare to Robinson, 8 Jan. 1832, Dr Williams's Library, H.C. Robinson Papers; Robinson, *On Books*, I, p. 401.

Chapter 6

1. First series May 1827, revised by Julius Hare 1838 and 1840; second series 1848. Citations here are to the 1866 edition. Julius Hare's contributions in later editions of the first series are signed "U." *NCBEL*, III, pp. 1282–83; *CHEL*, XII, p. 301. McF/B, pp. 168–74, has the best summary of the *Guesses*. For analysis of the romantic theory in the *Guesses*, see R.O. Preyer, "Julius Hare and Coleridgean Criticism," *Journal of Aesthetics and Art Criticism*, XV, no. 4 (June 1957), 449–60.

2. McF/B, pp. 169–70; Sanders, *Coleridge and the Broad Church Movement*, pp. 123–24 *et passim*.

3. McF/B, pp. 165, 168–69.

4. Augustus Hare to Taylor [early 1826], RLEMS 1238:79; *cf.* McF/B, p. 169.

5. *Guesses,* pp. ix–xi.

6. Wordsworth to Hare [postmarked 29 May 1838], B-PP.

7. *Guesses*, p. xiii.

8. Hare to Lucy Hare [1838?], in *Memorials*, III, pp. 229–31.

9. Hare to Taylor [1826], RLEMS 1238:36, 50, 52; Augustus Hare to Taylor [1826], *ibid.,* 1238:76, 79.

10. Sheepshanks to Whewell, 2 June 1827, WP/TCL Add. MS. a213.81; *cf.* Hare to Whewell [May 1827], *ibid.,* 0.18.H2.6; Hare to Taylor [1827], RLEMS 1238:60; McF/B, pp. 169 and n. 3, 174.

11. Southey to C.W.W. Wynn, M.P., 16 Nov. 1827, in Southey, *Letters,* II, p. 72; *cf.* R. Southey, *New Letters of Robert Southey*, ed. K. Curry (New York, 1965), II, p. 326.

12. Hare to Taylor [postmarked 14 Nov. 1828], RLEMS 1238:26.

13. [F.D. Maurice], "Guesses at Truth," *Athenaeum*, II, no. 42 (13 Aug. 1828), 656–57.

14. McF/B, p. 174.

15. Hare, MS. Commonplace Book, ff. 11, 18, 39–42, 44, 52 *et passim,* B-PP.

16. See my "The *Philological Museum* of 1831–1833," *Victorian Periodicals Newsletter*, no. 18 (Dec. 1972), 27–30; J.E.B. Mayer, "Adversaria, I: Julius Charles Hare," *Journal of Classical and Sacred Philology*, II (1855), 330–33; Clarke, *Greek Studies in England*, p. 101; McF/B, pp. 184–85; *Thirlwall*, pp. 63–65.

17. Hare, MS. Commonplace Book, ff. 168 *verso*, 170, B-PP; Clarke, *Greek Studies in England*, p. 101; K. Dockhorn, *Der Deutschen Historismus in England* (Göttingen, 1950), p. 22.

18. [Hare], "Preface," *Philological Museum*, I, no. 1 (Nov. 1831), ii–iv.

19. Thirlwall to Bunsen, 21 Nov. 1831, TCL MS. 0.15.44.4 [emphasis added].

20. [Hare], "On English Orthography," *Philological Museum*, I, no. 3 (May 1832), 654, 662–64.

21. *Ibid.,* pp. 672–74, 677–78.

22. W.S. Landor, *Complete Works of Walter Savage Landor*, ed. T.E.

Welby (London, 1927–36), VI, pp. 12–13. This late dialogue appeared first in Landor's *Last Fruit off an Old Tree* (1853), and Hare acknowledged it as a fair statement of his orthographic discipleship. Hare to Landor, 8 Nov. 1853, FP/V.&A. MS. 247–48.E.2:19.

23. Hare to Taylor [spring 1823], RLEMS 1238:58.
24. [Hare], "English Orthography," p. 645; Landor, *Works*, VI, p. 16. See Stanley, p. 17; C. Fox, *Memories of Old Friends* (London, 1882), I, p. 239; A.F. Hort, *Life and Letters of Fenton John Anthony Hort* (London, 1896), I, p. 55; *Memorials*, I, p. 200.
25. Henry Alford, *Life, Journals and Letters of Henry Alford*, 2nd ed. (London, 1873), p. 85.
26. My thanks to Professors J. Clive and T. Pinney for identifying Ellis.
27. Lewis disputed Hare's interpretation of the genitive elision in "On English Preterites and Genitives," *Philological Museum*, II no. 1 (Nov. 1832), 224–62.
28. Arnold to Hare, 9 Nov. 1831, B-PP.
29. Arnold to Hare, 16 March 1832, *ibid*.
30. Thirlwall to Bunsen, 18 Dec. 1832, TCL MS. 0.15.44.5.
31. Thirlwall to Bunsen, 5 May 1833, *ibid.*, 0.15.44.6.
32. Thirlwall to Bunsen, 10 Oct. 1833, *ibid.*, 0.15.44.1.
33. Thirlwall to M.C.L., c/o W. Ogilvie, Bookseller, Glasgow, 17 Feb., 6 March, and 30 July 1834, National Library of Scotland MSS. 4947, ff. 221–22, 223–24, 227.
34. *Classical Museum: A Journal of Philology and of Ancient History and Literature*, 7 vols. (London, 1844–50). The trustees of the journal were Blakesley, Bunsen, Thirlwall, Hare, Stanley, Henry Labouchere, and A.C. Tait. Hare solicited contributions from John Kenrick. Hare to Kenrick, 10 Nov. 1843, Dr Williams's Library MS. 24.81.34.
35. Stanley, p. 4.
36. J.W. Burrow, "The Uses of Philology in Victorian England," in *Ideas and Institutions of Victorian Britain*, pp. 181–84 *et passim;* Rothblatt, *Tradition and Change*, pp. 166–68.

Chapter 7

1. McF/A, pp. 56–57.
2. McF/B, p. 165.
3. [Hare], "Preface," *Philological Museum*, I, no. 1 (Nov. 1831), ii.
4. Thirlwall to Bunsen, 20 Jan. 1823, TCL MS. 0.15.44.3, and in *Thirlwall*, p. 27.
5. Hare, *The Mission of the Comforter*, 4th ed. (London, 1877), pp. iii, xii; *Guesses, passim;* T. Carlyle, *Early Letters of Thomas Carlyle*, ed. C.E. Norton (London, 1886), II, p. 201; Sanders, *Coleridge and the Broad Church Movement*, pp. 126–28, 131; Willey, *Coleridge*, pp. 252–53, 257; S. Prickett, *Coleridge and Wordsworth: The Poetry of Growth* (Cambridge, 1970), pp. 3, 188; *idem., Romanticism and Religion: The*

Tradition of Coleridge and Wordsworth in the Victorian Church (Cambridge, 1976), passim.

6. McF/A, p. 59; E.H. Zeydel, *Ludwig Tieck: The German Romanticist* (Princeton, 1935), p. v; Morgan and Hohlfeld, *German Literature*, p. 107.

7. Hare to Charles Ollier [1820], Beinecke Library, Yale University, MS. Lloyd (Tinker) 1501.

8. Hare to Taylor, 21 July 1824, RLEMS 1238:11; cf. Hare to Taylor, 4 March and 19 April 1823, and 3 May 1824, ibid., 1238:2, 5, 21; McF/A, pp. 69–71; Morgan and Hohlfeld, *German Literature*, pp. 52, 59–60, 99; Stockley, *German Literature*, pp. 292–93.

9. *London Magazine*, X, nos. 2 and 3 (Aug. and Sept. 1824), 189–97, 291–307; Stockley, *German Literature*, p. 293; McF/A, p. 71; S. Howe, *Wilhelm Meister and His English Kinsmen: Apprentices to Life* (New York, 1930), pp. 98–99.

10. Susanna Howe claimed that Hare's reply, "feeble enough," appeared in the October 1824 issue of the *London Magazine*, but neither Professor McFarland nor I have been able to locate or identify it. Howe, *Wilhelm Meister*, p. 99; McF/A, pp. 71, 73 n. 1.

11. Howe, *Wilhelm Meister*, p. 99. See E.C. Want, "Frederick Denison Maurice and *Eustace Conway*," *Anglican Theological Review*, LIV, no. 4 (Oct. 1972), 330–42.

12. *Guesses*, p. 333; H.A. Page [pseud. of A.H. Japp], *Thomas De Quincey: His Life and Writings* (London, 1877), II, p. 239 and n.; Hare on De Quincey's plagiarism, National Library of Scotland MS. 1889, ff. 60–61.

13. *London Magazine*, IX, no. 5 (May 1824), 527–28. See L. Van T. Simmons, *Goethe's Lyric Poems in English Translation Prior to 1860* (Madison, 1919), pp. 41, 50, 128.

14. Hare to Taylor [autumn 1824], RLEMS 1238:6.

15. Hare to Taylor [spring 1825], ibid., 1238:37; Blunden, *Keats' Publisher*, pp. 123, 133; McF/A, pp. 72–73. For Hare's defence of Coleridge, see chap. XII

16. McF/A, pp. 74–76 ff., is an expert reconstruction of his whole episode.

17. C. Knight, *Passages of a Working Life during Half a Century* (London, 1864), I, pp. 280–82, 295 ff.; Coleridge, *Praed*, I, pp. xxxvi–xxxvii; McF/A, p. 74.

18. Plumptre, p. xxiv; McF/A, pp. 74–75.

19. Quoted in McF/A, pp. 75–76, from Clowe's *Charles Knight* (London, 1892). Hare told Taylor about finding another outlet for the Goethe essay. Hare to Taylor [spring 1825], RLEMS 1238:37. Hare also asked Taylor if he would publish the essay as a pamphlet. Hare to Taylor [spring 1825], New York Public Library, Berg Collection MS. 57B5708.

20. H.G. Merriam, *Edward Moxon: Publisher of Poets* (New York, 1939), p. 36; E.H. Zeydel, *Ludwig Tieck and England: A Study in the*

Literary Relations of Germany and England (Princeton, 1931), p. 154; McF/A, p. 76.

21. *Fraser's Magazine*, IV, no. 4 (Nov. 1831), 446–60. The *Wellesley Index* suggests that Sarah Austin may have been the reviewer.

22. Zeydel, *Ludwig Tieck and England*, pp. 154, 177, 219, 243; idem., *Ludwig Tieck: The German Romanticist*, pp. 289–90, 297.

23. H.K. Galinsky, "Is Thomas De Quincey the Author of *The Love-Charm?*" *Modern Language Notes*, LII, no. 6 (June 1937), 389–94; McF/A, pp. 77–81.

24. Morgan, *Critical Bibliography*, item 9376 p. 483; McF/A, p. 77.

25. *Thirlwall*, pp. 29–34; Brilioth, *Anglican Revival*, p. 92; McF/A, p. 57; Clark, *Old Friends*, p. 100.

26. O. Pfleiderer, *The Development of Theology in Germany since Kant, and Its Progress in Great Britain since 1825* (London, 1890), pp. 209–11.

27. P. Hazard, *The European Mind, 1680–1715* (Cleveland, 1963), pp. 40–48, 180–97.

28. Brilioth, *Anglican Revival*, p. 92; *Thirlwall*, pp. 225–36.

29. V.F. Storr, *Development of English Theology in the Nineteenth Century, 1800–1860* (London, 1913), pp. 183–85; T.P. Peardon, *Transition in English Historical Writing, 1760–1830* (New York, 1933), pp. 166–67.

30. Dockhorn, *Deutschen Historismus*, p. 19; *Thirlwall*, p. 29; Thirlwall, *Letters*, p. 76; Storr, *Development of English Theology*, pp. 183–84.

31. J.K.L. Gieseler, *Historisch-kritischer Versuch über die Entstehung des Evangelien* (1818).

32. F. Schleiermacher, *A Critical Essay on the Gospel of St. Luke* [trans. C. Thirlwall] (London, 1825), pp. 6–7, 10–15.

33. Thirlwall to Hare, 5 May 1824, National Library of Wales MS., and in Thirlwall, *Letters*, pp. 71–72 and n.; cf. Storr, *Development of English Theology*, pp. 186–87.

34. Storr, *Development of English Theology*, p. 111.

35. [Thirlwall], introd. to *A Critical Essay on . . . St. Luke*, by Schleiermacher, pp. xiii–ix, ix; cf. *Thirlwall*, p. 31.

36. S.T. Coleridge to E. Coleridge, 19 Jan. 1826, RLEMS 732:41.

37. Sermons published as H.J. Rose, *Discourses on the State of the Protestant Religion in Germany* (1825); Burgon, *Twelve Good Men*, I, p. 133; Newman, *Apologia*, pp. 153–54; *Thirlwall*, pp. 32–33.

38. Maurice to C. Fox, 25 Feb. 1848, in *Maurice*, I, pp. 453–54; cf. *Thirlwall*, pp. 32, 178.

39. *Thirlwall*, pp. 31–33.

40. Maria Hare to C. Stanley, 22 Dec. 1829, in *Memorials*, I, p. 328. *Thirlwall*, p. 33, incorrectly attributes this letter to A.W. Hare.

41. Robinson, *Diary*, III, pp. 90–92; cf. *Thirlwall*, p. 34.

42. Quoted in *Thirlwall*, p. 34, which gives the date as 1829; cf. Schleiermacher, *Life of Schleiermacher as Unfolded in His Autobiography and Letters*, trans. F. Rowan (London, 1860), II, pp. 316–17.

43. Thirlwall to Hare, 29 May 1823, TCL MS. 0.15.44.13, and in Thirlwall, *Letters*, pp. 69–70; Thirlwall to Hare, 5 May 1824, National Library of Wales MS., and in Thirlwall, *Letters*, pp. 71–72 and n.
44. Thirlwall to Hare, 28 July 1824, National Library of Wales MS., and in Thirlwall, *Letters* p. 72.
45. Thirlwall to Hare, 10 Oct. 1824, in Thirlwall, *Letters*, pp. 72–74.
46. Thirlwall to Hare, 16 Oct. 1824, in *ibid.*, p. 74.
47. Thirlwall to Hare, 31 Oct. 1824, in *ibid.*, pp. 74–76 [emphasis added].
48. Thirlwall to Hare, 1 Nov. 1824, in *ibid.*, p. 77.
49. Thirlwall to Hare, 12 Nov. 1824, in *ibid.*, pp. 78–79 [emphasis added].
50. Thirlwall to Hare, 26 Nov. 1824, in *ibid.*, pp. 79–80; Hare to Taylor [winter 1824–25], RLEMS 1238:6, 56. Curious typos nonetheless deface Thirlwall's book, *e.g.*, p. 16, line 29.
51. Hare to Taylor [late 1824], RLEMS 1238:6.
52. Hare to Whewell, 17 Oct. [1846], WP/TCL MS. 0.18.H2.28; *cf.* Hare, MS. Commonplace Book, f. 99, B-PP.

Chapter 8

1. Peardon, *English Historical Writing*, pp. 19–33; G.P. Gooch, *History and Historians in the Nineteenth Century*, rev. ed. (Boston, 1959), chap. 1.
2. Gooch, *History and Historians*, chap. 3; Dockhorn, *Deutschen Historismus*, pp. 22–23.
3. In addition to Dockhorn two works are essential to this topic: D. Forbes, *The Liberal Anglican Idea of History* (Cambridge, 1950), pp. vii–ix *et passim*; R.O. Preyer, *Bentham, Coleridge, and the Science of History* (Bochum-Langendreer, 1958), pp. 1–5 *et passim*. See also Forbes, "Historismus in England," *Cambridge Journal*, IV, no. 7 (April 1951), 387–400, a review of Dockhorn.
4. Gooch, *History and Historians*, pp. 14, 22–23; Preyer, *Science of History*, p. 28; *CHEL*, XII, p. 301.
5. B.G. Niebuhr, *History of Rome*, new ed. (London, 1851–55), III, pp. 213 *et passim*, I, pp. 54–56 *et passim*; Preyer, *Science of History*, p. 32 and n. 15; Forbes, *Liberal Anglican Idea*, pp. 15–17 *et passim*.
6. Hazard, *European Mind*, pp. 37–40.
7. G. Vico, *The New Science of Giambattista Vico*, ed. and trans. T.G. Bergin and M.H. Fisch (Ithaca, N.Y., 1968), is the standard English edition.
8. B. Croce, *Philosophy of Giambattista Vico*, trans. R.G. Collingwood (New York, 1964), pp. 122–33, 150–63 *et passim*; R.G. Collingwood, *The Idea of History* (New York, 1956), pp. 67–71.
9. For Pouilly's *Dissertation sur l'incertitude de l'histoire des quatre premier siècles de Rome* (1722) and Sallier's *Sur la certitude de l'his-*

NOTES TO CHAPTER 8

toire . . . , see R. Flint, *Historical Philosophy in France and French Belgium and Switzerland* (Edinburgh, 1893), pp. 254–60.

10. L. de Beaufort, *Dissertation sur l'incertitude des cinq premier siècles de l'histoire Romaine* (Utrecht, 1738); Flint, *Historical Philosophy*, pp. 260–61.

11. Peardon, *English Historical Writing*, pp. 12–33; Forbes, *Liberal Anglican Idea*, p. 41

12. Hare, *Mission of the Comforter*, n. "H," p. 270; *cf.* Forbes, *Liberal Anglican Idea*, p. 137.

13. Forbes, *Liberal Anglican Idea*, p. 29.

14. " 'Civilization' meant at that time not a form of society, but a process. There were degrees of civilization, but not civilizations." *Ibid.*, p. 51. See also Rothblatt, *Tradition and Change*, pp. 17–22; *Guesses*, pp. 309–48.

15. *Guesses*, pp. 305, 186.

16. *Ibid.*, pp. 170–71; *cf.* Forbes, *Liberal Anglican Idea*, p. 129.

17. Forbes, *Liberal Anglican Idea*, p. 4.

18. Preyer, *Science of History*, pp. 21–22, 27; Forbes, *Liberal Anglican Idea*, pp. 7, 131.

19. Peardon, *English Historical Writing*, pp. 221–23, 331–33, 277–83.

20. Forbes, *Liberal Anglican Idea*, pp. 8–9.

21. *Guesses*, pp. 334–35 [emphasis added]; *cf.* Preyer, *Science of History*, p. 38.

22. Forbes, *Liberal Anglican Idea*, p. 10; Preyer, *Science of History*, p. 38.

23. *Guesses*, p. 337.

24. Preyer, *Science of History*, p. 34.

25. *Guesses*, pp. 276–77, 278–79.

26. *Ibid.*, pp. 265–89, 309–48 *et passim;* Forbes, *Liberal Anglican Idea*, pp. 15–17, 29, 53.

27. *Guesses*, pp. 309, 459; *cf.* Forbes, *Liberal Anglican Idea*, pp. 56, 98, 101.

28. *Guesses*, p. 338.

29. *Ibid.*, p. 203; *cf.* Preyer, *Science of History*, p. 41.

30. Forbes, *Liberal Anglican Idea*, pp. 30 ff., 43–44 ff.

31. Hare, *Mission of the Comforter*, n. "G," p. 206; *cf.* Forbes *Liberal Anglican Idea*, p. 30.

32. *Guesses*, pp. 406–07; Forbes, *Liberal Anglican Idea*, pp. 29, 40, 50–51.

33. Forbes, *Liberal Anglican Idea*, pp. 36, 30–31; Preyer, *Science of History*, pp. 36, 28.

34. *Guesses*, p. 270; *cf.* Forbes, *Liberal Anglican Idea*, p. 125.

35. Preyer, *Science of History*, p. 35; Forbes, *Liberal Anglican Idea*, p. 139.

36. *Guesses*, p. 525; *cf.* Forbes, *Liberal Anglican Idea*, p. 138.

37. *Guesses*, pp. 269–70, 284; *cf.* Preyer, *Science of History*, pp. 20, 34.

38. Collingwood, *Idea of History*, pp. 213–17 *et passim*.
39. *Guesses*, pp. 280–81; *cf.* Forbes, *Liberal Anglican Idea*, p. 50.
40. Forbes, *Liberal Anglican Idea*, p. 56.
41. Preyer, *Science of History*, pp. 37–38; Forbes, *Liberal Anglican Idea*, p. 60.
42. Forbes, *Liberal Anglican Idea*, pp. 58, 61, 70–71.
43. Hare, *Mission of the Comforter*, n. "H," p. 274, n. "I," p. 300; Forbes, *Liberal Anglican Idea*, pp. 96–97; Preyer, *Science of History*, pp. 43–44, 46–47.
44. Preyer, *Science of History*, pp. 38–39.
45. E.L. Williamson, *The Liberalism of Thomas Arnold: A Study of His Religious and Political Writings* (Birmingham, Ala., 1964), pp. 73–74, *cf.* pp. 53, 73; Arnold to Hare, 1824–42, twenty-four letters, B-PP. Stanley published only excerpts from these in his best-selling *Life and Correspondence of Thomas Arnold* (1844). Citations hereafter are to Murray's single-volume "popular edition": Stanley, *Life of Arnold* (London, 1904).
46. *Memorials*, I, pp. 168–71; Stanley, *Life of Arnold*, p. 18 and n.; A. Whitridge, *Dr Arnold of Rugby* (London, 1928), p. 26.
47. N. Wymer, *Dr Arnold of Rugby* (London, 1953), p. 77; R.J. Campbell, *Thomas Arnold* (London, 1927), p. 37; Stanley, *Life of Arnold*, pp. 39 ff.
48. Arnold to Hare, 4 July 1824, B-PP; *cf.* Hare, "Preface," *History of Rome*, by Thomas Arnold, 2nd ed. (London, 1845), III, pp. [iii]–iv; Arnold to Hare, 5 Aug. 1824 and 13 Feb. 1827, B-PP; Sanders, *Coleridge and the Broad Church Movement*, pp. 124 *et passim*; [Maurice], Introduction," pp. iv–v; Cannon, "Role of the Cambridge Movement," p. 318.
49. Arnold to Hare, 13 Feb. 1827, B-PP; *cf.* Whitridge, *Dr Arnold*, pp. 15–16; Stanley, *Life of Arnold*, pp. 39 *et passim*.
50. Quoted in Campbell, *Thomas Arnold*, p. 121; *cf.* Arnold to Hare, 30 Aug. and 12 Nov. 1830, and 30 May 1831, B-PP.
51. Arnold to Hare, 30 Aug. and 12 Nov. 1830, 9 Nov. 1831, and 21 June 1839, B-PP. For Lee, see D. Newsome, *Godliness and Good Learning: Four Studies on a Victorian Ideal* (London, 1961).
52. Stanley, *Life of Arnold*, pp. 210 *et passim*; Wordsworth to Hare, 28 Aug. [1832], B-PP; W. Knight, ed., *Letters of the Wordsworth Family* (Boston, 1907), II, pp. 500–01; D.W. Rannie, *Wordsworth and His Circle* (London, 1907), pp. 299–300; W. and D. Wordsworth, *Letters, . . . 1821–50*, II, p. 628, III, p. 1213.
53. Hare, "Preface," *History of Rome*, by Arnold, III, pp. xii–xiii; Mary Arnold to Hare, July 1842–June 1844, eight letters regarding Arnold's literary remains, B-PP; Thomas Arnold, Jr to Hare, 15 July 1842, *ibid.*; Mary Arnold to Maria Hare, 2 July 1842, Brotherton Library MS., no. 33.
54. Hare to John Kenrick, 10 Nov. 1843, Dr Williams's Library MS. 24.81.34.

Chapter 9

1. Hare to Taylor [1827/8], RLEMS 1238:60; *cf.* McF/A, p. 176.
2. Hare to Taylor [Nov./Dec. 1827], RLEMS 1238:35; *cf.* B. Niebuhr, *Life and Letters of Barthold George Niebuhr*, ed. and trans. S. Winkworth (London, 1852), II, letter CCCLIX.
3. Taylor to Hare, 1 March 1828, RLEMS 1238:70. Taylor volunteered to paste advertisements for the *Guesses* and Schleiermacher's *Saint Luke* into the Niebuhr volume.
4. B. Niebuhr, *Life and Letters of Niebuhr*, ed. and trans. S. Winkworth (New York, 1854), p. 508.
5. *Ibid.*, pp. 508–11; *cf.* McF/B, pp. 176–77.
6. Hare to Taylor, 14 Nov. [1828], RLEMS 1238:26; Taylor to J. Mackintosh, in Blunden, *Keats' Publisher*, pp. 185–86.
7. [T. Keightley], "Niebuhr's Roman History . . . ," *Foreign Quarterly Review*, II, no. 2 (June 1828), 554, *cf.* pp. 512–13, 516.
8. [T.J. Hogg], "Niebuhr's *History of Rome*," *Edinburgh Review*, 51 no. 2 (July 1830), 358–96; Robinson, *On Books*, I, p. 398.
9. Quoted in G.O. Trevelyan, *Life and Times of Lord Macaulay* (New York, 1876), I, p. 181.
10. *Guesses*, pp. 445, 459; *cf. Thirlwall*, p. 43; Southey, *Letters*, IV, pp. 219–20.
11. Quoted in Robinson, *Diary*, III, p. 16. Schlegel attacked Niebuhr's history in 1812 in the *Jena Literatur Zeitung*. Niebuhr, *Life and Letters* [American edition], p. 332.
12. [J. Barrow], "Dr Granville's Travels; Russia," *Quarterly Review*, 39, no. 1 (Jan. 1829), 1–41, quoted in McF/B, 117, and in *Thirlwall*, p. 44.
13. [T. Arnold], "Early Roman History," *Quarterly Review*, 32, no. 1 (June 1825), 67–92; McF/B, p. 177–78; *Thirlwall*, pp. 43–44.
14. Arnold to Hare, 16 March 1832, B-PP. Arnold was referring to Karl Otfried Müller's *History and Antiquities of the Doric Race* (English trans. 1830).
15. Hare, *A Vindication of Niebuhr's* History of Rome (Cambridge, 1829). See favourable review in *Athenaeum*, III, no. 74 (25 March 1829), 183–84; *Thirlwall*, p. 44. The "bark and bite" epithet appears on the endpaper of Whewell's copy of the *Vindication*, apparently in the hand of W. Aldis Wright (1831–1914), Vice-Master of Trinity College, Cambridge. TCL W.4.134.
16. Hare, *Vindication of Niebuhr*, pp. [1]–5, 17–19, 24, 34–42, 59–60, 62–63.
17. *Ibid.*, p. 60.
18. Thirlwall, postscript to *ibid.*, pp. 62–63.
19. Niebuhr, *Life and Letters* [American edition], p. 513; *cf.* Stanley, pp. 24–25; *Memorials*, I, pp. 198–200.
20. Wordsworth to Hare, 20 March [1829], B-PP.
21. Arnold to Hare, 30 March 1829, B-PP; *cf.* Stanley, *Life of Arnold*, pp. 222–23.

NOTES TO CHAPTER 9

22. G.C. Lewis, *An Inquiry into the Credibility of the Early Roman History* (London, 1855), I, p. 12, *cf.* pp. 112 and n. 29, 13 and n. 30.

23. *CHEL*, XII, pp. 302–05, 307–09; Thirlwall, pp. 96–107.

24. At age twenty-two Lewis published a translation of Boeckh's *Public Economy of Athens* (1828) and two years later translated Müller's *History and Antiquities of the Doric Race* (1830). Dockhorn, *Deutschen Historismus*, pp. 22–23.

25. Lewis, *Inquiry into the Credibility*, I, pp. 13, 14–16.

26. MS. fragment in Hare's hand, author's collection. Thanks to Professor William Baker for sharing his "marbles."

27. Dockhorn, *Deutschen Historismus*, pp. 21–23, 25, 42–49, 59, 88, *et passim;* Brookfield, *Apostles*, pp. 8, 13–14; *CHEL*, XII, pp. 305–07.

28. H. Kozicki, "Philosophy of History in Tennyson's Poetry to the 1842 Poems," *Journal of English Literary History*, XLII (1975), 88–106.

29. Dockhorn, *Deutschen Historismus*, p. 26.

30. Arnold to Hare, 21 June 1839, B-PP, and in Stanley, *Life of Arnold*, p. 509; *cf.* Hare to Taylor [postmarked 9 Feb. 1831], New York Public Library, Berg Collection MS. 57B5709; Arnold to Hare, 30 Aug. 1830, 7 Oct. 1833, and 1 April, 21 April, and [May] 1841, B-PP; Stanley, *Life of Arnold*, p. 317.

31. Schmitz later edited the *Classical Museum*. Dockhorn, *Deutschen Historismus*, pp. 25, 68.

32. Forbes, *Liberal Anglican Idea*, pp. 118–19; Preyer, *Science of History*, pp. 77–80.

33. Maurice, I, pp. 78–79; R.E. Turner, *James Silk Buckingham* (London, 1934), pp. 236–37; L.A. Marchand, *The Athenaeum: A Mirror of Victorian Culture* (Chapel Hill, 1941), pp. 2 and n. 2, 3 and n. 4, 4–5.

34. Quoted in Marchand, *The Athenaeum*, pp. 10–11, 7–9, *cf.* pp. 5, 6 and n. 12; *Maurice*, I, p. 79; Hare, "Life of Sterling" prefixed to *Essays and Tales* by John Sterling (London, 1848), I, pp. xxxii–xxxvi *et passim*.

35. Hare, "Sterling," p. xxxiv. For Maurice's reviews, see chap 6, n. 13, and chap. 4, n. 18.

36. Maurice to Hare, 20 March 1829, in *Maurice*, I, pp. 96–97, *cf.* p. 52; F.M. McClain, *Maurice: Man and Moralist* (London, 1972), pp. 20–21.

37. [Hare, trans.], "Richter's 'Vision of a Godless World,'" *Athenaeum*, III, no. 67 (4 Feb. 1829), 65–66.

38. F.D. Maurice, "Christmas Thoughts on Renan's *Vie de Jésus*," *Macmillans Magazine*, IX (Jan. 1864), 190–97. Thanks to Professor E.C. Want for calling this to my attention.

39. Hare, "Museum of Thought," *Athenaeum*, III, no. 73 (18 March 1829), 169–70; no. 74 (25 March 1829), 187–90; no. 75 (1 April 1829), 201–07; no. 76 (8 April 1829), 217–18; no. 78 (22 April 1829), 241–43; McF/B, pp. 183–84.

40. [Hare, trans.], "Goethe's First and Second Poetic Epistles," *Athenaeum*, III, no. 80 (6 May 1829), 280; no. 81 (13 May 1829), 297–98;

[Hare, trans.], "Goethe's 'Alexis & Dora,'" *Athenaeum*, IV, no. 105 (28 Oct. 1829), 677–78; McF/B, pp. 183–84.

41. [W. Whewell, ed.], *English Hexameter Translations from Schiller, Göthe, Homer, Callinus, and Meleager* (London, 1847), pp. 41–57, 204–28; Hare to Whewell, 11 Nov. and 24 Dec. 1846, and 30 March 1847, WP/TCL MSS. R.18.14.13–15; Whewell to Hare, 22 Jan. 1847, *ibid.*, 0.18.W2.92; Hare to Whewell, 29 Oct. 1849, *ibid.*, Add. MS a64.114. Morgan, *Critical Bibliography*, pp. 596–97, rates Hare's translations "excellent."

Chapter 10

1. Ordination certificates as Deacon and Priest, 26 March and 1 May 1826, B-PP; Southey, *Letters*, III, p. 538.
2. Hare to Whewell, 30 April [1822], WP/TCL Add. MS. a77.126.
3. Hare to the sixth Duke of Devonshire, 16 March 1829, Chatsworth MS. 1741; *cf.* Appointment as Domestic Chaplain to William Spencer, Duke of Devonshire, 7 March 1829, B-PP.
4. *Memorials*, I, pp. 408–10, 414 *et passim*.
5. *Ibid.*, I, pp. 175, 187–88, 215; 284–88; 409–15 *et passim*.
6. Hare to Maria Hare, 30 Aug. 1831, in *ibid.*, I, p. 411.
7. Maria Hare to C. Stanley, 6 Jan. 1830, in *ibid.*, I, pp. 329–30.
8. Maria Hare's diary, 10 Jan. 1830, in *ibid.*, I, pp. 348–49.
9. Maria Hare to Lucy Stanley, 29 Feb. 1832, in *ibid.*, I, p. 415.
10. Hare to Maria Hare, 30 Aug. 1831, in *ibid.*, I, pp. 413–14.
11. *Memorials*, I, pp. 308 *et passim;* Wordsworth to Hare on A.W. Hare's posthumously published sermons [postmarked 29 May 1838], B-PP; *Story*, I, pp. 156, 240.
12. Hare to Maria Hare, 9 March 1831, in *Memorials*, I, p. 417.
13. *Memorials*, I, p. 414; Super, *Landor*, pp. 226–27.
14. Maria Hare to Lucy Stanley, 26 May 1832, in *Memorials*, I, p. 434. The "Madonna" of the school of Raphael was a gift from Landor. Landor to Hare, n.d., B-PP; *cf. Memorials*, I, pp. 430–31; Robinson, *Diary*, III, p. 8; *idem; On Books*, I, p. 406; Super, *Landor*, pp. 226–27.
15. Wordsworth to Hare, 8 Aug. [1832], B-PP; Robinson *On Books*, I, pp. 410–11, 413–15; Super, *Landor*, pp. 231–33; Forster, *Landor*, II, p. 248; *Memorials*, I, p. 458; Certificate of Admission to the Living of Herstmonceux, 18 June 1832; Certificate of Subscription to the Articles and Prayer Book, 18 June 1832; Declaration of Subscription to the Liturgy, 18 June 1832; Certificate of Investiture as Rector, 22–23 June 1832; Declaration of Conformity to the Articles, 24 June 1832; License to be absent from his benefice until 25 December 1833 [dated] 25 July 1832, B-PP.
16. Hare, MS. Travel Diary, pp. 16, 7, 28, 33, B-PP.
17. Landor to Crabb Robinson, 20 Oct. 1832, Dr Williams's Library, Crabb Robinson Papers; *cf.* Robinson, *Diary*, III, p. 16; Super, *Landor*,

NOTES TO CHAPTER 10

pp. 233–34; Hare to Maria Hare, 4 April 1832, in *Memorials*, I, pp 429–30.

18. Hare, MS. Travel Diary, pp. 20, 30, 52, 55, 63, 176, B-PP; *idem.* to Augustus Hare from Italy, in *Memorials*, I, pp. 458–62.

19. Hare, MS. Travel Diary, pp. 17, 59–61, 82–83, 86, B-PP; W. Ward, *Life and Times of Cardinal Wiseman*, new ed. (London, 1912), I, p. 93.

20. Hare, MS. Travel Diary, pp. 70, 73, 75, 77, 79, 80, 81, 92, 133, 134, 136, 145, 147, 148, 150–51, 154, 155, 156–58, B-PP; A.J.C. Hare, *Life and Letters of Frances, Baroness Bunsen* (London 1879), I, pp. 397–99; Plumptre, p. xxxi.

21. Blakesley to R.C. Trench, 5 March 1835, in Trench, *Richard Chenevix Trench, Archbishop: Letters and Memorials* (London, 1888), I, p. 188. *cf.* B. Disraeli, *Disraeli's Reminiscences*, ed. H.M. and M. Swartz (London, 1975), p. 88.

22. Hare, MS. Travel Diary, pp. 91, 158, B-PP; *idem.*, to Augustus Hare, Jan. 1833, in *Memorials*, I, pp. 463–64.

23. The sermon was published as "The Prophet in the Wilderness," in *Sermons Preacht*, pp. 117–46; Robinson, *Diary*, III, p. 36; *Memorials*, I, pp. 462–63.

24. Hare, MS. Travel Diary, pp. 94, 113, 115, 120, 123 *et passim*, B-PP.

25. *Ibid.*, pp. 64, 65–66, 88, 126–27, 105 *et passim*, 51, 78, 25, *cf.* pp. 140–42, 186; Super, *Landor*, p. 234; [Maurice], "Introduction," p. xxvi.

26. Hare, MS. Travel Diary, pp. 160, 139–40, 167–68, *cf.* pp. 128, 133, 137, 163, 165, B-PP; *Memorials*, I, p. 459; Plumptre, p. xxxi; J.W. Goodison and G.H. Robertson, *Fitzwilliam Museum, Cambridge, Catalogue of Paintings*, vol. II: *Italian Schools* (Cambridge, 1967), nos. 107, 110, 120, 133, 145, 156, 160, 162. Hare's widow sold these paintings to the Fitzwilliam for £1,000.

27. Hare, MS. Travel Diary, pp. 170–73 *et passim*, B-PP; R.W. Emerson, *Journals and Miscellaneous Notebooks of Ralph Waldo Emerson*, ed. A.R. Ferguson (Cambridge, Mass., 1964), IV, pp. 172–73, 273 n., 276 n., 433; R.W. Emerson, *Letters of Ralph Waldo Emerson*, ed. R. Rusk (New York, 1939), I, pp. 282–83; L. Whiting, *The Florence of Landor* (Boston, 1905), pp. 23–24, 30–31, 46; Super, *Landor*, pp. 235–36. Emerson often quoted from the *Guesses*.

28. Hare, MS. Travel Diary, pp. 187, 190 ff., 198–201, 204, 209, 218, 219–20, B-PP.

29. Sterling to J.S. Mill, 10 June 1833, King's College, Cambridge, Keynes MS. 154.7; Hare, "Sterling," p. xlvii; Carlyle, *Sterling*, pp. 95–96.

30. Hare, MS. Travel Diary, p. 220, B-PP; *Memorials*, I, p. 488.

31. Ordnance Survey, one-inch series, Eastbourne, sheet 183; Hare to an applicant for a curacy, 30 July 1853, National Library of Scotland MS. 7178, no. 85; *Memorials*, II, p. 74; Horsfield, *History of Sussex*, II, appendices, pp. 84, 87.

32. *Memorials*, I, pp. 458, 486–89; *Story*, I, pp. 154, 190.

33. Maria Hare to Lucy Stanley, 22 July 1834, in *Memorials*, II, p. 94.

NOTES TO CHAPTER 10

34. Stanley, pp. 8–9; cf. Plumptre, p. xlv; *Memorials*, II, pp. 75–76, 81.
35. Hare to Taylor, 21 July 1824, RLEMS 1238:11; Plumptre, p. xlv; Stanley, p. 8; *Story*, I. p. 81.
36. Robinson, *Diary*, II, pp. 292–93.
37. Plumptre, p. xlv; cf. Lucy Stanley's description in *Memorials*, II, p. 119.
38. Stanley, p. 9; cf. *Story*, I, pp. 80–81; Forster, *Landor*, II, p. 254.
39. *Memorials*, II, pp. 80–81, 275, 87; Stanley, p. 9; Plumptre, p. xlvi.
40. Hare to Whewell, 13 Dec. 1833, 1 June 1834, 31 Jan. 1835, and 6 June 1835, WP/TCL MSS. 0.18.H2.8, 9, 13–14; Hare to Henry Havelock, 6 June 1851, North Yorkshire County Record Office, Havelock-Allan Papers.
41. *Story*, I, pp. 165–67; *Memorials*, II, pp. 226–27; Bateman, *Life of Elliott*, pp. 98, 153, 233, 259–60; S.A. Brook, *Life and Letters of F.W. Robertson* (London, 1865), *passim;* Plumptre, pp. xlv–xlvi.
42. My thanks to Reverend R.G.H. Horne, late Rector of Herstmonceux, who reconstructed a list of Hare's curates from the parish registers.
43. Hare to Whewell, 1 June 1834, WP/TCL MS. 0.18.H2.9; Sterling to J.S. Mill, 10 June 1833, King's College, Cambridge, Keynes MS. 154.7; Hare, "Sterling," pp. xlvi–xlvii ff.; Carlyle, *Sterling*, pp. 95–105; A. Tuell, *John Sterling: A Representative Victorian* (New York, 1941), pp. 57–58, 118; Trench, *Letters and Memorials*, I, pp. 149–50, 157, 159 *et passim;* Fox, *Memorials of Old Friends*, I, p. 110, II, pp. 95, 97; *Memorials*, II, pp. 89–91, 96; *Story*, I, p. 70; Plumptre, pp. xxxv–xxxvi. Sterling to Maurice, 2 May 1834, B-PP, establishes Sterling's presence at "Herstmonceux near Battle" a month earlier than other sources.
44. Hare to Venables, 29 Aug. 1844, in *Memorials*, III, pp. 247–49.
45. Hare to Venables, 6 Sept. 1844, in *ibid.*, III, pp. 249–50.
46. *Ibid.*, III, pp. 250–51.
47. Hare to Augustus Hare, 15 Oct. 1833, in *ibid.*, I, pp. 497, 496.
48. Quoted in Prothero, *Life of Stanley*, I, pp. 115, 118–19; cf. Stanley to Hare [1849/50], Cheshire County Record Office, D.S.A. 80/6.
49. C. Whibley, *Lord John Manners and His Friends* (Edinburgh, 1925), II, pp. 89–91; Hare to Whewell [postmarked 13 July 1835], WP/TCL MS. 0.18.H2.15.
50. Whibley, *Lord John Manners*, I, p. 133, II, p. 91 and n.; R. Blake, *Disraeli* (New York, 1967), p. 168.
51. J.N. Simpkinson, *Memoir of the Rev. George Wagner*, 2nd ed. (Cambridge, 1858), pp. 2, 4–5; Hare to Whewell, Oct. [1834] and [postmarked 24 Oct. 1834], WP/TCL MSS. 0.18.H2.12 and 12+1.
52. Hare to Whewell [postmarked 13 July 1835] and n.d., WP/TCL MSS. 0.18.H2.15 and 18+1; cf. Simpkinson, *Memoir of Wagner*, pp. 5, 25–27.
53. Simpkinson, *Memoir of Wagner*, pp. 16, 74–75, 79, 92, 146–47, 180–82, 182–83, 208–10, 252; *Memorials*, III, pp. 238, 242 and n.; *Story*, I, pp. 79–80.
54. Maria Hare's diary, 29 July 1834, in *Memorials*, II, p. 93, cf. II,

pp. 1, 28–31, 54–55, 73, I, pp. 475, 489–91, 496; *Story*, I, p. 49; A.J.C. Hare, *Baroness Bunsen*, I, p. 417.
55. *Memorials*, II, pp. 78–80, 89–91, 123, 137–39, 147, 168, 222–24; *Story*, I, pp. 56–59, 60, 67, 99.
56. *Memorials*, II, pp. 228–30.
57. Anna Hare to Maria Hare [1834/5], in *Story*, I, p. 51; *cf*. pp. 42, 53; *Memorials* II, pp. 45, 104–08, 143–44, 185–86.

Chapter 11

1. [Maurice], "Introduction," p. viii; *cf. Maurice*, I, p. 175.
2. Maurice to Hare, 3 Dec. 1829, in *Maurice*, I, p. 103, *cf*. pp. 97, 99–101, 102.
3. *Maurice*, I, p. 209; Hare to Whewell, 21 Oct. and 12 Nov. [1843], WP/TCL Add. MSS. a77.135–36; Hare to John Allen, 7 Nov. 1843, B-PP; Hare to S. Wilberforce [1841/2], Bodleian Library MS. Wilberforce c.7, ff. 239–40, 241–43.
4. *Memorials*, II, pp. 202–04, 227, 185–86, I, p. 416; *Story*, I, pp. 70–72 ff., 112–13, 82–83, 179, 280; L. Powell, "Annals of a Family Who Were All Led by a Right Way to the City of Habitation[,] Whose Faith Follow, 1873" [typescript], p. 88, B-PP, and Xerox copy in CUL; Hare, MS. Travel Diary, p. 102, B-PP; F.M. McClain, "Maurice: Man and Moralist," Cambridge Ph.D. Dissertation 6590 (1968), pp. 40–41 *et passim*.
5. *Story*, I, p. 73, *cf*. p. 74; *Memorials*, II, pp. 223, 227, 272.
6. *Story*, I, pp. 73, 203, *cf*. pp. 70–73, 179–80.
7. *Ibid.*, I, pp. 178–90; Powell, "Annals of a Family," p. 92, B-PP.
8. *Story*, I, p. 176; *cf. Memorials*, II, p. 227, 272–73.
9. Hare to Marcus Hare, 27 Sept. 1844, in *Memorials*, III, p. 252, *cf*. II, pp. 276, 288; Powell, "Annals of a Family," pp. 94, 96, B-PP; Hare to Thirlwall, 22 Nov. 1844, *ibid.*; Trench to Whewell, 22 Nov. 1844, WP/TCL Add. MS. c91.23; *Maurice*, I, pp. 376–81.
10. Lucy Hare to Maria Hare, 27 Aug. 1844, in *Memorials*, II, p. 274; *cf. Maurice*, I, pp. 386–88.
11. Thirlwall to Hare, 15 Nov. 1844; B-PP; Whewell to Hare, 20 Oct. 1844; *ibid.*, Sedgwick to Hare, 14 Nov. 1844, *ibid.*
12. Sterling to Hare, 26 Aug. 1844, *ibid.*
13. Wordsworth to Hare [1844], *ibid.*
14. Hare to Whewell, 2 Nov. [1844], WP/TCL Add. MS. a77.139.
15. Maria Hare to Lucy Hare, 26 March 1845, in *Memorials*, II, p. 288, *cf*. p. 277; *Story*, I, p. 180.
16. *Memorials*, II, p. 304.
17. *Story*, I, pp. 179, 318 *et passim*.
18. *Ibid.*, I, p. 67, *cf*. pp. 178–79; *Memorials*, II, pp. 224–25, 277.
19. *Story*, I, p. 109, *cf*. p. 102.
20. *Ibid.*, I, pp. 179, 181–87, 238–40, *cf*. pp. 202–03, 210.

21. Hare to Henry Manning, 17 Sept. 1844, MA/SMA Hare-Manning Correspondence, ff. 143–46.
22. Hare to Landor, 14 May 1852, FP/V.&A. MS. 247–8.E.2.17–18; cf. J.B. Mozley, *Letters of J.B. Mozley* (London, 1885), p. 329; *Memorials,* II, pp. 292–93, 225, 242, 201–04; *Story,* I, pp. 160–62, 194–96, 260–61.
23. *Story,* I, pp. 162–63, 175; *Memorials,* II, p. 228, III, pp. 234–36; C.K.J. Bunsen, *Memoirs of Baron Bunsen,* ed. F. Bunsen, 2nd ed. (London, 1869), II, pp. 19, 21, 27; A.J.C. Hare, *Baroness Bunsen,* II, p. 49; Hare to Manning [1841], MA/SMA, f. 66.
24. *Story,* I, pp. 164–65; cf. C.C. Abbott, *Life and Letters of George Darley* (Oxford, 1967), pp. 233, 208, 234, 263–64; Hare to Whewell, 18 March 1841, WP/TCL MS. 0.18.H2.24; Whewell to Hare, 16 and 20 Aug. 1845, and 3 Nov. 1845, *ibid.,* 0.18.W2.82–83, 85; Blunden, *Keats' Publisher,* p. 210; Clark and Hughes, *Life of Sedgwick,* II, pp. 113, 148.
25. N. Mitford, ed., *Ladies of Alderley, Being the Letters between Maria Josepha, Lady Stanley of Alderley and Her Daughter-in-Law Henrietta Maria Stanley during the Years 1841–1850* (London, 1939), p. 98; cf. J. Pope-Hennessy, *Monckton Milnes: The Years of Promise, 1809– 51* (London, 1949), p. 154 n. 1; Trench, *Letters and Memorials,* I, p. 218.
26. T. Carlyle, *New Letters of Thomas Carlyle,* ed. A. Carlyle (London, 1904), I, pp. 6–7.
27. Hare to Whewell, 4 Jan. 1838, WP/TCL MS. 0.18.H2.17.
28. Quoted in W. Allingham, *William Allingham: A Diary,* ed. H. Allingham and D. Radford (London, 1907), p. 218; cf. Carlyle, *New Letters,* II, p. 292.
29. Hare to Whewell, 17 April [1840], WP/TCL MS. 0.18.H2.29; cf. Carlyle to Sterling, 21 July 1838, B-PP; *Story,* I, pp. 166–71.
30. Hare to Landor, three letters, 1852–53, FP/V.&A. MSS. 247– 8.E.2.23; Landor to Esther Hare, five letters [c. 1847–52], B-PP; *Memorials,* II, p. 350; Super, *Landor,* p. 596 n. 39.
31. *Story,* I, p. 251; cf. *Memorials,* II, p. 310.
32. *Story,* I, p. 251; cf. Landor to Esther Hare, n.d. and 10 Aug. 1852, B-PP.
33. *Story,* I, p. 357; cf. 469, 249–50, 357.
34. *Memorials,* II, pp. 221, 284, 287, 81–83; *Story,* I, pp. 109, 156; Hare to prospective curate, 30 July 1853, National Library of Scotland MS. 7178 no. 85; Stanley, p. 11, Plumptre, pp. xxxiv–xxxv; A.R. Vidler, *F.D. Maurice and Company* (London, 1966), pp. 225–26, 227–28.
35. *Story,* I, pp. 252–53; cf. *Memorials,* I, pp. 348–49, II, pp. 83–84; A.J.C. Hare, *Baroness Bunsen,* II, p. 154.
36. W.H. Thompson to G.S. Venables, 13 March [1840], National Library of Wales, Venables Papers. Thanks to Professor P.R. Allen for providing me with this letter.
37. *Story,* I, pp. 109–10; *Memorials,* I, p. 191; MS. letters from parishioners to Hare, n.d., B-PP.
38. *Guesses,* pp. 28–31; G. Kitson Clark, *Churchmen and the Condition of England* (London, 1973), pp. 36–37 ff.

39. *Memorials*, II, p. 139; Minutes of the Hailsham Union Board of Guardians of the Poor, East Sussex County Record Office, 05/la/1–6, 1836–47. The Records from 1847 to 1857 are lost.

40. *Story*, I, p. 155; Distad, "Hare and the 'Broad Church' Ideal," pp. 55–57.

41. Quoted in Clark and Hughes, *Life of Sedgwick*, II, p. 115. Hare's hesitance was probably over qualms regarding the Athanasian Creed; *cf.* [Maurice], "Introduction," p. xli.

42. W.R.W. Stephens, *The South Saxon Diocese, Selsey-Chichester* (London, 1881), pp. 261–64; Declaration of Conformity, 10 April 1840; Certificate of Subscription, 10 April 1840; Memorandum of Archidiaconal Investiture, 10 April 1840; Certificate of Investiture as Archdeacon of Lewes, affixed with pendant seal of the Bishop of Chichester and £20 tax-paid revenue stamp, 10 April 1840, B-PP.

43. Hare to Marcus Hare, 15 March 1840, in *Memorials*, III, pp. 233–34.

44. Maria Hare to Mrs Pile, 24 April 1840, in *ibid.*, II, p. 214.

45. Hare to Manning, 26 Dec. [1840], MA/SMA, f. 23b; *cf.* Bishop Shuttleworth to Manning, 24 Dec. 1840, *ibid.*, f. 227; *Memorials*, III, pp. 235–36, II, pp. 216–18, 230–31.

46. Hare to Manning, 26 Dec. [1840], MA/SMA, f. 23b; *cf.* E.S. Purcell, *Life of Cardinal Manning* (London, 1895), I, pp. 171, 174–75, 179–80; S. Leslie, *Henry Edward Manning* (London, 1921), pp. 69–73; G.L. Strachey, *Eminent Victorians* (Harmondsworth, 1971), pp. 30–31. Manning has been ill-served by three biographers; none provides a trustworthy account.

47. Manning to Hare, 24 Aug. 1840, in Purcell, *Manning*, I, p. 167; *cf.* Manning to Hare [24 Aug. 1842] and 25 Sept. 1840, MA/SMA, ff. 10, 12; Hare to Manning, 26 Jan. and 3 Sept. 1842, and 15 Aug. [1843], *ibid.*, ff. 106–08, 123–24, 137–38. F. 10, the letter quoted from Purcell, is but a fragment; the rest of the manuscript has been removed.

48. Hare to Manning, 3 Sept. 1842, MA/SMA, ff. 123–24.

49. Hare to Manning [Feb. 1841], *ibid.*, f. 32; *cf.* Manning to Hare, 16 Feb. 1841, *ibid.*, ff. 30–31; Hare to Manning, 6 March [1841], *ibid.*, ff. 36–37; [Maurice], "Introduction," pp. lxiv–lxv.

50. Bishop Gilbert to Hare, 1842–55, 178 letters, West Sussex County and Diocesan Record Office, Add. MS. 1867, Ep. I/63; *cf.* Cause Papers, *ibid.*, Ep. I/48/3, 5; Church Fabric Papers, *ibid.*, Ep. I/49/7.

51. Gilbert to Hare, 10 Feb. 1846, *ibid.*, Add. MS. 1867:84.

52. Gilbert to Hare, 22 Dec. 1845 and 2 Jan. 1847, *ibid.*, Add. MS. 1867:83, 104; Cause Papers, *ibid.*, Ep. I/48/5; "Shoreham, More Puseyism," *Brighton Herald*, 2 Jan. 1847.

53. Gilbert to Hare, various dates, West Sussex County and Diocesan Record Office, Add. MS. 1867:3–5, 8, 10 *et passim;* Cause Papers, *ibid.*, Ep. I/48/3, 9.

54. Hare to S. Wilberforce, 28 April [1843], Bodleian Library MS.

Wilberforce c.7, ff. 204–05; Hare to Whewell, 29 March [1843], WP/TCL MS. 0.18.H2.26; Plumptre, p. xliii.

55. Thirlwall to Hare, 4 March [1841], Columbia University Library MS. X823 T34 S6, vol. 2, ff. 11–12; Fox, *Memories of Old Friends,* II p. 75.

56. *Story,* I, p. 122; *Memorials,* II, p. 245; Plumptre, pp. xl–xlii.

57. Hare, "Education the Necessity of Mankind," p. 9, preached at the opening of a Woodard school in Sussex in 1851; W.B.D. Heeney, *Mission to the Middle Classes: The Woodard Schools, 1848–1891* (London, 1969), pp. 61–62, 75–76.

58. Hare, "The Worth of Knowledge," in *Sermons Preacht,* pp. 215, 220–23.

59. Hare, MS. Commonplace Book, f. 121, B-PP; Hare, "The Children of Light," p. 22. On Hare's use of the Coleridgean "Reason and Understanding," see J.H. Rigg, *Modern Anglican Theology* (London, 1857), pp. 57–61; C.R. Sanders, "Coleridge, F.D. Maurice, and the Distinction between the Reason and the Understanding," *PMLA,* LI, no. 2 (June 1936), 459–75.

60. Hare, MS. Commonplace Book, ff. 121, 171, B-PP; *cf.* Hare to Whewell [postmarked 13 May 1822], WP/TCL Add. MS. a77.127.

61. Hare, "Education the Necessity of Mankind," pp. 10–13; *cf. idem.,* "Christ's Promise the Strength of the World," in *Sermons Preacht,* pp. 177–78; *idem.,* "Privileges Imply Duties," in *Charges,* pp. 21–28.

62. Hare to the clergy of the Archdeaconry of Lewes, 24 July 1843, printed letter, B-PP, *cf.* Hare, "Education the Necessity of Mankind," pp. 10–13.

63. *Idem.,* "Education the Necessity of Mankind," pp. 15–16; *cf. idem.,* "The Worth of Knowledge," pp. 228, 232–33.

64. *Idem.,* "Privileges Imply Duties," p. 34; *cf. idem.,* "Education the Necessity of Mankind," p. 14; *idem.,* "The Worth of Knowledge," pp. 231–32.

65. *Idem.,* printed archidiaconal letter, 24 July 1843, B-PP; *cf.* Kitson Clark, *Churchmen and the Condition of England,* pp. 62–68 *et passim.*

66. Hare, "The Church the Light of the World," in *Sermons Preacht,* p. 199; *idem.,* "Christ's Promise," pp. 170–72.

67. *Idem.,* MS. Commonplace Book, f. 166, B-PP.

68. *Idem.,* "Better Prospects of the Church," in *Charges,* pp. 2–3, 89; Kitson Clark, *Churchmen and the Condition of England,* pp. 44–47, 53–55, 59–60 *et passim.*

69. Hare, "Education the Necessity of Mankind," p. 17; *cf. idem.,* "Christ's Promise," pp. 149–56.

70. Hare to Whewell, 13 Dec. 1833, WP/TCL MS. 0.18.H2.8.

71. For this controversy, see *Thirlwall,* pp. 66–84; Winstanley, *Early Victorian Cambridge,* pp. 73–78.

72. Hare to Whewell, 1 June 1834, WP/TCL MS. 0.18.H2.9.

73. Hare to Maria Hare, 17 Jan. 1841, in *Memorials,* III, pp. 235–36.

74. Stephens, *South Saxon Diocese,* p. 263; *Story,* I, p. 113; *Memorials,* II, p. 211; West Sussex County and Diocesan Record Office, Church

Fabric Papers, Ep. I/49/7; Hare to Charles Thorp, n.d., Bodleian Library, MS. Eng. Lett. e.86, ff. 98–99, 100–01, 112–19; Whewell to Hare, 27 Sept. and 13 Oct. 1840, and 26 May [1841], WP/TCL MSS. 0.18.W2. 48–49, 58.

75. Hare to Charles Thorp. n.d., Bodleian Library MS. Eng. Lett. e.86, ff. 112–19; Hare, "Better Prospects," pp. 12–13; *idem.*, "Privileges Imply Duties," pp. 62 and n. "M," 107–09.

76. *Story*, I, p. 113; *cf.* Mitford, ed., *Ladies of Alderley*, p. 37.

77. Hare to Manning, 28 Feb. [1841], MA/SMA, f. 35; Manning to Hare, 16 Oct. 1840, *ibid.*, f. 15; Hare to Manning, 30 July [1841], *ibid.*, f. 65; Purcell, *Manning*, I, pp. 177–78.

78. Hare, "Privileges Imply Duties," pp. 61 and n. "L," 105–07.

79. *Ibid.*, pp. 49–53; Hare to Manning, on the propriety of matins [1840/41], MA/SMA, ff. 20–21, 24, 27–28.

80. Hare, "Privileges Imply Duties," pp. 43 ff., 54–56; Bishop Shuttleworth to Hare, Appointment as Member of Revived Convocation of Canterbury, 26 July 1842, B-PP; [Maurice], "Introduction," pp. liv–lv.

81. [Maurice], "Preface," in *Sermons Preacht*, p. x; Hare to Mr Hoper, 15 Nov. 1849, MS. in the author's collection. On Broad Church nationalism, see R.J. Helmstadter, "Julius Hare's *Apologia Pro Patria Sua*," *Ontario Victorian Studies Association Newsletter*, no. 8 (Oct. 1971), 18–21; R.T. Shannon, "John Robert Seeley and the Idea of a National Church," in *Ideas and Institutions of Victorian Britain*, pp. 236–67.

82. Hare to Whewell, 24 April 1848, WP/TCL MS. 0.18.H2.30.

83. Hare, "The Purpose of Man's Creation," in *Sermons Preacht*, p. 294.

84. *Idem.*, "The Heathen the Inheritance of the World," in *Sermons Preacht*, pp. 372–73, delivered at the jubilee of the Church Missionary Society; *cf.* Gilbert to Hare, 16 April 1842, West Sussex County and Diocesan Record Office, Add. MS. 1867:9a.

85. Hare, "The Duty of Preparing the Way for the Lord," in *Sermons Preacht*, p. 266.

86. *Idem.*, "The Heathen the Inheritance," p. 378.

87. *Idem.*, "The True End of War," in *Sermons Preacht*, pp. 475–87; [Maurice], "Introduction," p. lx; Sanders, *Coleridge and the Broad Church Movement*, p. 144.

88. [Maurice], "Introduction," p. xlix; C.K. Gloyn, *The Church in the Social Order* (Forest Grove, Ore. 1942), pp. 8, 6, 15–44; D. Bowen, *The Idea of the Victorian Church* (Montreal, 1968), pp. 364–66; Sanders, *Coleridge and the Broad Church Movement*, pp. 139–41, 143–46; Prickett, *Romanticism and Religion, passim;* Storr, *Development of English Theology* pp. 337–40; Kitson Clark, *Churchmen and the Condition of England*, pp. 78–82.

Chapter 12

1. Hare, *Portions of the Psalms in English Verse* (London, 1839); *idem.*, ed., *Sermons to a County Congregation*, by A.W. Hare (London, 1836); Hare to Whewell, 12 Oct. 1834 and 25 Oct. 1838, WP/TCL MSS.

0.18.H2.12, 19; *Memorials*, II, p. 138. Carlyle likened Hare's rendering of the Psalms to the "Scotch" version. Carlyle to Hare, 4 April 1842, B-PP.

2. Julius Hare to Marcus Hare, 17 Jan. 1836, in *Memorials*, III, p. 229; *cf*. Hare to Worsley, 20 Feb. [1838?], WP/TCL MS. 0.18.H2.35.

3. Hare to Charles Thorp, n.d. Bodleian Library MS. Eng. Lett. e.86, ff. 102–09.

4. Sussex Archaeological Society records, Lewes. My thanks to Miss Verena Smith.

5. F. Max Müller, *Life and Letters of F. Max Müller* (London, 1902), I, pp. 28, 30, 52–53, 55, 59, 61; Bunsen, *Memoirs*, I, p. 49 and n.

6. S. and C. Winkworth, *Memorials of Two Sisters: Susanna and Catherine Winkworth*, ed. M.J. Shaen (London, 1908), pp. 108, 123–27.

7. Whewell to Hare, 15 Dec. 1840, WP/TCL MS. 0.18.W2.53.

8. Hare to Whewell, 17 Dec. 1840, *ibid*., 0.18.H2.23.

9. *Ibid*.

10. Whewell to Hare, 26 Dec. 1840, and 26 Feb. [1841], *ibid*., 0.18.W2. 54, 56; Hare to Whewell, 3 Dec. [1841], *ibid*., Add. MS. a77.131.

11. Daniel Macmillan to Hare, 22 Sept. 1840, BL Add. MS. 55109, f. 2; *cf*. T. Hughes, *Memoir of Daniel Macmillan* (London, 1883), p. 117 *et passim;* C.L. Graves, *Life and Letters of Alexander Macmillan* (London, 1910), pp. 23–25 ff.; C. Morgan, *The House of Macmillan, 1843–1943* (London, 1944), pp. 22–34. Some of the Hare-Macmillan correspondence is reprinted in Hughes' *Memoir of D. Macmillan,* and in S. Nowell-Smith, ed., *Letters to Macmillan* (London, 1967).

12. D. Macmillan to Hare, 17 June and 25 July 1842, BL Add. MSS. 55109, ff. 4, 10–18; Hare to D. Macmillan, 16 and 20 Aug. 1842, *ibid.,* ff. 19–23; D. Macmillan to Maurice, 31 Aug. 1842, *ibid*., 55090, ff. 1–2; Graves, *Alexander Macmillan,* pp. 23–25; Morgan, *House of Macmillan,* pp. 23–49; *Maurice,* I, pp. 288 *et passim.*

13. Hare to D. Macmillan, 6 March 1843, BL Add. MS. 55109, ff. 26–27; Hare and D. Macmillan, 19 Aug. 1843–27 May 1844, eight letters, *ibid*., ff. 38–56, 63–65, 70–71, 84–85 *et passim;* Hare to Whewell, 21 Oct. [1843], WP/TCL Add. MS. a77.135.

14. A. Macmillan, *Letters of Alexander Macmillan,* ed. G.A. Macmillan (London, 1908), pp. 216–17; *cf*. Morgan, *House of Macmillan,* p. 82; Graves, *Alexander Macmillan,* pp. 84, 87; D. Macmillan to Hare, 31 March 1843, 21 June 1844, and 28 Aug. 1847, BL Add. MSS. 55109, ff. 32–33, 89–92, 119.

15. D. Macmillan to Hare, 25 June 1853, BL Add. MS. 55109, f. 142 ff.; Hughes, *Memoir of D. Macmillan,* pp. 174–76; Graves, *Alexander Macmillan,* p. 75; A. Macmillan to L. Powell, regarding repayment of the principal of the £500 loan, 23 March 1864, B-PP; Morgan, *House of Macmillan,* pp. 36–37; E.C. Mack and W.H.G. Armytage, *Thomas Hughes* (London, 1952), pp. 87–88.

16. Prospectus for Coleridge Prize in Hare's hand, Oct. 1834, and Hare to Whewell, 12 Oct. [1834], WP/TCL MSS. 0.18.H2.11–12.

17. Hare to Whewell [postmarked 24 Oct. 1834], *ibid.*, 0.18.H2.12+2; *cf.* McF/B, p. 188.

18. Whewell to Hare, 19 Oct. [1834], WP/TCL MS. 0.18.W2.35.

19. Revised Prospectus and Hare to Whewell [postmarked 24 Oct. 1834], *ibid.*, 0.18.H2.12+1; Whewell to Hare, 27 Oct. 1834 and 13 Feb. 1835, *ibid.*, 0.18.W2.36, 39; Trench, *Letters and Memorials,* I, p. 164.

20. Sara Coleridge, *Memoirs and Letters of Sara Coleridge* (London, 1873), I, p. 111; E.L. Griggs, *Coleridge Fille: A Biography of Sara Coleridge* (London, 1940), p. 182; McF/B, p. 189.

21. Arnold to Hare [postmarked 14 Oct. 1834], B-PP.

22. Griggs, *Coleridge Fille,* p. 182; McF/B, p. 189; Fox, *Memories of Old Friends,* II, p. 131.

23. Articles reprinted in De Quincey, *Collected Writings of De Quincey,* ed. D. Masson (Edinburgh, 1889–90), II, pp. 138–228; M. Lefebvre, *Samuel Taylor Coleridge: The Bondage of Opium* (London, 1974), p. 29; McF/B, pp. 189–90.

24. Hare, "Samuel Taylor Coleridge and the English Opium-Eater," *British Magazine and Monthly Register,* VII, no. 1 (1 Jan. 1835), 19–21, 24; *cf.* S.T. Coleridge, *Specimens of the Table-Talk of S.T. Coleridge* (London, 1835), I, p. lxv; McF/B, pp. 191–95.

25. Sara Coleridge to Hare [1848], B-PP; *cf.* Sara Coleridge to Hare, 31 March 1846, 4 April [1846], and other letters, B-PP; Griggs, *Coleridge Fille,* pp. 109–11, 146 and n. 3, 147–48, 164; McF/B, pp. 195–96.

26. Sanders, *Coleridge and the Broad Church Movement, passim;* E.S. Shaffer, *Kubla Khan and the Fall of Jerusalem* (Cambridge, 1975), *passim;* Prickett, *Romanticism and Religion, passim;* Rigg, *Modern Anglican Theology,* pp. 49–57; J. Tulloch, *Movements of Religious Thought in Britain during the 19th Century* (London, 1885), p. 34; Storr, *Development of English Theology,* p. 337 ff.; B.M.G. Reardon, *From Coleridge to Gore* (London, 1971), pp. 161–62; J. Barrell, "Introduction," in *On the Constitution of Church and State,* by S.T. Coleridge, Everyman edition (London, 1972), pp. xxiv–xxv; McF/B, pp. 173, 197.

27. Hare later called De Quincey "a great benefactor of our literature, intellectually among the foremost of the present day," and expressed the hope that he would receive a government pension. Hare to unknown correspondent, 8 June 1848, National Library of Scotland MS. 1889, ff. 60–61.

28. Hare to Worsley, 1 March 1834, in *Memorials,* III, p. 229; *cf.* McF/B, p. 191.

29. [A.P. Stanley], "Report on the Judgement of the Judicial Committee of the Privy Council in the Case of Gorham *versus* the Bishop of Exeter," *Edinburgh Review,* XCII (July 1850), 266.

30. [W.J. Conybeare], "Church Parties," *Edinburgh Review,* XCVIII (Oct. 1853), 273, 330, 334 *et passim; cf.* W.O. Chadwick, *The Victorian Church* (London, 1966–70), I, p. 544 n. 2.

31. C. Thirlwall, "On the Broad Church," in Thirlwall, *Remains Literary and Theological,* ed. J.J.S. Perowne (London, 1877–78), III, pp.

481 ff.; cf. Thirlwall to Plumptre, 17 Oct. 1874, in Thirlwall, *Letters,* p. 384.

32. C.R. Sanders, "Was Frederick Denison Maurice a Broad-Churchman?" *Church History,* III (1934), 222–31; *Maurice,* I, pp. 20–31; Powell, "Annals of a Family," pp. 36–38, 45–47 *et passim,* B-PP.

33. *Maurice,* II, p. 632; *cf.* C.R. Sanders, "Coleridge, Maurice, and the Church Universal," *Journal of Religion,* XXI, no. 1 (Jan. 1941), 34–36 *et passim.*

34. *Maurice,* II, p. 359, I, p. 239, *cf.* pp. 183–84 *et passim.*

35. [Maurice], "Introduction," pp. lx–lxi; *cf.* Vidler, *Maurice and Company,* p. 233.

36. Robinson, *Diary,* II, p. 292; *cf.* Storr, *Development of English Theology,* pp. 338–39; Rigg, *Modern Anglican Theology,* pp. 36–37; Reardon, *From Coleridge to Gore,* pp. 160–62.

37. Vidler, *Maurice and Company,* pp. 229–31; *Maurice,* I, pp. 307–09, II, p. 255; [Maurice], "Introduction," pp. liv–lv; Hare, "The Contest with Rome," in *Charges,* pp. 56–58 *et passim.*

38. Maurice to Georgiana Hare, 24 Feb. 1849, in *Maurice,* I, p. 509.

39. Vidler, *Maurice and Company,* p. 232.

40. Maurice, "Introduction," p. viii.

41. Maurice to J.M.F. Ludlow [Dec. 1849], CUL Add. MS. 7348/8, no. 21, and in *Maurice,* II, p. 30; *cf,* T. Christensen, *The Divine Order: A Study of F.D. Maurice's Theology* (Leiden, 1973), pp. 294–98 *et passim.* Although this is a controversial book, the Platonic element in Maurice's theology has not been disputed by other Maurice scholars. McClain, *Maurice,* p. 3; O. Brose, *Frederick Denison Maurice: Rebellious Conformist* (Athens, Ohio, 1971), pp. 26–27; A.M. Ramsey, *F.D. Maurice and the Conflicts of Modern Theology* (Cambridge, 1951), pp. 11–21.

Chapter 13

1. Chadwick, *Victorian Church,* I, pp. 189–91; Bunsen, *Memoirs,* I, pp. 373–74; Hare to Maria Hare, 18 Aug. [1840], in *Memorials,* III, pp. 234–35; *Story,* I, p. 163; *Maurice,* I, p. 320.

2. Stanley, *Life of Arnold,* pp. 612–13; *cf.* T. Arnold, *Principles of Church Reform,* ed. M.J. Jackson and J. Rogan (London, 1962).

3. E. Hodder, *Life and Work of the Seventh Earl of Shaftesbury* (London, 1887), I, pp. 362–82; Chadwick, *Victorian Church,* I, pp. 189–90.

4. W. Ward, *The Life of John Henry Cardinal Newman, Based on His Private Journals and Correspondence* (London, 1912), I, p. 74; Purcell, *Manning,* I, pp. 272–73; J. Morley, *Life of W.E. Gladstone,* new ed. (New York, 1911), I, pp. 308–09; Chadwick, *Victorian Church,* I, pp. 191–92.

5. Manning to Hare, 28 Oct. 1841, MA/SMA, ff. 78–79.

6. Chadwick, *Victorian Church,* I, p. 190; *Story,* I, p. 163; Bunsen, *Memoirs,* I, p. 383.

NOTES TO CHAPTER 13

7. Quoted in Chadwick, *Victorian Church*, I, p. 192.
8. Hare to Manning, 23 Nov. [1841], MA/SMA. ff. 91–92; *cf*. Bunsen to Arnold, 14 July 1835, in Bunsen, *Memoirs*, I, p. 252.
9. Hare to Manning, 30 Dec. [1841], MA/SMA, ff. 95–96.
10. *Ibid.; cf*. Arnold to Hare, 7 Oct. 1833, B-PP.
11. Hare, *Vindication of Luther against His Recent English Assailants*, 2nd ed. (London, 1855), pp. 74–97; L.O. Frappell, "Coleridge and the 'Coleridgeans' on Luther," *Journal of Religious History*, VII, no. 4 (Dec. 1973), 316.
12. Hare, *The Victory of Faith* (Cambridge, 1840), *passim;* W.J. Baker, "Julius Charles Hare: A Victorian Interpreter of Luther," *South Atlantic Quarterly*, LXX, no. 1 (winter 1971), 95.
13. Baker, "Victorian Interpreter," pp. 96–98; Frappell, "Coleridgeans on Luther," p. 316. One of the assailants was a Scot.
14. MS. shelflist of the Hare Collection, TCL; Hare, "Sterling," pp. xvi–xvii; S.T. Coleridge, *Confessions of an Inquiring Spirit* (London, 1840), pp. 92–93; [Maurice], "Introduction," pp. xxvii–xxx; Frappell, "Coleridgeans on Luther," pp. 307–15; Ramsey, *Maurice*, p. 28 n. 1.
15. Hare, *Vindication of Luther*, p. 2; *cf*. Baker, "Victorian Interpreter," pp. 88, 91, 93.
16. Hare, *Vindication of Luther*, pp. 6–7; Baker, "Victorian Interpreter," pp. 96–97; Frappell, "Coleridgeans on Luther," pp. 316–18.
17. Hare, *Vindication of Luther*, pp. 8, 213, *cf*. pp. 8–73, 165–94, 213–15; Hare and D. Macmillan on the character of Sir William Hamilton, March 1846, BL Add. MSS. 55109, ff. 107, 109–11.
18. Hare, *Vindication of Luther*, pp. 74–75.
19. Baker, "Victorian Interpreter," p. 101; *cf*. Frappell, "Coleridgeans on Luther," pp. 322–23.
20. Hare to Whewell, 17 Oct. [1846], WP/TCL MS. 0.18.H2.28.
21. Reardon, *From Coleridge to Gore*, pp. 251–52.
22. Hare to Francis Hare, 26 Dec. 1837, in *Memorials*, II, pp. 185–86.
23. Coleridge, *Confessions*, pp. 27, 30–33, *cf*. pp. 15–22; Plumptre, p. xlviii.
24. Bunsen to Hare, 17 Sept. 1846, B-PP.
25. Hare to H.M. Frederic William IV, King of Prussia, undated draft, B-PP.
26. Hort, *Life and Letters of Hort*, I, p. 46; Whewell to Hare, 26 Oct. 1846, WP/TCL MS. 0.18.W2.87.
27. Hare to John Kenrick, 3 March 1846, Dr Williams's Library MS. 24.81.35.
28. Quoted in [Hare], *Vindication of the Chevalier Bunsen from the Charges of the* Christian Remembrancer, *From the* British Magazine *for September, 1846* (London [1846]), pp. 3–4.
29. Hare to Whewell, 11 Sept. [1846], WP/TCL MS. 0.18.M6.22.
30. Hare, *Vindication of Bunsen*, pp. 5, 6, *cf*. p. 7.
31. *Ibid.*, pp. 13–14, 10–11, 24–27; *cf*. Hare to Whewell regarding the

latter's support for the vindication, 17 Oct. [1846], WP/TCL MS. 0.18.H2.28.

32. Hare, "The Romanizing Tendencies of the Age," in *Charges*, pp. 123–24, *cf.* pp. 115 ff.; *idem.*, "Romanizing Fallacies," in *ibid.*, pp. 69–70, 75 ff., 79 ff.

33. See G. Best, "Popular Protestantism in Victorian Britain," in *Ideas and Institutions of Victorian Britain*, pp. 118–23 *et passim*.

34. Chadwick, *Victorian Church*, I, pp. 112–21.

35. *Ibid.*, I, p. 238, *cf.* pp. 237–47; J. Prest, *Lord John Russell* (London, 1972), pp. 275–77.

36. Chadwick, *Victorian Church*, I, pp. 241–46.

37. Hare to Whewell, 20 Dec [1847], WP/TCL Add. MS. a77.148; *cf.* Hare, *A Letter to the Very Reverend the Dean of Chichester, On the Agitation Excited by the Appointment of Dr Hampden to the See of Hereford*, 2nd ed. (London, 1848), p. 1; Vidler, *Maurice and Company*, pp. 234–35.

38. Prest, *Russell*, p. 278; *cf.* Prothero, *Life of Stanley*, I, p. 349.

39. Hare, *Letter to the Dean of Chichester*, pp. 2–4, 6–11, 23.

40. Hort, *Life and Letters of Hort*, I, pp. 62–63; *cf.* [Anon.], *An Attempt to Justify the Agitation against Dr Hampden to the See of Hereford, A Letter to Archdeacon Hare, By a Tutor of a College* (London, 1848); W.J. Trower, *An Address to the General Committee of the Chichester Diocesan Association, Occasioned by the . . . Letter of Archdeacon Hare* (London, 1848); *idem.*, *The Hampden Controversy: Plain Remarks on Archdeacon Hare's Letter* (London, 1848).

41. Hare to Whewell, 4 Feb. 1848, WP/TCL Add. MS. a77.150; Hare, *Letter to the Dean of Chichester*, p. 77.

42. C.C.F. Greville. *The Greville Memoirs*, ed. G.L. Strachey and R. Fulford (London, 1938), VI, p. 3.

43. J.H. Newman, *Letters and Diaries of John Henry Newman*, ed. C.S. Dessain (London, 1961–), XII, pp. 158–59.

44. Stanley, pp. 24–25; *Memorials*, I, pp. 198–200.

Chapter 14

1. Fox, *Memories of Old Friends*, II, p. 95; *cf.* Carlyle, *Sterling*, pp. vii–ix, 1–2; Tuell, *Sterling*, pp. 11, 14–15.

2. See Chadwick, *Victorian Church*, II, p. 112 ff.; B. Willey, *More Nineteenth Century Studies: A Group of Honest Doubters* (New York, 1956), *passim*.

3. Hare, "Sterling," pp. cxxxiii–cxxxvii.

4. *Ibid.*, pp. cxliii, cli–clii, clx–clxi.

5. *Ibid.*, pp. ccxix–ccxx, ccxxi, ccxxvii, ccxxviii.

6. W. Palmer, "On Tendencies towards the Subversion of Faith," *English Review*, X, no. 20 (Dec. 1848), article VIII, 399–444; *Maurice*, I, pp. 504–05; Tuell, *Sterling*, pp. 353–54 ff.; Vidler, *Maurice and Company*, pp. 236–37; Chadwick, *Victorian Church*, I, pp. 539–42.

7. Palmer, "Subversion of Faith," pp. 401, 427, 431.
8. *Ibid.*, p. 409.
9. Hare, *Thou Shalt Not Bear False Witness against Thy Neighbour: A Letter to the Editor of the* English Review (London, 1849), pp. 3–4, 20, 5.
10. *Ibid.*, pp. 11–12, 16–17, 18–19, 20, 22, 58, 26–27, 29–32, 34; *cf.* Plumptre, p. xlviii.
11. Hare, *Thou Shalt Not*, p. 38; *cf.* Hare to D. Macmillan, 22 May [1848], BL Add. MS. 55109, f. 122.
12. Hort, *Life and Letters of Hort*, I, p. 95.
13. Chadwick, *Victorian Church*, I, p. 541 nn. 2, 4; Tuell, *Sterling*, pp. 13–14.
14. *Record*, 1 March 1849.
15. Carlyle, *Sterling*, pp. 148–49; *cf.* Sterling to J.S. Mill [14 June 1838], King's College, Cambridge, Keynes MS. 154.7; J.S. Mill, *Later Letters of J.S. Mill, 1849–1873*, ed. F.E. Mineka and D.N. Lindley (Toronto, 1972), I, pp. 22–23, *cf.* p. 16 n. 13; Tuell, *Sterling*, pp. 365–67; M. St J. Packe, *Life of John Stuart Mill* (London, 1954), p. 229.
16. *Record*, 8 March 1849. For membership lists, see Carlyle, *Sterling*, p. 159; A.R. Ashwell and R.G. Wilberforce, *Life of Bishop Wilberforce* (London, 1880–82), I, p. 142 n. 8; *Maurice*, I, p. 516.
17. *Record*, 19 March 1849. The issue of 26 March 1849 attacked Thirlwall for having translated Schleiermacher.
18. Carlyle, *Sterling*, p. 159; *cf.* Tuell, *Sterling*, pp. 351–71, for a summary of the attacks; R.M. Grier, *John Allen, Vicar of Prees and Archdeacon of Salop: A Memoir* (London, 1889), pp. 127–32; Manning to S. Wilberforce, 21 March 1849, Chichester Diocesan Record Office, Wilberforce MS. 96/7, f. 65; *cf.* version in Ashwell and Wilberforce, *Life of Wilberforce*, I, pp. 142–43.
19. C. Thirlwall, *Letters to a Friend by Connop Thirlwall*, ed A.P. Stanley (London, 1881), p. 57, *cf.* p. 14; Brook, *Life of Robertson*, II, pp. 75–76.
20. Carlyle, *Sterling*, pp. vii–xi; Tuell, *Sterling*, pp. 16–23; Chadwick, *Victorian Church*, I, pp. 542–44.
21. Carlyle's copy survives in the Widener Collection at Harvard University, shelf mark 1.10.3. The marginalia run from p. xiv to p. lxxv. Many illustrate Carlyle's disdain for Coleridge, *e.g.* pp. xiv, xxiv, xxviii, *cf.* pp. xvii, xx–xxi, xxiii, xxvi, xxx. Curiously, Hare's own author's copy of the "Sterling" is also at Harvard.
22. Fox, *Memories of Old Friends*, II, p. 128; *cf.* Tuell, *Sterling*, p. 16.
23. Tuell, *Sterling*, p. 16; Packe, *Life of Mill*, p. 287.
24. Sanders, *Coleridge and the Broad Church Movement*, p. 137.
25. Packe, *Life of Mill*, p. 287; *cf.* Tuell, *Sterling*, pp. 21–23.
26. Hare to John Allen [3 Dec. 1851], B-PP; *cf. Maurice*, I, p. 548.
27. Packe, *Life of Mill*, p. 287; Tuell, *Sterling*, pp. 18–21; Carlyle, *New Letters*, II, pp. 117–18.

Chapter 15

1. Ludlow, "Autobiography of J.M.F. Ludlow" [typescript], CUL Add. MS. 7450.5, III, chaps. 18 and 19; *Maurice*, I, pp. 430–31, 457–61, 472; C. Kingsley, *Charles Kingsley: His Letters and Memories of His Life*, ed. F. Kingsley (London, 1877), I, pp. 154–56; N.C. Masterman, *John Malcolm Ludlow. Builder of Christian Socialism* (Cambridge, 1963), pp. 62–63.

2. Major studies are C.E. Raven, *Christian Socialism, 1848–1854* (London, 1920), and T. Christensen, *Origin and History of Christian Socialism, 1848–1854* (Aarhus, 1962). For revisions, see P.R. Allen, "F.D. Maurice and J.M. Ludlow: A Reassessment of the Leaders of Christian Socialism," *Victorian Studies*, XI, no. 4 (June 1968), 461–82; idem., "Christian Socialism and the Broad Church Circle," *Dalhousie Review*, XLIX, no. 1 (spring 1969), 58–68.

3. Maurice to Ludlow, 13 April 1848, CUL Add. MS. 7348/8, no. 5; and in *Maurice*, I, pp. 460–61.

4. Kingsley, *Charles Kingsley*, I, p. 157; Ludlow, "Autobiography," CUL Add. MS. 7450.5, III, chap. 19. Both misdate the meeting at Parker's. For contributions, see Raven, *Christian Socialism*, pp. 370–75; *Maurice*, I, p. 475.

5. Hare to Macmillan, 22 May [1848], BL Add. MS. 55109, f. 122.

6. Hare to Kingsley, 31 May 1848, Kingsley Papers, BL Add. MS. 41299, III, f. 7; *cf.* "Parson Lot," *Politics for the People*, nos. 1 and 4 (6 and 27 May 1848); Raven, *Christian Socialism*, p. 115; Christensen, *Origin and History*, pp. 83–84.

7. Maurice to Hare, 28 May 1848, in *Maurice*, I, pp. 476–77; Allen, "Maurice and Ludlow," pp. 468–69.

8. Ludlow, "Autobiography," CUL Add. MS. 7450.5, III, chap. 19, pp. 31–32 *et passim*, chap. 37, p. 12 n.; *cf.* Plumptre, p. lii; McClain, "Maurice: Man and Moralist," pp. 38–40, 56, 61; J.F.C. Harrison, *History of the Working Men's College, 1854–1954* (London, 1954), pp. 19–22 *et passim*.

9. Hare to Ludlow, 20 Feb. 1854, CUL Add. MS. 7348/10, no. 154.

10. *Maurice*, II, pp. 156 n., 163–64 ff.; Chadwick, *Victorian Church*, I, pp. 545–50.

11. Ramsey calls *Theological Essays* one of Maurice's weakest books. Ramsey, *Maurice*, p. 48; *cf.* Reardon, *From Coleridge to Gore*, pp. 186–94.

12. *Maurice*, I, pp. 451, 521–26, II, pp. 78–86, 90–96, 98–102, 164; Chadwick, *Victorian Church*, I, p. 547.

13. Hare to Thirlwall, 22 Aug. 1853, Columbia University Library MS. X825 T34 S6, vol. 2, ff. 21–22; *cf. Maurice*, II, pp. 174–76, 179–82; Chadwick, *Victorian Church*, I, p. 547.

14. *Maurice*, II, pp. 180–81; Chadwick, *Victorian Church*, I, p. 547. The whole controversy is thoroughly examined in G. Rowell, *Hell and the Victorians: A Study of the Nineteenth-Century Theological Con-*

troversies Concerning Eternal Punishment and the Future Life (Oxford, 1974), pp. 76–89 *et passim.* See also D. Cupitt, "The Language of Eschatology: F.D. Maurice's Treatment of Heaven and Hell," *Anglican Theological Review,* LIV, no. 4 (Oct. 1972), 305–17.

15. Maurice to Hare, 15 Sept. 1853, in *Maurice,* II, pp. 181–82.

16. Hare to unknown correspondent, 4 Oct. 1853, in *ibid.,* II, pp. 182–83; *cf.* S. Wilberforce to Dr Jelf, n.d., Bodleian Library MS. Wilberforce c.10, ff. 255–56. Wilberforce's biographers date the letter 27 August 1853 and print an expurgated version. Ashwell and Wilberforce, *Life of Wilberforce,* II, pp. 209–10.

17. *Maurice,* II, pp. 190–94; [Anon.], "King's College Council and the Fortieth Article," *Spectator,* XXVI (1853), 1113–14.

18. Kingsley to Maurice, n.d., Hove Public Library, Sussex; *cf.* Kingsley to Maurice, 21 July 1853, BL Add. MS. 41297, I, f. 42; Kingsley to Ludlow, 1 April 1849, denounced Maurice's critics as "quill-driving cowards and bigots." CUL Add. MS. 7348/5, no. 22; Merivale, *Autobiography,* pp. 272 ff.; Chadwick, *Victorian Church,* I, pp. 548–49; Robinson, *Diary,* III, pp. 415, 418.

19. Hare to Derwent Coleridge, 10 Dec. 1853, King's College, London.

20. *Maurice,* II, pp. 210–33. Tennyson summarized the anguish felt by Maurice's friends in his "To Maurice," the unexpurgated MS. version of which begins, "With loathsome, loveless prate of Hell,/Each bigot makes his infidel/Claps Calvin in God's chair and bids us/Honour the Devil & all is well." TCL MS. 0.15.36, Tennyson notebook no. 36: "Maud."

21. Robinson, *Diary,* III, p. 407.

22. Hare to Whewell, 31 Oct. 1849, WP/TCL Add. MS. a64.112.

23. Whewell to Hare, 1 and 11 Nov. 1849, *ibid.,* MSS. 0.18.W2.101–02; Hare to Sedgwick, 17 Nov. 1849, CUL Archives and Registrary MS., vol. 39.2, f. 16.12; Hare to Trench, 9 Nov. 1849, Royal Archives, Windsor Castle, MS. F.33.

24. Trench, Blakesley, and Alford. Hare to Whewell, 3 and 9 Nov. 1849, WP/TCL Add. MSS. a64.117, 113; Whewell to Hare, 19 Nov. 1849, *ibid.,* MS. 0.18.W2.103.

25. Robinson, *Diary,* III, pp. 359–60.

26. Hare to Havelock, 1850–51, Havelock-Allan Papers, North Yorkshire County Record Office; Marshman, *Havelock,* pp. 191–92, 196–201, 223.

27. Hare to Havelock [July 1850], North Yorkshire County Record Office.

28. *Memorials,* II, p. 329; *Story,* I, p. 98; Plumptre, p. xliii.

29. Hare to Manning, 3 Feb. 1849, MA/SMA, ff. 172–74.

30. Manning to Hare, 22 March 1851, *ibid.,* f. 178.

31. Hare to Manning, 25 March 1851, *ibid.,* f. 177.

32. *Memorials,* II, p. 332.

33. Leslie, *Manning,* p. 98; *cf.* Purcell, *Manning,* I, p. 634

34. Hare, *A Letter to the Hon. Richard Cavendish, On the Recent Judgement of the Court of Appeal, as Affecting the Doctrine of the*

Church, 2nd ed. (London, 1850), p. 10, *cf.* pp. 4, 6, 7–10, 12–14, 20, 30, 107 *et passim.*

35. R. Cavendish, *A Letter to Archdeacon Hare on the Judgement in the Gorham Case* (London, 1850), pp. 5–6, 9, 13 *et passim; cf.* J.M. Neale, *A Letter to Archdeacon Hare with Respect to His Pamphlets on the Gorham Question* (London, 1850), pp. 15, 17, 23–24; R. French, *A Letter to a Friend upon Certain Suggestions . . . by Archdeacon Hare . . . for the Removal of Doubts on the Doctrine of Regeneration* (Oxford, 1850), pp. 3–4, 50 *et passim.*

36. Hare, *A Few Words on the Rejection of the Episcopal Bill to Amend the Ecclesiastical Court of Appeal* (London, 1850), pp. 3–4, 7–8, 13–14, 19.

37. Hare to Manning, 25 March 1851, MA/SMA, f. 177.

38. Powell, "Annals of a Family," p. 109, B-PP; *cf. Memorials,* II, pp. 329, 331, 351.

39. MS. Declaration from Hare's parishioners, n.d., B-PP; Powell, "Annals of a Family," p. 109, *ibid.*

40. J. Campbell, Marquis of Breadalbane, Chamberlain of the Royal Household, to Hare, 3 June 1853, *ibid.*

41. Hare to Lord Breadalbane, 6 June 1853, *ibid.*

42. L. Powell, "Annals of a Family," pp. 122, *cf.* pp. 120–21, *ibid.; Memorials,* II, pp. 361–62; *Story,* I, pp. 480–81.

43. Powell, "Annals of a Family," p. 123, B-PP.

44. H.V. Elliott and J.N. Simpkinson, *Two Sermons Preached in Herstmonceux Church* (Cambridge, 1855), p. 18. Stanley, Plumptre, and A.J.C. Hare all repeated this account with slight variations. A.O.J. Cockshut, *Truth to Life: The Art of Biography in the Nineteenth Century* (London, 1974), pp. 43, 49–50, doubts the credibility of these last words. Yet Elliott recounted them before eye-witnesses, who must have been his informants. On the other hand, Lucilla Powell, an avid collector of death-bed scenes, did not record this one in her "Annals of a Family."

45. Powell, "Annals of a Family," pp. 123–24, B-PP; Bateman, *Life of Elliott,* pp. 259–62; *Memorials,* II, p. 363; *Story,* I, pp. 481–84. On Thirlwall's grief at Hare's death, see Hort, *Life and Letters of Hort,* I, p. 308.

Selected Bibliography

Space does not permit the recapitulation of all the titles cited in the notes. Included here are collections of manuscript sources, Julius Hare's own works, and printed primary and secondary sources which contain material such as Hare letters or a significant amount of information about Hare. Many biographical works are listed as primary sources because their principal value lies in the original correspondence which they contain.

The labour of research was lightened by such indispensable reference works as the *Dictionary of National Biography, Oxford English Dictionary, Oxford Dictionary of the Christian Church, New Cambridge Bibliography of English Literature,* Venns' *Alumni Cantabrigiensis,* and the *Wellesley Index to Victorian Periodicals.*

For material on the general religious and social background, the reader should consult the volumes in the Oxford series of *Bibliographies of British History* edited by L. Brown and I. Christie (1789–1851) and by H.J. Hanham (1851–1914), as well as the bibliographical essay "The Victorian Churches" by R.J. Helmstadter in *Victorian Prose: A Guide to Research,* ed. D.J. DeLaura (New York, 1973), pp. 387–432.

Manuscripts

Bayne-Powell Papers, private collection of R.L. Bayne-Powell, great grand-nephew of J.C. Hare and F.D. Maurice: Of particular interest are Hare's manuscript commonplace book, 1816–18, and continental travel diary, 1832–33, Xerox copies of which I have deposited in the library of Trinity College, Cambridge.

Beinecke Library, Yale University, New Haven, Connecticut: A.L.ss. of Hare, Southey, Thirlwall, Bunsen, Milnes, Maurice, and Stanley.

Bodleian Library, Oxford University: English Letters MSS.; Wilberforce MSS.; and Autograph MSS., A.L.ss. of Hare, Maurice, Stanley, Thirlwall, and Samuel Wilberforce.

Boston Public Library, Boston, Massachusetts: 3 A.L.ss. from Hare to Charles Ollier.
British Library, London: Additional Manuscripts, Flaxman Papers, Kingsley Papers, Macmillan and Company Archives.
Brotherton Library, Leeds University: Thomas Arnold Papers, correspondence of Julius Hare and Mary Arnold.
Cambridge University Archives and Registrary: Registrary MSS. dealing with the Regius Professorships of Greek and Divinity, and with endowed prizes and scholarships.
Cambridge University Library: Cholmondeley-Houghton MSS.; Additional Manuscripts, MS. diary of Joseph Romilly, MS. and TS. autobiography of J.M.F. Ludlow, and A.L.ss. of Hare, Maurice, Kingsley, Hughes, and Ludlow.
Chatsworth, Derbyshire: Cavendish Papers, A.L.S. from Hare to the sixth Duke of Devonshire.
Cheshire County Record Office, Chester: Stanley of Alderley Papers.
Columbia University Library, New York City: A.L.ss. of Hare and Thirlwall.
East Sussex County Record Office, Lewes: Minutes of the Hailsham Union Board of Guardians of the Poor.
Essex County Record Office, Chelmsford: Essex Commission of the Peace, Quarter Sessions Rolls.
Henry E. Huntington Library and Art Gallery, San Marino, California: F.J. Furnival Papers, A.L.ss. of Hare and Thirlwall.
Houghton Library, Harvard University, Cambridge, Massachusetts: Carlyle's annotated copy of Hare's memoir of John Sterling.
Hove Public Library, Hove, Sussex: Wolseley Papers, A.L.ss. of A.J.C. Hare and Charles Kingsley.
University of Kansas Library, Lawrence, Kansas: 2 A.L.ss. of F.D. Maurice.
King's College Library, Cambridge: Keynes MSS., correspondence of John Sterling and J.S. Mill, A.L.S. of Bishop Francis Hare.
King's College Library, London: A.L.ss. of Hare, Maurice, and Sara Coleridge.
Lancing College, Lancing, Sussex: Woodard Papers, correspondence of Julius Hare and Nathaniel Woodard. I have not used these letters, but have relied upon the work of my friend Dr Brian Heeney (see below).
National Library of Scotland, Edinburgh: A.L.ss. of Hare, Maurice, and Thirlwall.
National Library of Wales, Aberystwyth: A.L.ss. of Thirlwall and W.H. Thompson.
New York Public Library, New York City: Henry W. and Albert A. Berg Collection, correspondence of Julius Hare and John Taylor.
North Riding of Yorkshire County Record Office, Northallerton: Havelock-Allan Papers, correspondence of Julius Hare and Sir Henry Havelock.
Oblates of St Charles, St Mary of the Angels, Moorhouse Road, Bays-

SELECTED BIBLIOGRAPHY 241

water, London: Cardinal Manning Archive, correspondence of Julius Hare and H.E. Manning.
Royal Archives, Windsor Castle, Berkshire: A.L.S. from Julius Hare to R.C. Trench.
John Rylands Library, University of Manchester: English MSS., Gaskell Collection, Landor Papers, correspondence of Julius Hare and John Taylor, A.L.ss. of Landor and S.T. Coleridge.
Trinity College Library, Cambridge: Whewell Papers; Houghton Papers; Thirlwall Papers; MS. diary of John Allen; MS. shelflist of the Hare Collection, and—by the gracious permission of the College Council—the Conclusion Books.
Victoria and Albert Museum Library, South Kensington, London: Forster Papers, A.L.ss. of Landor, Hare, and W. Wordsworth.
West Sussex County and Diocesan Record Office, Chichester: Wilberforce Archive; Papers of Bishop A.T. Gilbert; Diocesan Cause Papers; Diocesan Church Fabric Papers.
Dr Williams's Library, Gordon Square, London: Henry Crabb Robinson Papers; 2 A.L.ss. from Julius Hare to John Kenrick.
Author's collection: Hare A.L.S.; MS. fragment.

Julius Hare's Works in Chronological Order

[J.C. Hare, trans.]. *Sintram and His Companions: A Romance*, From the German of Frederic Baron De La Motte Fouqué, Author of *Undine*, &c. London: C. & J. Ollier, 1820.
[————, trans.]. "A.W. Schlegel on Shakspeare's [sic] *Romeo and Juliet*; with Remarks upon the Character of German Criticism." *Olliers Literary Miscellany in Prose and Verse*, no. 1 (1820), 1–39.
[————, trans.]. "The Siege of Ancona: A Romantic Idyll," from the German of La Motte Fouqué. *Olliers Literary Miscellany*, no. 1 (1820), 54–61.
[————]. "On the German Drama. No. I: Oehlenschlaeger." *Olliers Literary Miscellany*, no. 1 (1820), 90–153.
[————, with A.W. Hare]. *A Layman's Letters to the Author of the* Trial of the Witnesses. London: Hunt, 1824.
[————]. "On Walter Savage Landor's *Imaginary Conversations*." *London Magazine*, IX, no. 5 (May 1824), 523–41. [Contains Hare's translation of "Kennst du das Land," Mignon's song from *Wilhelm Meister*.]
[————, trans.]. "The Love-Charm," from the German of Tieck. *Quarterly Magazine*, 2nd series, I, no. 1 (Aug. 1825), 146–73.
[————, with A.W. Hare]. *Guesses at Truth by Two Brothers*, New Edition, with a Memoir by E.H. Plumptre. London: Macmillan, 1866. [First series, 2 vols. London: Taylor, 1827; Second series, London: Taylor and Walton, 1848; by 1905 nineteen other British and American editions had appeared.]
————. *The Children of Light: A Sermon Preached before the University*

of Cambridge at St Mary's Church on Advent Sunday, 1828. Cambridge: Smith, 1828.

———, trans., with C. Thirlwall. *The History of Rome,* by B.G. Niebuhr. New ed. 3 vols. London: Walton and Maberley, 1851–55. [Vols. I and II first published London: Taylor, 1828–32; vol. III translated by L. Schmitz and W. Smith.]

———. *A Vindication of Niebuhr's* History of Rome *from the Charges of the Quarterly Reviewer.* Cambridge: Taylor, 1829.

[———, trans.]. "Richter's 'Vision of a Godless World.'" *Athenaeum,* III, no. 67 (4 Feb. 1829), 65–66.

[———]. "Museum of Thought I–V." *Athenaeum, III,* no. 73 (18 March 1829), 169–70; no. 74 (25 March 1829), 187–90; no. 75 (1 April 1829), 201–07; no. 76 (8 April 1829), 217–18; no. 78 (22 April 1829), 241–43.

[———, trans.]. "Goethe's First and Second Poetic Epistles." *Athenaeum,* III, no. 80 (6 May 1829), 280; no. 81 (13 May 1829), 297–98.

[———, trans.]. "Goethe's 'Alexis & Dora.'" *Athenaeum,* IV, no. 105 (28 Oct. 1829), 677–78.

[———, trans.]. *The Old Man of the Mountain; The Love Charm; and Pietro of Abano: Tales from the German of Tieck.* London: Moxon, 1831.

[———]. "Preface." *Philological Museum,* I, no. 1 (Nov. 1831), i–iv.

[———]. "On the Names of the Days of the Week." *Philological Museum,* I, no. 1 (Nov. 1831), 1–73.

[———, trans.]. "On the Origin and Growth of the Latini as a Peculiar Class in the Latin State and on the Jus Italicum," from the German of Savigny. *Philological Museum,* I, no. 1 (Nov. 1831), 150–73.

[———, trans.]. "On the Sicelians of the *Odyssey*," from the German of Niebuhr. *Philological Museum,* I, no. 1 (Nov. 1831), 174–76.

[———]. "Miscellaneous Observations: On a Passage of Thucydides, III, 91; Savigny and the *Edinburgh Review;* Hermann's *Opuscula;* Dobree's *Adversaria.*" *Philological Museum,* I, no. 1 (Nov. 1831), 188–208.

[———, trans.]. "On the Age of the Coast-Describer, Scylax of Caryanda," from the German of Niebuhr. *Philological Museum,* I, no. 2 (Feb. 1832), 245–79.

[———, trans.]. "On the Historical References, and the Allusions in Horace," from the German of Buttman. *Philological Museum,* I, no. 3 (May 1832), 439–84.

[———]. "On English Orthography." *Philological Museum,* I, no. 3 (May 1832), 640–78.

[———]. "Miscellaneous Observations: Sir William Joneses Division of the Day." *Philological Museum,* I, no. 3 (May 1832), 689–91.

[———, trans.]. "On the Roman *Coloni,*" from the German of Savigny. *Philological Museum,* II, no. 1 (Nov. 1832), 117–45.

[———]. "Comments on This Matter of the G[ree]k V[er]b." *Philological Museum,* II, no. 1 (Nov. 1832), 203–26.

SELECTED BIBLIOGRAPHY 243

[————]. "Miscellaneous Observations: On English Preterites and Genitives." *Philological Museum*, II, no. 1 (Nov. 1832), 243–62.

————. "Samuel Taylor Coleridge and the English Opium-Eater." *British Magazine and Monthly Register of Religious and Ecclesiastical Information, Parochial History, and Documents Respecting the State of the Poor, Progress of Education, &c.,* VII, no. 1 (1 Jan. 1835), 15–27.

[————, ed.]. *Sermons to a Country Congregation* by A.W. Hare. 2 vols. London: Hatchard, 1836. [Appeared in seven editions over the next four decades.]

————, trans. *Portions of the Psalms in English Verse, Selected for Public Worship*. London: J.W. Parker, 1839.

————. *The Victory of Faith, and Other Sermons*. Cambridge: Deighton [1840] [Third edition, London: Macmillan, 1874, contains reprints of F.D. Maurice's introduction to the *Charges* and of A.P. Stanley's obituary article on Hare from the *Quarterly Review*.]

————. *Sermons Preacht in Herstmonceux Church*. 2 vols. London: J.W. Parker, 1841–49.

————. "Preface." *History of Rome*, by Thomas Arnold, vol. III. 2nd ed. London: Fellowes, 1845.

————. *The Mission of the Comforter, and Other Sermons*. 2 vols. London: J.W. Parker, 1846. [Reissued three times by Macmillans.]

————. *Vindication of the Chevalier Bunsen from the Charges of the* Christian Remembrancer, *From the* British Magazine *for September 1846*. London: Thomas Savill [1846].

————. *A Letter to the Very Reverend the Dean of Chichester, On the Agitation Excited by the Appointment of Dr Hampden to the See of Hereford*. 2nd ed. London: J.W. Parker, 1848.

————, ed. *Essays and Tales*, by John Sterling, Corrected and Edited, With a Memoir of His Life. 2 vols. London: J.W. Parker, 1848.

————. *Thou Shalt Not Bear False Witness against Thy Neighbour: A Letter to the Editor of the* English Review, *With a Letter from Professor Maurice to the Author*. London: J.W. Parker, 1849.

————. *A Letter to the Hon. Richard Cavendish, On the Recent Judgement of the Court of Appeal, as Affecting the Doctrine of the Church*, Second Edition, With a Postscript. London: J.W. Parker, 1850.

————. *A Few Words on the Rejection of the Episcopal Bill to Amend the Ecclesiastical Court of Appeal*. London: J.W. Parker, 1850.

————. *The Life of Luther in 48 Historical Engravings by Gustav König*, With Explanations by Archdeacon Hare. Continued by S. Winkworth. London: Murray, 1855.

————. *Miscellaneous Pamphlets on Some of the Leading Questions Agitated in the Church during the Last Ten Years*. Cambridge: Macmillan, 1855. [Reprints seven charges, sermons, and other short pieces.]

————. *Vindication of Luther against His Recent English Assailants*, Second Edition, Reprinted and Enlarged from the Notes to *The Mission of the Comforter*. London: J.W. Parker, 1855.

————. *Charges to the Clergy of the Archdeaconry of Lewes, Delivered during the Ordinary Visitations from the Year 1840 to 1854, With Notes on the Principal Events Affecting the Church during that Period* . . . With an Introduction Explanatory of His Position in the Church with Reference to the Parties Which Divide It [by F.D. Maurice]. 3 vols. in 1 [each item separately paginated]. Cambridge: Macmillan, 1856.

———. *The Contest with Rome.* 2nd ed. Cambridge: Macmillan, 1856. [Reprint of Hare's 1851 charge.]

———. *Sermons Preacht on Particular Occasions.* Cambridge: Macmillan, 1858. [Preface by F.D. Maurice.]

———. *Fragments of Two Essays in English Philology,* ed. J.E.B. Mayer. London: Macmillan, 1873. [Contains "Words Derived from Names of Persons" and "Words Corrupted by False Analogy or False Derivation."]

Other Printed Primary Sources

Bunsen, C.K.J. *Memoirs of Baron Bunsen, Late Minister Plenipotentiary and Envoy Extraordinary of His Majesty Frederic William IV, At the Court of St. James.* Edited by F. Bunsen. 2nd ed. 2 vols. London: Longmans, 1869.

Bunsen, F. *Life and Letters of Frances, Baroness Bunsen.* Edited by A.J.C. Hare, 2 vols. London: Daldy, Isbister, 1879.

Clark, J.W., and T. McK. Hughes. *Life and Letters of the Reverend Adam Sedgwick.* 2 vols. Cambridge: Cambridge University Press, 1890.

Coleridge, Sara. *Memoirs and Letters of Sara Coleridge.* Edited by Her Daughter. 2 vols. London: H.S. King, 1873.

Conybeare, W.J. "Church Parties." *Edinburgh Review,* XCVIII (Oct. 1853), 273–342.

Elliott, H.V., and J.N. Simpkinson. *Two Sermons Preacht in Herstmonceux Church, ON SEPTUAGESIMA SUNDAY, February 4, 1855, Being the Sunday after the Funeral of Archdeacon Hare.* Cambridge: Macmillan, 1855.

Forster, J. *Walter Savage Landor: A Biography.* 2 vols. London: Chapman and Hall, 1869.

Graves, C.L. *Life and Letters of Alexander Macmillan.* London: Macmillan, 1910.

Hare, A.J.C. *Memorials of a Quiet Life.* 13th ed. 3 vols. London: Daldy, Isbister, 1876. [Earlier editions of this best seller were also published by Strahan, and some later ones by Smith, Elder.]

———. *The Story of My Life.* 6 vols. London: George Allen, 1896–1900.

———. *The Years with Mother* and *In My Solitary Life.* Edited by Malcolm Barnes. 2 vols. London: Allen and Unwin, 1952–53. [Abridgement of *Story of My Life.*]

Hughes, T. *Memoir of Daniel Macmillan.* London: Macmillan, 1883.

Macmillan, A. *Letters of Alexander Macmillan.* Edited by G.A. Macmillan. London: Privately printed, 1908.

Maurice, F.D. "The Children of Light." *Athenaeum*, II, no. 62 (31 Dec. 1828), 977–78.

———. "Guesses at Truth." *Athenaeum*, II, no. 42 (13 Aug. 1828), 656–58.

———. *Life of Frederick Denison Maurice Chiefly Told in His Own Letters.* Edited by F. Maurice. 3rd ed. 2 vols. London: Macmillan, 1884.

Niebuhr, B.G. *The Life and Letters of Barthold George Niebuhr, With Essays on His Character and Influence, by the Chevalier Bunsen and Professors Brandis and Lorbell.* Edited by S. Winkworth. New York: Harper, 1854. [First published in 2 vols., London: Chapman and Hall, 1852.]

Norris, W. *On the Meeting of Three Schoolfellows and Friends, After a Separation of Forty Years.* N.p.: Privately printed, 1850. [Norris, Havelock, and Hare; reminiscences in bad verse.]

Nowell-Smith, S., ed. *Letters to Macmillan.* London: Macmillan, 1967.

Palmer, W. "On Tendencies towards the Subversion of Faith." *English Review*, X, no. 20 (Dec. 1848), 399–444.

Prothero, R.E. *Life and Correspondence of Arthur Penrhyn Stanley.* 2 vols. London: John Murray, 1893.

Purcell, E.S. *Life of Cardinal Manning, Archbishop of Westminster.* 2 vols. London: Macmillan, 1895.

Rigg, J.H. *Modern Anglican Theology: Chapters on Coleridge, Hare, Maurice, Kingsley, and Jowett, and on the Doctrine of the Sacrifice and Atonement.* London: Heylin, 1857.

Robinson, H.C. *Diary, Reminiscences, and Correspondence of Henry Crabb Robinson,* Edited by T. Sadler. 3 vols. London: Macmillan, 1869.

———. *Henry Crabb Robinson on Books and Their Writers.* Edited by E.J. Morley. 3 vols. London: Dent, 1938.

Stanley, A.P. "Archdeacon Hare." *Quarterly Review*, XCVII, no. 2 (June 1855), 1–28.

———. *Life and Correspondence of Thomas Arnold.* 2nd ed. 2 vols. London: Fellowes, 1844. [One volume popular edition, London: John Murray, 1904.]

Stifler, J.M., ed. *"My Dear Girl": The Correspondence of Benjamin Franklin with Polly Stevenson, Georgiana and Catherine Shipley.* New York: Doran, 1927.

Thirlwall, C. *Letters Literary and Theological of Connop Thirlwall.* Edited by J.J.S. Perowne and L. Stokes. London: Bentley, 1881.

———. *Letters to a Friend by Connop Thirlwall.* Edited by A.P. Stanley. London: Bentley, 1881.

[Whewell, W., ed.]. *English Hexameter Translations from Schiller, Göthe, Homer, Callinus, and Meleager.* London: John Murray, 1847.

Life and Selections from the Correspondence of William Whewell. Edited by Mrs J.M. Stair Douglas. London: Kegan Paul, 1881.

———. *William Whewell, D.D.: An Account of His Writings with Selections from His Literary and Scientific Correspondence.* Edited by I. Todhunter. 2 vols. London: Macmillan, 1876.

Winkworth, S., and C. *Memorials of Two Sisters, Susanna and Catherine Winkworth.* Edited by M.J. Shaen. London: Longmans, 1908.

Secondary Sources

Allen, P.R. *The Cambridge Apostles: The Early Years.* Cambridge: Cambridge University Press, forthcoming.

Annan, N. "The Intellectual Aristocracy." In *Studies in Social History: A Tribute to G.M. Trevelyan,* edited by J.H. Plumb, pp. 243–87. London: Longmans, 1955.

Baker, W.J. "Julius Charles Hare: A Victorian Interpreter of Luther." *South Atlantic Quarterly,* LXX, no. 1 (winter 1971), 88–101.

Burrow, J.W. "The Uses of Philology in Victorian England." In *Ideas and Institutions of Victorian Britain: Essays in Honour of George Kitson Clark,* edited by R. Robson, pp. 180–204. London: Bell, 1967.

Cannon, W.F. "The Role of the Cambridge Movement in Early 19th Century Science." In *Acts of the 10th International Congress of the History of Science,* pp. 317–20. Ithaca, N.Y.: Cornell University Press, 1962.

———. "Scientists and Broad Churchmen: An Early Victorian Intellectual Network." *Journal of British Studies,* IV, no. 1 (Nov. 1964), 65–88.

Chadwick, W.O. *The Victorian Church.* 2 vols. London: Adam and Charles Black, 1966–70.

Distad, N.M. "Julius Charles Hare and the 'Broad Church' Ideal." In *The View from the Pulpit: Victorian Ministers and Society,* edited by P.T. Phillips, pp. 45–65. Toronto: Macmillan Canada, 1978.

———. "The *Philological Museum* of 1831–1833." *Victorian Periodicals Newsletter,* no. 18 (Dec. 1972), 27–30.

Dockhorn, K. *Der Deutschen Historismus in England: Ein Beitrag zur Englischen Geistesgeschichte des 19. Jahrhunderts.* Göttingen: Vanderhoeck and Ruprecht, 1950.

Forbes, D. *The Liberal Anglican Idea of History.* Cambridge: Cambridge University Press, 1950.

———. "*Historismus* in England." *Cambridge Journal,* IV, no. 7 (April 1951), 387–400.

Frappell, L.O. "Coleridge and the 'Coleridgeans' on Luther." *Journal of Religious History,* VII, no. 4 (Dec. 1973), 307–23.

Galinsky, H.K. "Is Thomas De Quincey the Author of *The Love-Charm?*" *Modern Language Notes,* LII, no. 6 (June 1937), 389–94.

Gloyn, C.K. *The Church in the Social Order: A Study of Anglican Social Theory from Coleridge to Maurice.* Forest Grove, Ore.: Pacific University Press, 1942.

Heeney, W.B.D. *Mission to the Middle Classes: The Woodard Schools, 1848–1891.* London: S.P.C.K., 1969.

Helmstadter, R.J. "Julius Hare's *Apologia Pro Patria Sua.*" *Ontario Victorian Studies Association Newsletter,* no. 8 (Oct. 1971), 18–21.

SELECTED BIBLIOGRAPHY

Kozicki, H. "Philosophy of History in Tennyson's Poetry to the 1842 Poems." *Journal of English Literary History,* XLII (1975), 88–106.
Leslie, S. *Henry Edward Manning: His Life and Labours.* 2nd ed. London: Burns, Oates and Washburne, 1921.
McClain, F.M. *Maurice: Man and Moralist.* London: S.P.C.K., 1972.
McFarland, G.F. "The Early Literary Career of Julius Charles Hare." *Bulletin of the John Rylands Library,* XLVI, no. 1 (Sept. 1963), 42–83.
———. "Julius Charles Hare, Coleridge, DeQuincey, and German Literature." *Bulletin of the John Rylands Library,* XLVII, no. 1 (Sept. 1964), 165–97.
Merriam, H.G. *Edward Moxon: Publisher of Poets.* New York: Columbia University Press, 1939.
Prasher, A.L. "The Censorship of Landor's *Imaginary Conversations.*" *Bulletin of the John Rylands Library,* XLIX, no. 2 (spring 1967), 427–63.
Preyer, R.O. *Bentham, Coleridge, and the Science of History.* Bochum-Langendreer: Pöppinghaus, 1958.
———. "Julius Hare and Coleridgean Criticism." *Journal of Aesthetics and Art Criticism,* XV, no. 4 (June 1957), 449–60.
Robson, R. "Trinity College in the Age of Peel." In *Ideas and Institutions of Victorian Britain: Essays in Honour of George Kitson Clark,* edited by R. Robson, pp. 312–35. London: Bell, 1967.
Sanders, C.R. *Coleridge and the Broad Church Movement: Studies in S.T. Coleridge, Dr. Arnold of Rugby, J.C. Hare, Thomas Carlyle, and F.D. Maurice.* Durham, N.C.: Duke University Press. 1942.
Storr, V.F. *Development of English Theology in the Nineteenth Century, 1800–1860.* London: Longmans, 1913.
Super, R.H. *The Publication of Landor's Works.* Supplement to the Bibliographical Society's *Transactions,* no. 18. London: Bibliographical Society, 1954.
———. *Walter Savage Landor: A Biography.* London: Calder, 1957. [First published by New York University Press in 1954.]
Thirlwall, J.C. *Connop Thirlwall: Historian and Theologian.* London: S.P.C.K., 1936.
Tuell, A. *John Sterling: A Representative Victorian.* New York: Macmillan, 1941.
Venables, E. "The Castle of Herstmonceux and Its Lords." *Sussex Archaeological Collections,* IV (1851), 125–202.
Vidler, A.R. *F.D. Maurice and Company: Nineteenth Century Studies.* London: S.C.M. Press, 1966.
Winstanley, D.A. *Early Victorian Cambridge.* Cambridge: Cambridge University Press, 1940.

Index

Please note that Cambridge, London, and Oxford have *not* been indexed as place-names. Titles of books and articles are listed under the names of single or principal authors where possible. Julius Hare is designated throughout as 'JCH'. In lieu of a genealogical table members of the Hare family are supplied with dates of birth and death and notes on kinship.

Ainsworth, William Harrison, 68
Airy, George Biddle, 51
Albert, Prince Consort, 195
Alexander, Mary Manning ["Ma-Man"], Mrs, 54–55, 56, 136
Alexander, Michael Solomon, 163
Alford, Henry, 77, 112
Allen, John, 181, 182
Altertumswissenschaft, 74 ff., 79–80, 100
Aponte, Emmanuele, 9, 11, 12–13
Apostles, see Cambridge Conversazione Society
Aristotle, 25, 41
Arnold, Mary, 104, 131
Arnold, Thomas, as Broad Churchman, 157, 176; JCH eulogizes, 104; JCH, friendship with, 102–104; as historian, 98, 102–104, 109; Jerusalem Bishopric, 162; Newman attacks, 164; Niebuhr, reviews, 108; on "Vindication of Niebuhr," 110; & *Philological Museum,* 77; mentioned, 112, 121, 127, 166, 176
Athenaeum, 30, 47, 48, 73, 114–115

Barrow, John, 108
Benthamism, 46, 47–48, 84, 101, 114
Blakesley, Joseph Williams, 52, 56, 121
Bonaparte, Napoleon, 10, 29
Bonn, 56, 74, 110, 119, 122–123; University of, 74, 113
British Critic & Theological Review, 109

British Magazine & Monthly Register, 168
Broad Church, & Benthamism, 48–49; & Bunsen, 120–121; & "Children of Light," 48, 51; definition, 157–158; divine punishment, 27, 187–190; Evangelicals attack, 180–182; freedom of expression, 58, 187–190; goals, viii, 143–145, 147–148, 157–158; JCH's role in, 48, 51, 148, 150, 158–161, (chap. 13) 162–173, 176–182; Maurice on, 159–160; National Church, 126, 144–145, 147–148; nationalism, 82, 147–148; Thirlwall on, 158–159; toleration, 86 ff., 126, 139–140, 145, 157–158, 190; Tractarians attack, 176–180
Buckingham, James Silk, 114
Bunsen, Christian Karl Josias, Chevalier von, *Ägyptens Stelle in der Weltgeschichte,* 168–170; & comparative linguistics, 79; JCH's decoration, 167; JCH defends, 86, 168–170; JCH meets, 120–121, 122; Herstmonceux, resides at, 135; Jerusalem Bishopric, 162–163; Max Müller & S. Winkworth, patron of, 150; on Niebuhr, 110; & *Philological Museum,* 75, 78; Thirlwall meets, 32; mentioned, 54, 82, 124, 176, 187, 195
Bunsen, Frances Waddington, Baroness, 32, 135
Byron, George Gordon, Lord, 26, 46

248

INDEX 249

Cambridge Conversazione Society ["Apostles"], 45–47, 114, 125, 191; see also Maurice, F. D. & Sterling, John

Cambridge Union Debating Society, 28–30, 31

Cambridge University, Benthamism at, 46–48; degree requirements, 32; intellectual network, 23–24, 112–113; ordination requirements, 40–41; political repression at, 29; social life, 51–55; reform, 23–24, 49, 145; religion at, 27–28, 40–41, 48, 86, 191

Cambridge University, Trinity College, viii, (chap. 2) 23–34; Benthamism at, 46–49; curriculum, 23, 25; fellowship examinations, 32; Fellows, Hurrell Froude on, 52–53, A. P. Stanley on, 52, remuneration of, 56; JCH's rooms at, 119; "Renaissance" at, 23; Roman Catholicism at, 52; social life, 51–55; students on, 45 ff.; Tutor's "sides," 43

Carlyle, Thomas, as Germanist, 30, 37, 83; JCH compared with, 96; & JCH, 135–136, 183; Herstmonceux, visits, 135–136; & Sterling, 174, *Life of John Sterling*, 182–183

Cary, Henry Francis, 40, 121

Cavendish, Richard, 193–194

Cavendish, Lord William, 116

Charterhouse school, 19–22

Christian Remembrancer, 168

Christian Socialism, 160, 184–187

Clare, John, 40

Classical Museum, 79, 213 n.34

Clinton, Henry Fynes, 77

Colburn, Henry, firm of, 68, 106, 114

Coleridge, Samuel Taylor, & Apostles, 46; Coleridge Prize, 154–155; as Germanist, 30, 155–157; & *Guesses at Truth,* 70–71; & JCH, 39–40, 56, 128; JCH defends, 155–157; historiography, (chap. 8) 93–104, N.B. 96; on inspiration, 167; as intellectual regenerator, 82; National Church, vision of, 148; papers, 155; works: *Aids to Reflection,* 70; *Biographia Literaria,* 156; *Essays of His Own Times,* 156; *Table-Talk,* 156; mentioned, 25, 26, 45, 47, 84, 127, 165, 176, 182

Coleridge, Sara, 155, 156

Conybeare, John Josias, 88

Conybeare, William John, 157–158, 159

Croft, John, 49–50

Darley, George, 135

Dashwood, Anna Mary Shipley, Mrs [first cousin of JCH], 18, 55, 116

Deighton, J., firm of, 77, 79, 103

DeQuincey, Thomas, 40, 83–84, 85, 127, 155–157, 175, 230 n.27; "Goethe as Reflected in His Novel *Wilhelm Meister,*" 83

DeStaël-Holstein, Germaine Necker, Baronne, 30; *De l'Allemagne,* 30

Devonshire, Georgiana Spencer Cavendish, Duchess of, 6, 7, 8, 116

Devonshire, William Spencer Cavendish, sixth Duke of, 116

Dictionary of Greek & Roman Biography and Mythology, 113

Digby, Kenelm Henry, 25, 52, 121, 127; *Broad Stone of Honour,* 52, 128, & Disraeli, 128

Donaldson, John William, 112–113; Bopp's *New Cratylus,* 112–113; *Theatre of the Greeks,* 113

Duncan, James, 69, 106

Edgeworth, Maria, 32–33, 203 n.61

Edinburgh Review, 26, 30, 63, 107

Elliott, Henry Venn, 24, 124, 196–197

Ellis, Thomas Flower, 88

Emerson, Ralph Waldo, 122, 176, 222 n.27

English Hexameter Translations, 115

English Review, 176, 180

Essays & Reviews, 86, 158

Essex, Hare family origins in, 3

Flaxman, John, 9, 10, 15, 16
Foreign Quarterly Review, 107, 109
Fouqué, Friedrich Heinrich Karl, Baron de la Motte, 82, 206 nn.12 & 15; works: "Siege of Ancona," 38; *Sintram & His Companions,* 17, 35–38, 81, 206 n.12; *Undine,* 36, 37
Fox, Caroline, 89, 142, 174, 182, 183
Franklin, Benjamin, 7–8
Fraser's Magazine, 85
Friedrich Wilhelm IV, King of Prussia, 162, 167–168
Froude, Richard Hurrell, 52–53

George I, King of England, 30, 31
German Language, English knowledge of, 30–32, 35–36 ff., 51, 74 ff., 81–92, 169
Germano-Coleridgean historiography, (chap. 8) 93–104, 113–114; see also Niebuhr and Roman history
Gifford, William, 61, 63
Gilbert, Ashurst Turner, 138, 141
Goethe, J.W. von, 15, 25, 83, 84, 115, 120, 156; works: "Alexis & Dora," 115; "Kennst du das Land," 83; "Poetic Epistles," 115; *Wilhelm Meister,* 37, 83
Gorham, George Cornelius, case of, 193
Green, Joseph Henry, 155
Greville, Charles Cavendish Fulke, 173

Hallam, Henry, 165
Hamilton, Sir William, 165
Hampden, Renn Dickson, 170–173
Hare, Anna-Maria Clementina (1799–1813) [fifth child of Francis & Georgiana Hare-Naylor], 13, 17
Hare, Anna Maria [formerly Mrs Mealey], Mrs (d.1849) [second wife of Francis Hare-Naylor], 17
Hare, Anna Paul ["Italima"] (1801–1864) [wife of Francis George Hare; mother of A. J. C. Hare], 129, 135
Hare, Augustus John Cuthbert (1834–1902) [son of Francis George & Anna Hare; adopted by Maria Leycester Hare], on Mrs Alexander, 54, 136; birth & adoption, 129; on Bunsen family, 135; on JCH, 133–134; on JCH's betrothal, 132–133; & "Italima," 135; Maurice family, hatred of, 131–135; suffers at hands of Esther Hare, 131, 134; visitors at Herstmonceux, 135; mentioned, 5, 14, 16, 17, 138, 141, 146, 192
Hare, Augustus William (1792–1834) [second child of Francis & Georgiana Hare-Naylor], adopted by Lady Jones, 11; Arnold, introduces JCH to, 102; birth, 8; clerical career, 116–117; death, 128; education, 15, 19; finances, 56; Herstmonceux, refuses living, 116; JCH & Cambridge post, 42; JCH's engagement, ended, 55; & Landor's dialogues, 62; as preacher, 118; *Alton Sermons,* 146, 149; *Guesses at Truth,* 70, 72, see under JCH
Hare, Francis (1671–1740) [Bishop of Chichester; great-grandfather of JCH], 3–5
Hare, Francis George (1786–1842) [eldest child of Francis & Georgiana Hare-Naylor], birth, 8; Bologna, letters from, 11, 12; character, 18–19; death, 135; education, 9, 12, 14, 15, 18; finances, 56; JCH visits, (in Paris) 33, (in Milan) 40; & Herstmonceux advowson, 116–117; & Landor, 58–59, 67
Hare, Jane Esther Maurice (1814–1864) [sister of F. D. Maurice; wife of JCH], 131–136; & Mrs Alexander, 136; A.J.C. Hare, hated by, 131, 134; JCH, devotion to, 133, 194–196; JCH on, 133, 134; Lucy Hare on, 132; & "Italima," 135; & Landor, 136; sells JCH's paintings, 222 n.26
Hare, Julius Charles (1795–1855) [third child of Francis & Georgiana Hare-Naylor], *chronologi-*

INDEX

cal sequence: parents, 5–17; birth, 9; appearance as infant, 9, 12; christened by Duchess of Brissac, 9; nursed, 11; early speech, 12; Tonbridge school, 15; taken to Weimar, 15; tutored by brother Francis, 15–16; Charterhouse school, 19–22; matriculates at Trinity College, Cambridge, 23–24; graduates B.A., 32; elected Fellow, 32; visits Paris, 33, 35; at Middle Temple, 33–34; literary labours, (chap. 3), 35–40, 58–74, 81 ff.; translates *Sintram,* 35–38; inspires *Olliers Literary Miscellany,* 38–39; contributes to *London Magazine,* 40, 63, 81 ff.; visits Milan, 40; agent & editor for Landor, 58–69; stands for Regius Professorship of Greek, 49–51; ordained, 116; preaches against "Children of Light," 47–48; translates Niebuhr's *Römische Geschichte,* 105–113; tours northern Europe, 55–56; appointed chaplain to sixth Duke of Devonshire, 116; contributes to *Athenaeum,* 114–115; edits *Philological Museum,* 74–78; Italian tour, 119–123; becomes Rector of Herstmonceux, 123–126; tutors private pupils, 127–128; shares Herstmonceux with Maria Hare, 128–129, 152; defends Coleridge, 155–157; betrothal & marriage, 131–133; appointed Archdeacon of Lewes, 137–148; Vice-President of Sussex Archaeological Society, 150; persuades Whewell to remain at Cambridge, 150–152; finances Macmillan brothers, 152–154; supports Jerusalem Bishopric, 162–164; defends Luther, 163–166; decorated by King of Prussia, 167–168; defends Bunsen, 168–170; defends Hampden, 172–173; writes memoir of Sterling, 174–176; defends Sterling, 177–182; proposes *Politics for the People,* 184–185; disheartened by Maurice's dismissal, 187–190; courts Regius Professorship of Divinity, 190–191; serves on Wordsworth Monument Committee, 191; reunited with Havelock, 191–192; upset by Manning's conversion, 192–193; appointed a Royal Chaplain, 195; succumbs to illness, 194–196; last words, 196, 237 n.44; death, 196; funeral, 196–197; *alphabetical sequence:*

Archdeacon of Lewes, (chap. 11) 137–148; on archidiaconal dress, 140; duties as, 141–142; persistence as, 194–196; pleasure in, 152; reform, sees need for, 160

art, appreciation for, 122, 124, 142; collection of, 119, 122, 124, 221 n.14, 222 n.26

Benthamism, opposition to, 47–49, 84, 101

bibliomania, 12, 18, 56–57, 123–124

bishopric, lack of ambition for, 138–139

Broad Churchmanship, 48, 51, 148, 150, 158–161, (chap. 13) 162–173, 176–182

Calvinism, horror of, 27

Cambridge Apostles, mentor to, 46–47, 114–115, 125, 191; see also Maurice, F.D. & Sterling, John

Cambridge Union, speech for, 28–30

Chartism, remedies for, 184–186

children, manner with, 133

church building & restoration, 138, 146

Church unity, desire for, 126, 127, 139–140, 143, 144–145, 147–148, 149, 157, 166, 179, 180–182, 189–190, 192–194

Coleridge & Coleridgeanism, affection for, 25, 26, 39–40, 46, 70–71, 96, 127, 128, 148, 154–157, 167

Convocation, support for, 147, 160

cosmopolitanism, vii, 13, 16, 18, 167–168, 195
education, ideas about, 41–44, 71–72, 96, 121, 139, 142–144, 148, 190–191
Enlightenment, the, opposes, 94–97, 101, 102
finances, 56–57, 123, 127
freedom of expression, belief in, 58, 61, 64, 86, 91–92, 165, 175–176, 185–186, 189
French Revolution, disdain for, 29
friends, devotion to, 58, 59, 66–67, 67–68, 84, 86, 148, 149–157, 162–170, 174–183, 188–190
German books, vii, 124, 156
German language, knowledge of, 15, 16, 17–18, 19, 25, 30–31, 35–40, 51, 81 ff., 96–97, 156
German thinkers, indebtedness to, 17–18, 25, 49, 81 ff., 96–97, 126, 160, 167–168
Germanizer, activities as a, 19, 30, 31, 35–39, 49, 74 ff., 81–85, 96–97, 105–115, 128, 179
Germany, affection for, 13, 117, 120
Gothic & Romantic, fondness for, 36–38, 52, 82–83, 84–85
government, thoughts on, 49, 137–138, 143
health, declining, 142, 187, 194–196; illnesses, (1804) 15, (1821) 40, (1832) 119, (1837) 131, (1851) 193, (1852–53) 194–195, (1854–55) 195–196
historiography, 94–101, 112
inspiration, biblical, 92, 109, 110–111, 161, 166–167, 168–170, 177–180
Italy, affection for, 13, 120–122
Law, dislike for, as profession, 35, 41
liturgy, reform of, 146–147
loneliness, 118, 124–125
lower classes, attitude toward, 118, 120, 137–138, 142–144, 147, 151
Luther, admiration for, 16, 150, 164–168
Mammon-worship, denunciations of, viii, 48–49, 95–96, 102, 143, 147–148, 185, 187
marriage prospects, 33, 54–55, 116–117, 131–133
mathematics & science, dislike of, 26, 32, 142
missions, calls for, 144, 147
nationalism, 76–77, 99, 143, 147, 170
outspokenness, 31, 34, 47–49, 64, 137, 140, 148, 157, 165–166, 175–176
pastor, discomfort as a, 127, 137, 151–152
Peace of Paris, critical of, 28–29
pews, suppression of, 141, 146
poetry, love of, 26, 46, 124
politics, 29, 51, 117, 208 n.29
preacher, effectiveness as a, 47–48, 96, 117, 121, 133, 137, 164, 186
Protestantism, devotion to, 125, 163–166, 170, 180
public schools, attitude toward, 21, 22, 203 n.61
religious faith, 17–18, 27–28, 47, 92, 125, 138, 165–167, 168–170, 178–179, 190–191, 193, 196
Roman Catholicism, attitude toward, 25, 121–122, 135, 166, 170, 204 n.15
rural deaneries, revival of, 142, 147
schools, building of, 141, 142
Scriptures, interpretation of, 13, 27–28, 109, 125, 138, 161, 165–167, 168–170, 177–180, 190–191, 226 n.41
sexuality, 21
spelling reforms, 75–77, 85, 212 n.22
teacher, influence as a, 42, 43, 44, 46–47, 114–115, 127–128, 152–153, 190–191
tourist, 55–56, 119–123
translator, 35–40, 81–85, 86–92, 105–113; translation, theory of, 36–37
vindicator & partisan, 33–34, 148, (chap. 12) 149–157, (chap. 13) 162–173, (chap. 14) 174–183; (Bunsen) 86, 168–170;

INDEX 253

(Coleridge) 84, 155–157; (Hampden) 172–173; (Luther) 164–168; (Niebuhr) 86, 109–111; (Sterling) 173–183

visits: Alton Barnes, 117; Antwerp, (1828) 56, (1832) 119; Bodryddan, 55; Bologna, 10–13; Bonn, (1828) 56, (1832) 119, (1833) 122–123; Brighton, 55, 195; Bruges, 56; Carrara, 122; Cologne, 119; Florence, 120, 122; Frankfurt, 119; Genoa, 122; Ghent, (1828) 56, (1832) 119; Hannibal's route retraced, 122; Heidelberg, 56; Lausanne, 16; Liège, 119; Lugano, 122; Milan, (1821) 40, (1833) 122; Monte Casino, 121; Munich, 119; Naples, 121–122; Ostend, (1828) 55, 56, (1832) 119; Paris, (1819) 33, 35, (1828) 56; Plymouth, 191; Pompeii & Herculaneum, 121; Reading, 132, Rome, 120–122, 164; Sienna, 120; Strasbourg, 56; Tunbridge Wells, 194; Valdagno, 9; Venice, 120; Ventnor, 132; Vesuvius, climbs Mount, 121; Wartburg, 16; Weimar, vii, 15–16; Westmoreland, 104, 119, 131; Wimbledon, 32; Worting, 17; Zurich, 122

women, attitude toward, 17, 29, 33, 35–36, 54–55, 69, 131–133, 144, 194

Wordsworth, devotion to, 25, 26, 39–40, 46, 56, 70–71, 77, 104, 110, 119, 124, 127, 131, 132, 191

work habits, 149–150, 151–152

works discussed in text: *Charges,* 142, 150, 170, 196; "Children of Light," 47–48, 51, 114, 142, 147, 186; MS. Commonplace Book, (1816–18), 25–28, 71, 74, 239; *Guesses at Truth,* 25, 40, 58, 70–74, 94–101, 102, 108, 114, 135, 149, 152–153, 212 n.1; *Mission of the Comforter,* 164, 167–168, 179; "On English Orthography," 75–77; *Portions of the Psalms in English Verse,* 149, 228 n.1; "Samuel Taylor Coleridge & the English Opium-Eater," 155–156; John Sterling, *Essays & Tales, with a Memoir of His Life,* 174–183; *Thou Shalt Not Bear False Witness against Thy Neighbour,* 177–180, 190; MS. Travel Diary (1832–33), 119–123, 239; *Victory of Faith,* 152–153, 164, 186; *Vindication of Luther,* 164–168; "Vindication of Niebuhr's *History of Rome,*" 109–110; "Vindication of the Chevalier Bunsen," 168–170

Hare, Lucy Stanley (1798–1869) [wife of Marcus Hare], 72, 119, 128, 132, 135

Hare, Marcus Theodore (1796–1845) [fourth child of Francis & Georgiana Hare-Naylor], abilities, 19; birth, 9; death, 135; marriage, 128; naval career, 19; Tonbridge school, 15; mentioned, 139, 149

Hare, Maria Leycester (1798–1870) [wife of Augustus Hare; adopted mother of A.J.C. Hare], 118; adopts A.J.C. Hare, 129; on JCH's politics, 117; on JCH's rooms, 119; on JCH's temperament, 89; life at Herstmonceux, 128–129, 133–134; marriage, 117; & Maurice family, 131–134; school building & church restoration, 146; on Schleiermacher, 89; widowed, 128

Hare, Robert (d. 1832) [brother of Francis Hare-Naylor; uncle of JCH], 5, 117

Hare-Naylor, Francis (d.1775) [eldest son of Bishop Hare], 4

Hare-Naylor, Francis (1753–1815) [father of JCH], anti-slavery sentiments, 13; birth, 5; bizarre courtship, 6–7; death, 58; elopement, 7, 9; estate, 56; JCH, accompanies to Cambridge, 23; literary work, 14, 15; republicanism, 11, 14, 29; works:

Age of Chivalry, 14; *Civil & Military History of Germany*, 30; *History of the Helvetic Republic*, 14; *Mirror*, 14; *Theodore, or the Enthusiast*, 15

Hare-Naylor, Georgiana Shipley (d.1806) [mother of JCH], America, wishes to emigrate to, 8; blindness, 14; death, 16; Ben Franklin, friend of, 7–8; scholarship, 9, 14, 144; painting, 7, 9, 14; poor health, 15–16; religious views, 13; republicanism, 10, 14, 16, 29; resides at or visits with family, Bath, 11, 13; Bologna, 9–11; Herstmonceux, 11, 13–14; Karlsruhe, 7; Lausanne, 16; Valdagno, 8; Vicenza, 8; Weimar, vii, 15–16

Hare-Naylor, Henrietta [formerly Mrs Henckell; second wife of Robert Hare-Naylor], cruelty, 5; extravagance, 5, 6; guts Herstmonceux Castle, 5–6, 11; loses Hurstmonceux Place, 11, 14; marriage to Hare-Naylor, 5

Hare-Naylor, Robert (1730–1799) [father of Francis Hare-Naylor; grandfather of JCH], 5, 7, 9, 11

Hargraves, Frank [pseud. of JCH], 63

Havelock, Sir Henry, 19, 20, 21, 22, 191–192

Hazlitt, William, 63, 65

Herodotus of Halicarnassus, 94, 100

Herstmonceux Castle, acquired by Bishop Hare, 4; painted by Georgiana Hare-Naylor, 14; ruined by Mrs Henckell Hare, 5–6; site of, 123; spelling of, 200 n.4

Herstmonceux, parish of, advowson, 116–117, 202 n.40; description, 123; Augustus Hare refuses living, 116; JCH accepts living, (chap. 10) 117–118, 119, 123–125 ff.; JCH unwilling to relinquish, 191; JCH, funeral of, 196–197; poor of, 137–138; spelling of, 200 n.4

Herstmonceux rectory, enlarged, 123; Maria Hare on, 123; library, A.P. Stanley on, 123–124; tone after JCH's marriage, 133–136; paintings in, 122, 124, 221 n.14, 222 n.26; portrait busts in, 124; JCH unwilling to relinquish, 191; visitors: 129, 135; Mrs Alexander, 55, 136; Bunsen, 135; Carlyle, 135; Darley, 135; Francis & Anna Hare, 135; Marcus & Lucy Hare, 135; Landor, 136; Manning, 139, 193; Maurice sisters, 131; Maurice, 130; Max Müller, 150; Sedgwick, 135; Thirlwall, 135; Whewell, 135; Worsley, 125

Hessey, John, 40, 59, 65, 83, 84

Higher criticism, (chap. 7) 85–92, 93, 109, 110–112, 137, 165–170, 174–182, 190–191

Hinds, Samuel, 19, 35

Hobbes, Thomas, 25, 47

Hogg, Thomas Jefferson, 107

Homer, 20, 25, 26, 93, 100, 167; Wolf's *Prolegomena ad Homerum*, 93

Hood, Thomas, 40

Hort, Fenton John Anthony, 173, 179–180

Hughes, Thomas, *Tom Brown's School Days*, 20

Hume, David, 25, 93, 94

Hurstmonceux Place, advowson, 116–117, 202 n.40; built by Mrs Henckell Hare, 6; Bunsen family occupies, 135; entailment, 6, 11, 14; JCH's parents inherit, 11; Hare-Naylor family occupies, 13, 14, 137; sold by Francis Hare-Naylor, 16–17; spelling of, 200 n.4; Wagner family occupies, 127–128

Hyde Hall, 53–54

Jeffrey, Francis, Lord, 63

Jelf, Richard William, 188–189

Jerusalem Bishopric, 162–164, 169, 195

Jones, Anna-Maria Shipley, Lady (d.1829) [sister of Georgiana Hare-Naylor; aunt of JCH], adopts Augustus & Anna-Maria Hare, 11, 17; appearance, 17;

INDEX

character, 17; death, 17, 56; dislike of things German, 17, 31, 124; finances, 56; Augustus Hare, wishes ordained, 117; JCH, opposes engagement of, 55; attachment for, by JCH, 17, 29, 55
Jones, Sir William, 7, 8, 79

Kant, Immanuel, 25, 27, 45, 46, 47
Keats, John, 38, 40
Keble, John, 48
Keightley, Thomas, 107
Kemble, John Mitchell, 45–46, 52, 77, 112, 114
Kenrick, John, 77, 104
Kingsley, Charles, 184, 185–186, 187, 189–190, 236 n.18
Knight, Charles, firm of, 84–85, 114, 186
Knight's Quarterly Magazine, 84
König, Gustav, *Life of Luther*, 150

Lamb, Charles, 40, 127
Landor, Walter Savage, JCH meets, 119; JCH tours with, 119–120; JCH visits, 122; Herstmonceux, visits, 136; *Imaginary Conversations*, (chap. 5) 59–69, 76, 77, 149; JCH characterized in, 76; controversies over figures characterized in, (Burke) 60, 61, (Chatham the Younger) 62, (Cromwell), 62, (Grenville) 60, (Magliabechi) 61, (Middleton) 61–63; in *Philological Museum*, 77; and Spelling reform, 76–77; mentioned, 9, 40, 54, 70, 149
Lee, James Prince, 103
Lewes, Sussex, 123, 146
Lewis, George Cornewall, 77, 111–112, 113, 220 n.24; *Inquiry into the Credibility of the Early Roman History*, 111–112
Lime Park, Herstmonceux, 128–129, 131, 133
Lincoln's Inn, 40, 186
Livy, Titus, 44, 93
Locke, John, 42, 94, 95, 99, 125
Lodge, John, 52
London Literary Chronicle, 115

London Magazine, 30, 40, 63, 83–84
London University, King's College, 163, 187–190
Long, George, 112
Longman, Thomas Norton, firm of, 59, 68
Ludlow, John Malcolm Forbes, 184, 186–187
Luke, Gospel of Saint, 85, 86, 87
Luther, Martin, 16, 150, 164–168, 188

Macaulay, Thomas Babington, 51, 52, 84, 107
McFarland, George F., 36, 38, 39, 70, 73–74, 81, 208 n.28, 214 n.10
Macmillan, Alexander, 153
Macmillan, Daniel, 152–154, 185
Malcolm, Sir John, 53–54
Malcolm, Lady, 54, 56
Malden, Henry, 77, 84
Manning, Henry Edward, becomes Archdeacon of Chichester, 139; conversion to Rome, 192–193; on Hampden, 173; JCH, agreement with, 141, 146; JCH, disagreement with, 139–140, 163–164, 192–193; Jerusalem Bishopric, 163; Newman, defends, 163–164; & Sterling Club, 181; mentioned, 145, 194, 226 n.46
Mark, Gospel of Saint, 86, 87
Marsh, Herbert, 31, 86–87
Matthew, Gospel of Saint, 86, 87
Matthews, George, 119
Maurice, John Frederick Denison, & Apostles, 45–47; & *Athenaeum*, 47–48, 73, 114–115; on Broad Church, 159–160; Christian Socialism, 184–187; & Coleridge, 39; JCH, his classes, 43–45; JCH, his cosmopolitanism, 16, 160; JCH, contrasted with, 159–161; JCH, friendship with, 130–131; JCH, officiates at wedding of, 132; on JCH's nationalism, 147–148, 159–160; JCH's would-be biographer, ix; Jerusalem Bishopric, 162; & Macmillan brothers, 152–153; reviews "Children of Light,"

48, *Guesses at Truth*, 73; on Thirlwall's Schleiermacher, 89; *Kingdom of Christ*, 153; *Theological Essays*, 187–190
Maurice, Georgiana Hare [half-sister of JCH; second wife of Maurice], 120, 122, 160, 187
Maurice, Priscilla, 131
Merivale, Charles, 46, 112; *History of the Romans under the Empire*, 112
Michaelis, Johann David, 86; *Introduction to the New Testament*, 86
Middle Temple, 33
Mill, John Stuart, 95, 174, 176, 181, 182
Monk, James Henry, 23, 25, 32
Moxon, Edward, firm of, 84–85
Müller, Friedrich Max, 79–80, 150
Müller, Karl Otfried, 93, 109, 113; *History and Antiquities of the Doric Race*, 220 n.24; *History of Greek Literature*, 113
Munro, Lady, 55, 117
Museum Criticum, 74

Napier, Macvey, 107
New Poor Law, 137–138
Newman, Francis, 175, 176
Newman, John Henry, attacks Arnold, 164; conversion to Rome, 168, 170; attacks Hampden, 171, 173; JCH on, 163–164; Jerusalem Bishopric, 163–164; *Lectures on Justification*, 164; attacks Luther, 164–166; mentioned, 48, 140, 175
Niebuhr, Barthold Georg, on England, 106–107; JCH defends, 86, 109–111; on JCH's "Vindication," 110; historiography, 93–102; *Römische Geschichte*, 93, 102–103, (chap. 9) 105–113, 122, see Roman history; mentioned, 56, 58, 74, 75, 104, 113, 120, 156, 164
Norris, Sir William, 19

Oehlenschlaeger, Adam Gottlob, 38, 39
Ollier, Charles, 37, 38, 39, 57, 81, 83

Olliers Literary Miscellany, 38–39, 81, 83
Otter, William, 138, 139
Oxford University, New College, 19, 117
Oxford Tractarian Movement, Arnold opposes, 104; Broad Church, compared with, 53; Broad Church, hostility toward, 168–173, 176–179; attacks Hampden, 170–173; JCH, hostility toward, 168; JCH opposes, 125–126, 141, 145, 147, 165–166, 172–173, 176–179; attacks Sterling, 176–179; mentioned, 48

Paley, William, 48, 125
Palmer, William, 176–180
Parker, John William, firm of, 153, 185–186
Parker of Oxford, firm of, 77, 172–173
Peacock, George, 24, 51
Peacock, Thomas Love, 38
Philological Museum, 58, 74–79, 100
philology, 74–80, 85–94, 100, 137
Plato, 25, 41, 43, 44, 45, 62, 161, 231 n.41; *Gorgias*, 44
Plumptre, Edward Hayes, 33, 47
Powell, Lucilla Maurice, 131, 194–195, 196, 237 n.44
Praed, Winthrop Mackworth, 52, 55–56, 84
Pusey, Edward Bouverie, attacks Bunsen, 168–170; Germanist, 31, 168; *Historical Enquiry into . . . the Rationalist . . . Theology of Germany*, 169; Tractarian leader, 141, 168; mentioned, 145, 171, 179

Quarterly Magazine, 84, 85
Quarterly Review, 61, 63, 83, 108–109

Raine, Matthew, 19–21
Raphael, 119, 120, 167, 221 n.14
Record, 180–182, 190
Regius Professorships, of Divinity, 190–191; of Greek, 25, 49–51; of History, 31
Rheinische Museum, 74

INDEX

Richter, Jean-Paul, 58; "Vision of a Godless World," 115
Rivington, firm of, 77, 105
Robinson, Henry Crabb, as Germanist, 30; on JCH's churchmanship, 160; on JCH's library, 124; on JCH's optimism, 190; on Thirlwall's Schleiermacher, 89; at Weimar with the Hare-Naylors, 15; on Wordsworth Monument Committee, 191; mentioned, 108
Roman history, 74, 93 ff.; compared with England, 98–99, 101–102; G. C. Lewis on, 111–112; Arnold's history, 104, 111; Niebuhr's history, 93, 102–103 (chap. 9) 105–113, 122
Romilly, Joseph, 51, 52, 53, 208 n.16
Rose, Hugh James, 24; Germanist, 31–32; Greek Professorship, 49–51, & JCH, 40; attacks higher criticism, 31–32, 51, 89, 110, 179; *State of the Protestant Religion in Germany*, 51; & Tractarian Movement, 52, 168
Rugby school, 103, 112
Russell, John, 21–22, 23

Schelling, F.W.J. von, 155–156
Schiller, Friedrich, 15, 83, 115
Schlegel, A.W. von, 38–39, 56, 108, 120
Schleiermacher, Friedrich, 56, 58, 75, 85, 87–92, 156; *Critical Essay on the Gospel of Saint Luke*, 85, 87–92, 127, 216 n.50
Schmitz, Leonhard, 113, 220 n.31
Scholefield, James, 49–51
Sedgwick, Adam, 25, 53, 54, 135, 191
Shakespeare, William, 25, 26, 38, 167
Sheepshanks, Richard, 24, 33, 51, 54, 72–73
Shelley, Percy Bysshe, 38, 39, 107
Shipley, Jonathan [grandfather of JCH], 6–8
Shipley, Louisa, of Bodryddan [aunt of JCH], 55, 56

Shuttleworth, Philip Nicolas, 138, 139
Simpkin & Marshall, firm of, 61
Simpkinson, John Neville, 197
Smythe, George A.F.P.S., 127–128
Soane, George, 30, 36, 37
Sophocles, 161; *Antigone*, 43, 127
Southey, Robert, 61, 62, 63, 64, 73, 107–108
Spedding, James, 46
Spineto, Elizabeth Campbell, Marchesa di, 53
Stanley, Arthur Penrhyn, Broad Churchmanship, 127, 157; on JCH, vii; JCH, pall bearer of, 197; JCH, library of, vii, 123–124; JCH, tutored by, 127; on *Philological Museum*, 79; on Trinity College Fellows, 52; mentioned, 102, 218 n.45
Sterling, John, as Apostle, 46–47; & *Athenaeum*, 47, 114–115; attacked, 173 (chap. 14) 174–183; biography by JCH, 175–176, by Carlyle, 182–183; & Carlyle, 135, 174; & Coleridge, 39, 154–155, 182; death, 132; *Essays & Tales*, ed. JCH, 174, 176, 234 n.21; Germanist, 122, 125; & JCH, 122, 132, 174; JCH defends, 177–180; Herstmonceux, curate of, 122–123, 125, 127, 223 n.43; A.P. Stanley on, 127; Sterling Club, 180–182, 188
Strauss, David Friedrich, 166–167; *Leben Jesu*, 166–167, 175
Sussex Archaeological Society, 150

Tait's Edinburgh Magazine, 155
Tambroni, Clotilda, 9, 11, 12–13
Taylor, John, & *Guesses at Truth*, 70–74; & *Imaginary Conversations*, 40, 59–69; & Niebuhr's history, 105–107; & Schleiermacher's *Saint Luke*, 90–92; mentioned, 83, 84, 85, 124, 214 n.19, 219 n.3
Taylor, William, of Norwich, 30, 83
Tennyson, Alfred, Lord, 45, 113, 127, 236 n.20

Thackeray, William Makepeace, 21–22, 45, 207 n.7; *Pendennis*, 22

Thirlwall, Connop, on Broad Church, 158–159; Cambridge Apostles, mentor to, 46, 49; at Charterhouse, 19, 20; consecration, JCH preaches at, 136; Fellow, 51; Germanist, 31, 37, 81–85, 86–92, 105–113, 234 n.17; JCH's early influence upon, 19; & JCH, 42, 132, 197, 237 n.45; Herstmonceux, visits, 135; *History of Greece*, 111; lawyer, 33–34, 207 n.26; translates Niebuhr's history, 105–113; edits *Philological Museum*, 74–79, 80; on *Record*, 182; spelling reform, 75; & John Taylor, 40, 90–92; university reform, 49, 79, 145; mentioned, 52, 53, 72, 98, 100, 102, 121, 142, 176, 188

Thirty-Nine Articles, 28, 127

Thompson, William Hepworth, 137

Thorp, Thomas, 24, 40–41, 51

Thorwaldsen, Bertal, 120

Thucydides, 96, 103

Tieck, Ludwig, 37, 56, 58, 82, 84–85, 90–91; works: *Betrothal*, 90–91; *Love Charm*, 84–85; *Old Man of the Mountain*, 84–85; *Pictures*, 90–91; *Pietro of Abano*, 84–85

Tonbridge, school, 15

Tractarianism, see Oxford Tractarian Movement

Trench, Richard Chenevix, 114, 125, 176

Urevangelium theory, 87–88

Utilitarianism, see Benthamism

Venables, Edmund, 125–126, 194

Vico, Giambattista, 94, 97, 98; *Principi Di Scienza Nova*, 94

Victoria, Queen of England, 195

Vienna Review, 38–39

Waddington, George, 24, 32

Wagner, George, 127–128, 194, 197

Walker, William Sidney, 25, 49–50, 51, 53

Warburton, William, 4, 25–26

Ward, William George, 165, 166

Whewell, William, 24; & Coleridge Prize, 154–155; Fellow, 32; Germanist, 31, 32, 115; & JCH, 33, 35; dissuades JCH from Divinity Professorship, 190–191; persuaded by JCH to remain at Cambridge, 150–152; secures JCH's return to Cambridge, 41–42, 152; Herstmonceux, visits, 135; Hyde Hall, 53–54; Master of Trinity, 152; & *Philological Museum*, 77; on *Sintram*, 36; spelling reform, 75; Tutor, 43; mentioned, 24, 25, 29, 32, 33, 40, 51, 52, 53, 72, 124, 128, 136, 145, 168, 172, 173

Whittaker, George Byrom, firm of, 90

Wilberforce, Samuel, 176, 181, 194

Winkworth, Susanna, 150; *Tauler's Life & Sermons*, 150; König's *Life of Luther*, 150

Wiseman, Nicholas, 120

Wood, James, 29, 49

Woodard, Nathaniel, 142, 143

Wordsworth, Christopher, 49–51, 52, 145, 152

Wordsworth, William, & Apostles, 46; death, 191; & *Guesses at Truth*, 70–71; & JCH, 26, 39–40, 56, 124, 127; on JCH's marriage, 132; JCH visits, 104, 119, 131; as intellectual regenerator, 82; & Landor's *Imaginary Conversations*, 61–63; on "Vindication of Niebuhr," 110; mentioned, 25, 157

Worsley, Thomas, 24–25, 54, 119–122, 125